THE

THE GOLDEN HORDE

Peter Morwood

LEGEND

First published by Legend Books in 1993

1 3 5 7 9 10 8 6 4 2

Copyright © Peter Morwood 1993

The right of Peter Morwood to be identified as the author
of this work has been asserted by him in accordance
with the Copyright, Designs and Patents Act, 1988

This paperback edition published in 1993

Legend Books
Random House, 20 Vauxhall Bridge Road, London SW1V 2SA

Random House Australia (Pty) Limited
20 Alfred Street, Milsons Point, Sydney,
New South Wales 2061, Australia

Random House New Zealand Limited
18 Poland Road, Glenfield
Auckland 10, New Zealand

Random House South Africa (Pty) Limited
PO Box 337, Bergvlei, South Africa

Random House UK Limited Reg. No. 954009

A CIP catalogue record for this book
is available from the British Library

ISBN 0 09 989840 3

Printed and bound in Great Britain by
Cox & Wyman Ltd, Reading, Berkshire

Chapter One

The Independent Tsardom of Khorlov;
June, AD 1243

'Papa, what are those bells?'

There was a wool-stuffed leather ball arching through the air towards him, and even though the catch was an easy one, Tsar Ivan Aleksandrovich Khorlovskiy came very close to missing it.

'Bells? What bells?' he said, and knew even as he spoke that he was lying. The bells were there, and had been there for several minutes past, and not all the feigned ignorance in the wide white world would wipe them from the hearing of a child.

Ivan set the ball down carefully and dusted off his hands, then peered over the kremlin battlements in the various directions wildly pointed by his son. Nikolai was seven and a half years old, as fair-haired and innocent-looking as both his parents, and even though sometimes he could be unsettlingly wise in the ways of the world, at other times he was no more than what he was: a little boy. This was one such time, and Ivan hated it as much as all the others.

Far off across the steppe, almost lost in the haze of distance and in the dust of his own speed, a rider thundered by. The man was leaning low across his horse's neck, almost crouching as he rode; Ivan could see that much from the vague silhouette. What he did not need to see was the high stirrups that gave such a stance in the saddle, or the fur hat that was no doubt flapping in the wind of the horseman's speed. Or the curved sword, or the bow, or the quiver crammed with arrows. The sound of the crossed belts of bells told him that all those things were there, as necessary to a courier of the Great Khan as his very horse.

'A messenger, that's all,' he said, as if the messenger, and the Tatars, and even the Great Khan Ögotäi himself, were of no importance. To emphasise his lack of interest, he nonchalantly stroked the golden sweep of moustache and close-cropped beard

1

that he had cultivated in the seven years since he became Tsar. Ivan fancied they made him look older and wiser. His loving wife Mar'ya Morevna had said several other things on the subject, but short of attacking him in his sleep with a razor and a lathered brush, could do nothing more about it. Then he grinned and picked up the ball again, tossing it invitingly from hand to hand to resume the game of catch. Or indeed, to do anything at all rather than discuss the matter further. With a younger child it might have worked, while an older might have detected the edge in his father's voice and veered from mentioning the evident source of such displeasure.

Nikolai was neither young enough nor old enough; he could play ball at any time, and the finer tones of voice were still a mystery to him. But he had seldom in his short life seen anyone riding so fast, and certainly had never heard anyone wear bells so that mere folk on foot could hear him coming and get out of his way. The boy was sharp enough to realise what the harsh, bright noise was for, and to say as much. And innocent enough to add the words that sank a knife into his father's heart. 'Those bells must mean he's very important, *batyushka*. Do they mean he's as important as you? Or even Grandpapa?'

Ivan glanced at his son, then gazed out at the Tatar messenger in the way a man might watch an annoying insect that buzzed just out of reach. He did not reply, and Nikolai Ivanovich lost interest, seized the ball from his father's hands and ran off with it.

As important as Grandpapa? thought Ivan sourly, turning his back on the racing horseman as if by doing so he could make the Tatar – all Tatars – cease to exist. *More important. So much more important that you can't yet grasp it. And sometimes, neither can I . . .*

The Independent Tsardom of Khorlov; March, AD 1236

The waiting was the worst. Ivan, Tsarevich and heir to the crown of Khorlov, wouldn't have believed it had anyone told him as much. At least, he wouldn't have believed it an hour ago. Now . . .

Now he wasn't so sure.

There could be very few things worse than waiting in the grinding cold of the early spring of Russia, glancing apprehensively every now and then at the kremlin's Lesser Council Chamber. When your own father had summoned you to attend him there, and had given only a time but not a reason – and when you got there to find the huge double doors closed and locked and guarded against even you, the Tsar's own and only son – then listening to the ebb and flow of raised voices inside the high wooden hall had an added piquancy which was very far from pleasant.

The sound was blurred and muffled enough that Ivan could make no sense from the individual words, but the tone of each outcry was unmistakable. Tsar Aleksandr's councillors did not like what he was telling them.

Ivan stopped pacing to and fro, listened harder as if that might make some difference – which it didn't – and scuffed the toes of his boots into the handspan's depth of snow that still remained in the kremlin courtyard. He wanted to be inside the Council Chamber, to stand at his father's side during whatever turmoil the old man had stirred up among the *boyaryy*. And at the same time he wanted to be a long way from Khorlov; certainly not standing in the chilly courtyard with a far-from-specific royal summons hanging over his head.

Ivan was one of the many who preferred to know, rather than be kept in suspense. The only concern right now was, what was it he should know?

Tsar Aleksandr had been behaving strangely in the past year, a strangeness that had begun only a few months after the Teutonic Knights had been turned back at the River Nemen. There had been erratic flashes of violence and foul temper that Ivan had never seen before, and at the same time there had been the constant feeling that even at the height of his softly sneering rages, Tsar Aleksandr had been watching his son and coldly gauging his responses to each unreasonable insult. Ivan had taken care to control his reactions: Tsars' sons had been killed by their own fathers, or by their command, for nothing more than an eyebrow lifted in disapproval at the wrong time. He had gained small reassurance from the presumed well-wishers who had suggested it was nothing more than a manifestation of his father's great age. Ivan felt certain that it was something more, but the matter was not one that could be discussed either in the open or behind closed doors. If their words had been meant as a comfort, then one and all had a great deal to learn about the art – and if they intended more than comfort, then their opinions were not only lacking in subtlety, but dangerously close to treason.

Their suggestions were dangerous not merely for themselves, as Ivan well knew. Whatever was troubling Tsar Aleksandr, he was capable of lashing out in any direction, but if he suspected some sort of conspiracy between the lords and warriors of his *druzina* retinue and his own son and heir, then there was one very specific target for the old man's wrath. Ivan did not much relish whatever interview awaited him within the noisy Council Chamber. In such delicate situations as this, mere innocence was hardly a defence. Enough tsars' sons had learnt that lesson abruptly, fatally, and far too late to gain any profit from it.

Ivan wished that Mar'ya Morevna could have been here by his side. That, however, was out of the question. Two six-month-old children had proven themselves capable, singly and together, of making more demands on her time than ruling a princely domain had ever done. Being both the wife of the Tsarevich and a liege lady in her own right had provided certain advantages, mostly in the shape of an unlimited supply of servants, wet-nurses and most especially, clean nappy-cloths. For all of that, Mar'ya Morevna had made it plain that her – their – son and daughter were not going to suffer the usual fate of royal children, of being kept in a nursery and only seeing their parents at convenient times. Convenient for the parents, anyway. It had happened to her, and to a lesser degree to Ivan; she was determined that it would not happen to Nikolai and Anastasya.

When the court surgeons had come to him and told him that, all things progressing to a satisfactory conclusion, he would be the father of twins, Ivan had stared at them and refused to believe his own ears. He had actually said, 'Twin what?' and after his wife's somewhat shocked personal physicians had finished with him, was thoroughly convinced that they were men who valued their dignity more than the chance of a cheap joke. Besides which, they didn't know. If Mar'ya Morevna's occasional use of the Art Magic had told her anything, she hadn't bothered to pass on the information to her servants.

But she had told Ivan.

Twins! Not just a son or a daughter, but one of each.

A son, an heir to the Tsardom, would have been more than sufficient. Even a daughter would have been entirely acceptable; useful things could be done with daughters, things involving dowries, and politically expedient marriages, and favourable alliances . . .

But *twins*. . . ?

Tsarevich Ivan had given way to a most unprincely fit of chuckling, because he could remember his own childhood only too well. Prince Nikolai would never know just how lucky he was. They could so easily have been twin daughters, a combination as perilous as a matched pair of daggers, and totally unfair to any later son. Ivan had grown up with not one, not two, but three elder sisters, and he liked to claim that the bruises still twinged when the weather changed. It was a joke, but those who heard it could not help but notice that it was never one he uttered when any of those sisters were within hearing. They were not well known for their sense of humour.

Nor just now, by the sound of another outburst of shouting from the Council Chamber, was his father. Ivan's wandering mind was twitched abruptly back from certain family matters to other family matters, because Tsar Aleksandr seldom raised his voice in anger but when he did, the sound was most distinctive. His son was hearing that sound now, and not liking it. The roar still fell short of that bellow of real rage which Ivan had heard only once before in his life, but there was a disturbing edge to it, the fury held in check and overlaid with a mellow persuasiveness that Mar'ya Morevna had once described as broken glass stirred into butter. It was an accurate enough description: the voice of a man who had the power to make sure that his orders were obeyed, but who was trying – maybe for the last time – to gain that obedience by something other than direct command. Either those direct commands were too easy or, and the thought insinuated itself unpleasantly into Ivan's mind, no longer sufficiently reliable.

Prince Ivan felt again that it would be better to be well away from Khorlov, hunting something safe like bear or boar, than standing out here waiting to find out what was wrong. He muttered something inaudible, kicked at the snow, and turned from the Council Chamber and towards the kremlin's stables. Then stopped in his tracks as the doors, not one of them but both, were flung open and a double file of Captain Akimov's troopers came out. They formed a guard of honour, flanking either side of the stairs and right up to the dark oblong of the doorway. And equally, they formed a picket line through which Prince Ivan could not pass without making his departure look more like an escape than it already was.

Petr Mikhailovich Akimov stood at the top of the stairs in full armour, even to the shield and helmet, and stared down at Ivan. The Guard-Captain said not a word, but Ivan felt embarrassed nonetheless that he should have been seen looking less than eager for his father's summons. He retraced his steps carefully, grateful that the snow was trampled enough not to betray how he had been pacing to and fro, and looked up at the Cossack Captain.

'Now?' he said.

'Now, Highness,' said Akimov.

As Ivan mounted the cut-stone stairs with all the eagerness of a man ascending a scaffold, the Captain flipped one hand palm-outwards in a gesture so fast that Ivan almost missed it. He slackened his pace as he came within earshot of Akimov, and as he did so noticed that the Guard-Captain had placed himself in a position – square in the middle of the staircase – that was not only imposing but also somewhat out of earshot of the guardsmen who stood to right and left. It didn't encourage Ivan particularly, but it provided a quick jab of curiosity that briefly blunted the edge of his nervousness.

'What is it?' Prince Ivan spoke in a way he had learned from Mar'ya Morevna, a quick, slipshod mumble that didn't move his lips. All of a sudden, every subtlety his wife had ever used to conceal her dealings with spies and informers seemed significant and important. Akimov blinked, managing by that small gesture to convey a nod of satisfaction.

'Your father, Highness,' he said quietly, 'has made announce-ments that do not meet with his Council's approval.'

'I had already guessed that much all by myself,' said Ivan. 'But you could tell me something useful. *What* announcements?'

'About you and how you are to become – '

'Captain Akimov, enough!' The interruption was accompanied by a quick rapping of boot-heels on the wooden floor of the Council Chamber, and a richly dressed *boyar* emerged scowling from the shadows of the hall into the dull daylight.

Even though he couldn't put a name to the face at first, Ivan knew the man who spoke was a member of the Tsar's *druzina* retinue. The *boyar* was staring at Guard-Captain Akimov as though waiting for an explanation, but Ivan stared at the nobleman in his turn until the man shifted his attention, and held the stare for a good minute more while the *boyar*'s discomfort became apparent.

'Is it customary,' Ivan said at last, 'for one servant of the Tsar of Khorlov to interrupt another, when that other is speaking to the Tsarevich of Khorlov?' He smiled, a slow, careful, nasty expression, while his eyes never left those of the *boyar* and the man's name dropped at last into his mind. 'Let me put it another way. A way even you can understand, Count Danyil Fedorovich. Since when do my father's servants break into my conversations without asking my permission?'

That was his own fear talking, taking refuge in pride and unpleasantness. If he couldn't put himself at ease, then he was more than willing to spread his unease around, and maybe dilute it a little. It worked on Danyil Fedorovich, and more than Ivan had expected, because the nobleman's anger-flushed face went pale. Ivan raised his eyebrows in curiosity at that, only to have it taken for irritable impatience. The *boyar* stammered uselessly for a few seconds without saying anything worthy of note, then bowed low enough that he seemed almost to grovel on the threshold of the Council Chamber.

'Highness, I – that is, your pardon, Highness! My apologies! I didn't mean – '

'Then what did you mean?' Prince Ivan gazed thoughtfully at the *boyar* for another few seconds as if committing the man's name and face to memory, then waved his hand, dismissing the matter. 'Never mind. If it was to say that my presence is required at last, then Captain Akimov had already conveyed the information. With a deal more courtesy and respect. Thank you for that, Captain.'

And thank you, he thought, *for at least trying to warn me of what to expect inside. Even if you were a damned sight too slow over it.*

As he stepped through the door and into the Lesser Council Chamber, Prince Ivan shivered slightly. It might have been because of the hostile atmosphere within, something he could feel as heads turned and eyes stared, but that shiver had a more mundane cause as well. Despite the number of fur-clad people inside, despite the fact that the Lesser Chamber had been chosen instead of the Great as being the warmer of the two, the place was bitterly cold.

As his breath fumed from his mouth in whorls of grey vapour, Ivan felt sure that despite the braziers set along the tapestry-hung walls, the place was colder inside than out. Khorlov's Lesser Council Chamber was built in the customary Russian style, with wooden walls and floor and ceiling. The Great Chamber, part of the structure of the kremlin fortress, was walled in stone, floored with marble and roofed with tile. For all that it was the most impressive single room in the kremlin, unless it was needed to impress visiting dignitaries, it was never used in winter. Even in the muggy heat of high summer the great vault breathed a stealthy cool from its very structure, and in winter that coolness dropped down to a brutal, barely tolerable cold.

Perhaps, thought Ivan as he strode towards the elevated daïs where his father sat, *holding this meeting in the Great Hall might have been a better idea after all.* He glanced from one side of the hall to the other and saw more, too many more, bad-tempered faces like the one which Danyil Fedorovich had worn. *The place would have kept your tempers from growing so heated, my lords, if it did nothing else.*

Ivan Aleksandrovich squared his shoulders and his heavy furred robe, straightened his back and the set of his handsome egret-plumed hat. He drew a deep breath, slowly, so that it wouldn't be noticed, then with a deliberately arrogant hammering of red-heeled boots on inlaid flooring, walked the gauntlet of unfriendly eyes all that long way from the doors of the Council Chamber to where his father the Tsar awaited him.

Tsar Aleksandr was sitting bolt upright in the Chair of State, long, lean hands hooked like talons around the carven armrests, watching as his only son stalked proudly towards him. Ivan focused all his attention on the old man's regal features, so that no member of the hostile *druzina* retinue could claim to have attracted any notice. Until he found out more of what had been happening behind those closed and bolted doors, Ivan intended to treat all of his father's councillors with equal disdain – and equal distrust.

All, perhaps, except one. There was no great love between Ivan and Dmitriy Vasil'yevich Strel'tsin, but his father's High Steward and First Minister – and his grandfather's and great-grandfather's, come to that – had proven himself honest over so many years that doubting his good faith was tantamount to doubting that the sun would rise in the east. Strel'tsin stood now to the right of the Tsar's chair, a place of honour that he would vacate for Tsarevich Ivan and no-one else. His long silver-grey beard hung down below his waist; his white hair was precisely parted in the middle so that it framed his lean, clever face; and he looked so much all that typified a minister and a wise advisor that Ivan, for the thousandth time, felt certain that something, somewhere about him, had to be false.

Except that there was nothing. Ivan's impression – his mistake – was one that had been made by a succession of envoys down the years, and Dmitriy Vasil'yevich used his appearance like a weapon against them. It was only when the treaty, pledge or whatever had been irrevocably signed and sealed that those envoys realised that every now and again, someone who looked as intelligent as that might just turn out to be so.

Strel'tsin bowed slightly as Prince Ivan approached, and was about to move aside when Tsar Aleksandr lifted one hand, index finger extended, and stopped him. 'Stay where you are, Dmitriy Vasil'yevich,' the Tsar said.

Ivan blinked, and his confident stride faltered just ever so slightly. Not to be granted his proper place at his father's right hand sounded like some sort of insult, and not an overly subtle one. The Tsar glanced at him and inclined his head a fraction in a gesture that might have been an acknowledgement either of Ivan's presence, or of the expression that had flickered briefly across his face.

'Not by my side, Vanya,' said Aleksandr of Khorlov in a voice too quiet to carry beyond the foot of the daïs. The Tsar's hand flicked a gesture so quick and small that Ivan barely saw it, then swooped back to rest once more on the arm of the Chair of State as though it had never moved. 'Stand at my back. Guard it.'

There was a curved Cossack *shashka* sabre hanging from Ivan's belt, and a long Circassian dagger thrust through the belt itself, just across the centre of his stomach. Neither weapon had been more than ornaments for his clothing until now, but suddenly Ivan felt very grateful for the present fashion that said gentlemen of quality should go armed about their everyday affairs. Though instinct and reflex and simple fear twitched at his hands, he managed to keep them from checking the blades, from loosening them in their scabbards, even from drawing them and resting the slim curve of the sabre comfortably on one shoulder.

'Well done, Highness,' said Strel'tsin as Ivan passed him, a reasonable indication that the old courtier had seen and identified that flurry of indecision. 'Stand quietly. Watch, listen, but say and do nothing unless the Tsar's Majesty bids it.'

Ivan nodded, observing with the mild surprise of one who has always known it, but never taken notice, that Dmitriy Vasil'yevich Strel'tsin had taken Mar'ya Morevna's art of speaking without the bother of moving his lips, and had refined it so that every word he said was – within a certain and very limited radius – quite plain. For Ivan's own part, he could only utter murmurs that he hoped Strel'tsin could hear. Ivan could barely hear them himself, because another of the Tsar's councillors was on his feet by now, holding forth with the orotund phrases of one in love with the sound of his own voice. *I'll be your Tsar one day, gentlemen*, Ivan thought as he listened to the fine, rolling words of which one in seven had any relevance, *and you'll learn to speak plainer, that I promise*.

'What concerns the Council?' he tried again, a little more loudly. This time Strel'tsin heard him, and jerked his head ever so slightly towards the gorgeously clad men whose complexions so closely matched the popular shade of scarlet velvet most of them were wearing.

'The succession,' Strel'tsin replied. '*Your* succession, which . . .'

Ivan went white, and lost the rest of what the High Steward was saying amid the hissing tide of blood in his own ears. If the Council and the *druzina* were disputing what was the most basic of Khorlov's laws, then they were talking something close to treason. And if that was the case, why was the Tsar his father allowing them to get away with it? Why were Guard-Captain Akimov and his soldiers standing idle, when every law of every realm in all the Russias, down to the smallest independent principality, said that they would be within their rights to harvest traitorous heads like scythe-wielding peasants in a field of standing barley?

Instead, these people were getting a more than fair hearing; their complaints were being considered as though there was something of note in them; and even Tsar Aleksandr, whose temper of late had been far from certain, as Ivan knew to his own discomfort, was nodding his head and waving his hand in invitation for this latest traitor to continue with his lies!

'Highness? *Highness!*' Dmitriy Vasil'yevich Strel'tsin's voice was no longer a subtle murmur for the conveyance of secrets, but a snap of caution, of warning, of command.

Ivan's head jerked around, his mouth twisting automatically into a snarl of disapproval at being addressed by a Crown servant in such a manner for the second time in five minutes. Then he pulled himself back under control with an audible click of teeth, writhed the snarl a little wider until it might just pass for a crooked sort of smile, and said, 'Yes?'

'I said, stand quietly. Watch and listen. Highness, each change of mood is written plain across your face for every man to see! I beg you, be more circumspect, please!'

Ivan nodded and cleared his throat, feeling no end of a fool. Then he tried, with rather more difficulty, to clear his face of expression and his mind of reaction to each councillor's words. Hardest of all, as it had always been, was just listening, without letting his personal views of rhetoric or delivery – never mind content – lend their own colour and interpretation to what was being said. And – as it had always been – once he started paying something like attention, Prince Ivan found that he was gaining information rather than just losing his temper every few minutes.

It wasn't treason. Treason would have been easy to deal with. This was honest concern for the Tsardom of Khorlov, and the reason for that concern was on the Tsar's own head. Ivan stared at his own father, and wondered what was going on in that wise, wily, wickedly convoluted mind. Because the matter under discussion was Tsar Aleksandr's immediate abdication in favour of his son, in favour of Tsarevich Ivan, his children, his heirs and assigns, and those he should choose to set in authority.

Tsar Ivan of Khorlov . . .

Ivan felt his stomach drop. It was one thing to know that you would some day become Tsar when your father died, and another thing entirely to discover that your father had decided for some reason of his own not to wait that long. The prospect was both a flattering display of confidence in his ability – from his father – and an unsettling demonstration of what Khorlov's High Council really thought of the prospect of Prince Ivan as their Tsar, when they were still in a position to express opinions to the living ears of their previous lord. If he was indeed previous, rather than still current.

Swallowing quietly enough that he hoped nobody, not even Strel'tsin, might hear such a sound of undiluted apprehension, Ivan started to listen a great deal more closely than he had done so far. When all the hyperbole was stripped away, it was all very simple: the nobles of the Council and the *druzina* opposed any thought of abdication, on the grounds that Prince Ivan was neither old enough nor experienced enough to be their Tsar. Tsar Aleksandr, on the other hand, took the increasingly irritable view that if he suddenly dropped dead over dinner one fine evening, they would have a great deal less choice in the matter than now, which was not much. For all their loudly stated reasons, neither side had seen fit to consult Ivan, any more than they would have consulted him had the Tsar indeed died without advance warning.

The revelation that he was intended to become the next Tsar of Khorlov rather sooner than anticipated, and with his father still in perfect health, came as something of a shock. It was assumed, in a tradition that had developed over the generations, that a new Tsar would succeed only on the death of his predecessor, and that a father would be followed by his eldest son. But that was only by tradition, and only in Khorlov. Primogeniture, the passing of property or title from father to eldest son, was still not established throughout the realms of all the Russias, even though it had long been a custom among the North people who were their common ancestors. Nor was it generally assumed that a ruler would continue to rule until he or she died in office; lords and ladies, tsars and princes, were all people of power, and among other things that power gave them the right to make up their own minds. If they decided they had suffered the complaints of their subjects long enough, they could either silence those subjects once and for all – which had been done on more than one occasion – or they could take off the crown, lay down the sceptre, and leave their troublesome people to complain amongst themselves.

In the city-states of Kiev and Vladimir, the great families of Yaroslavich and Vsevolodovich had taken turns keeping the throne-cushions warm over something like fifteen years. They had passed the title of *Velikiy knyaz'*, meaning something like 'Great Prince' or 'Grand Duke', from father to son, son to father, brother to brother and finally back and forth between uncles, nephews and relatives of increasingly obscure degree as though it had been an overly hot meat pie.

Yuriy Vladimirovich, not even a distant cousin of either family, had become Great Prince of Kiev almost by accident, apparently slipping onto the throne while the other half-dozen contenders weren't looking. He had remained there for almost four years now, which was commonly considered something of a record.

In the same time there had been not one, not two, but three Princes of Vladimir before *their* Prince Yuriy, this one a Vsevolodovich, had taken the obvious if ruthless step of arranging accidents for his most immediate potential rivals. It didn't matter whether they were rivals in truth or not: the potentiality was sufficient. The accidents weren't fatal, of course: that would have been too much. Slaughtering the peasantry was an acceptable demonstration of noble annoyance; slaughtering those of equal rank was considered boorish at best. Even so, those accidents were enough to take two of Yuriy's own brothers out of circulation, along with Ingvar and Andrey Yaroslavich and five of their major supporters. By the time those worthies returned to court life, Great Prince Yuriy had ensconced himself firmly, bribed the unswerving support of every *boyar* not already aligned to someone else, and re-enacted the ancient law which stated that a liege lord must be sound and whole in all his parts, thus neatly

13

excluding those who might have challenged him from doing so, at least until their injuries were healed and the scars no longer visible.

Khorlov's political life was boringly straightforward by comparison – or at least, it had been until now. Ivan stared through the vaulted shadows of the Council Chamber, studied the faces of *boyar* and *bogatyr'*, nobleman and warrior, and began compiling a mental list of who spoke in his favour, and who spoke against. It came as a reassuring surprise to discover that the Council was equally divided, more or less: there was little difference in the tone of voice of a man shouting disapproval at the Tsar, and the shouted disapproval of his neighbour that he should dare to do so. Most, indeed almost all, of the *bogatyri* warrior-heroes who had fought last winter against the Teutonic Knights were on Ivan's side, and that too was a comfort. He knew from his tutoring in the history of the antique Romans that a man backed by the army could survive –at least for a time – without the Senate. If Khorlov's High Council was no Roman Senate, its part-time army was likewise no Praetorian Guard: but the booty that army had earned from plundering the enemy camp was as good as any Caesar's bribe. The Knights of the Teutonic Order were a great deal less austere than their image as crusaders might have led anyone to believe, so that the loot taken from their tents had paid the bride-price of several daughters, and augmented the inheritance of several sons. It was those fathers and those sons who were cheering for Ivan now. Their cheers were strong and lusty, drowning out the reedy, reasoned cries of older men, and they would last . . .

. . . As long as the money did.

Ivan grimaced slightly, then forced himself to relax. He suspected that he could already see what would happen when all the shouting and complaints died down. What *always* happened. Both sides and the undecided would sit down together, drink a great deal too much wine and vodka, agree to differ, then do what Tsar Aleksandr had wanted all along, even though they would do it for the good of the realm rather than at the Tsar's command.

At least nobody had raised the subject of sorcery. For that at least Ivan was grateful, since it meant that Khorlov's Metropolitan Archbishop was not in the Council Chamber. Had he been there, Levon Popovich would never have let such a golden opportunity go by without expressing his views on Tsarevich Ivan and the Art Magic, on Mar'ya Morevna and the Art Magic, and on the Church's view of them both. It mattered not a whit to the Archbishop that it was mostly magic in the shape of the Firebird – together with courage, military skill and more than a little luck – which had saved him from being burned as a heretic if the Teutonic Knights and their inquisitors had managed to reach Khorlov. Ivan, his father the Tsar, Mar'ya Morevna and quite possibly Dmitriy Vasil'yevich Strel'tsin had all spoken to Metropolitan Levon, with varying degrees of severity and varying degrees of success. Those lectures had changed only the way he spoke aloud, not the way he thought inside. It was an unsettling truth that the Archbishop of Khorlov and the Holy Inquisition could well have become fast friends. At least, when they were not busy trying to burn one another as heretics or lapsed schismatics, or using the rack and the boot and the choking-pear to reinforce their own opinions of some obscure point of doctrine.

Ivan shrugged inwardly. The Metropolitan Archbishop, whoever he might be, was just one more weight around any Tsar of Khorlov's neck, and his father had successfully borne – or should that be tolerated? – Levon Popovich for almost his entire reign. There was one comfort: the Archbishop was old enough that he wouldn't plague more than a very few years of Ivan's reign, and after that, Ivan intended to appoint someone either more sensible in the ways of the world, or more amenable to the Tsar's suggestions.

Someone younger, anyway.

He was growing very tired of listening to the old voices uttering old opinions, refusing to change them because, like the Archbishop, not one of the old men on the Council had enough expectation of life left in him that any change would matter a damn. Ivan suspected that they knew the way his mind was working, and that was why they were so reluctant to have a new tsar forced on them by anything less permanent than the death of the last one.

'Father,' said Ivan quietly under cover of three yelling councillors who were all venerable enough to have learned better manners, 'Father, this is, er, a great honour you want to confer on me. But could you not have asked what *I* thought about it, before giving orders to the Council?'

15

Tsar Aleksandr glanced at the squabbling men in the body of the chamber; the argument, no longer anything to do with the succession, was spreading fast, and becoming more partisan with every *boyar* and *bogatyr'* who became involved in it. Then he swung around in his great chair and eyed his son from head to heels in much the way that Ivan had seen potential buyers eye their purchase. Speculative; wondering if it was worthwhile; suspecting it might be a waste of money. It was uncomfortable, and made him feel as much like a slave on the bidding-block as the Tsar had sometimes complained the responsibilities of the crown made *him* feel.

'No, my son, I could not. You might have refused the honour – and then I would have had to force you. This way, the councillors do it for me.'

Ivan was shocked at such duplicity. 'Force me? What makes you think that I would need to be forced?'

'The fact that you haven't accepted my bidding without question, for one,' said Tsar Aleksandr, a touch cool. 'I hadn't thought that you might prefer to become Tsar in the usual fashion, after my death. Are you so keen to see me in my grave?'

'Dear God, no! I just . . . I don't want to be the Tsar of Khorlov until I have to, that's all.'

'And that time is now, Vanya. You are my only son, and the child of my heart. But you are also bound to obey the command of your lord; I say you will be Tsar, and so you have to.'

Ivan took note that the Council had resolved its differences, at least for the present moment, and lowered his voice as the noise in the hall died down to a more normal murmur. 'But why do I have to? You're well, in good health, your . . .'

'. . . Mind is sound? Was that it?' The Tsar smiled faintly, the smile of a man enjoying a very private joke. 'Since you married Mar'ya Morevna, and she brought her spy service as part of her dowry, your simple, trusting old *batyushka* has known a great deal more of what's been going on in his domains and kremlin than he ever did before. I know what's been said about me over the past year. But you – bless you, Ivan, you refused to believe it.' The smile stretched briefly wider. 'Or at least, you made sure that nobody could report back that you *did* believe it.'

'You were testing me,' said Ivan slowly, feeling stupid that of all the possibilities, this one hadn't occurred to him. His eyes narrowed as he bit down on a surge of anger that left a taste like acid at the back of his throat. 'You were putting me through some sort of examination, to see if I was suitable to be made Tsar before I had no choice about it.'

'Yes.'

'Your idea?'

'Mine and Strel'tsin's. But mostly mine.'

'Then damn you.' Ivan shifted his glare to Dmitriy Vasil'yevich, who met it with equanimity. 'Damn you both.'

The High Steward bowed slightly, as though he had been complimented on some masterful piece of statecraft. Which, in a crooked way, he had. Certainly both the Tsar and his Steward had been more than satisfied with what they had learned about their Tsarevich – otherwise he wouldn't be standing here right now, about to be acclaimed as Tsar for all that he was bristling with outrage like a tail-trodden cat.

'Damn away, Ivan,' said Tsar Aleksandr, completely unruffled. 'It won't change a thing. At least you'll have good and trustworthy advisors to help you. Dmitriy Vasil'yevich knows more about how this realm should be run than both you and I together, and your wife has reigned alone in Koldunov since her father died. Never be so proud and confident that you won't ask them for advice. You have another advantage: a better relationship with the other Princes of the Rus than I could ever gain.'

'Have I?' said Ivan, and laughed hollowly. 'There's no love lost between me and Aleksandr Nevskiy, and as for Kiev and Novgorod – '

'Peace, Vanya. I have already told you that I know more than I take credit for. Trust me on this. There is a wariness among the other domains, true; but not the active dislike directed towards me. You stood side by side with Yuriy of Kiev and the Mikhaylovichi of Novgorod in the battle on the ice. More to the point, you were instrumental in that battle being a notable victory, and regardless of how Nevskiy's tame bookmen slant the history in his favour, they know it. They were there. Don't sell yourself short in the marketplace of alliances, my boy.'

The Council Chamber was almost completely silent now. It was not because the councillors and the *druzina* retinue were trying to listen in on the Tsar's conversation. Rather, they knew that those soft, murmured exchanges between Aleksandr and his son represented a crucial turning point in this whole affair, and they held still like men awaiting judgement in a court of law. Ivan leaned closer and spoke so quietly that not even Strel'tsin could hear him.

'One last question. Why now, and not later?'

It seemed as if Tsar Aleksandr had not heard the question, because he stared not at Ivan but past him for several seconds. Then his eyes focused on those of his son, and to Ivan's surprise and discomfort, their expression was one of shame. 'I am an old man, Ivan. One more old man among all these others. Khorlov will need a young man before long.'

'I don't understand.'

'You do not have the Sight.'

And Ivan understood. It was an ability that appeared now and then in the male line of the Khorlovskiy, just as some families occasionally produced children with red hair. Dmitriy Vasil'-yevich Strel'tsin had claimed to trace it back to the pagan priests of Uppsala, when all the Rus were just one tribe or clan among the North people, the Vikings. Not that the Sight was of any great use, to hear the stories go. It was of no use for finding lost things, or for seeing accurate events in the future. But it could cast a brightness or a shadow, an imitation of something good or bad waiting to happen. Even had it been more useful, the Sight was no gift to be wished on anyone. If one was minded to be that way, it was possible to worry about what that impending light or darkness might mean to the exclusion of all else, even sanity. That was the tale, anyway. If Tsar Aleksandr felt that a young tsar was needed to face whatever might come to pass tomorrow, next month, next year or whenever, then even though his reasoning might be almost impossible to explain to one without the Sight, that reasoning would be sound.

Ivan felt his courage shrivel up inside him, as it sometimes did when he stood on the open brink of a tall place, but rather than step back from the precipice, he jumped. 'I accept the charge,' he said, clearly enough to be heard all the way to the back of the Council Chamber, 'and I will be such a tsar as my father would wish.'

18

The words were simple; generations of ritual had not yet encrusted them with elaborate phrases of acceptance. But once those words were spoken, whether here and now in front of the Council and the *druzina*, or more usually intoned softly beside the bed wherein the last Tsar lay newly dead, the Prince who uttered them was Prince no longer.

Ivan was Tsar, by birth, by decree and – after an uncomfortable few seconds of hesitation among the councillors, and glances exchanged by the *boyaryy* and *bogatyri* of the Tsar's retinue – by popular acclaim. There was nothing else for them to do except stand up and cheer, or be attainted traitor. Despite the cold of the great wooden hall, roofed even now with a layer of snow that would not thaw for weeks, Ivan felt drops of sweat forming and flowing in the hollow of his back.

It was not entirely because of the too-apparent reluctance of his own Council to see him as Tsar, though that had a part in it. But Ivan had been watching his father's face as he took the plunge into the sea of monarchy, with all the shallows, rocks and sharks that waited for him there, and the expression he had glimpsed on his father's face was more than anything else responsible for the sweat and shivers down his spine. Because the relief on Tsar Aleksandr's face had been a terrible thing to see.

The Independent Tsardom of Khorlov;
June, AD 1237

'I think,' said Tsar Ivan wearily as he sprinkled sand on the wet ink of the last sheet of parchment and pushed it aside, 'that my father has to be commended.'

'I'd be the last to deny it,' said Mar'ya Morevna, pouring him a cup of wine without being asked and sliding it between his pen-cramped fingers. 'But why this time especially?'

Ivan drank the cup empty in three swallows and held it out for a refill before he replied. 'For not abdicating years ago. I'm sure that – Oh no you don't!'

This last was addressed to the Tsarevna Anastasya Ivanovna, who was in the process of trying to chew his most recently completed document to a malleable consistency. Mar'ya Morevna had brought the eighteen-month-old twins down to keep their father company and watch him at work, but this had proven of little interest to them. Far more interesting was what he was working with: pens with newly sharpened points that could be broken off with a satisfying snapping sound, molten sealing-wax simmering over alcohol lamps, a heavy silver inkwell containing reputedly indelible black ink and a bottle to refill it, containers of fine silver sand that could be rubbed into their own or preferably someone else's eyes, and the many sheets of paper that might prove edible if it was gummed and dribbled on for long enough. Ivan had never realised before how much entertainment could be extracted from the secretarial impedimenta of the realm, nor how dangerous to small fingers it could be.

He reached over and extracted his daughter from the middle of the next six months' legislation for the Tsardom of Khorlov, more than half inclined to leave her there just to see what might happen. Setting the child onto the floor, where she immediately toddled off to do something horrible to her brother, he slapped the stack of paperwork on which he had been working for the most part of the afternoon back into something resembling order. There was a similar stack waiting for the morning, but some servant had shown the sense to cover them all with a cloth and put a block of crystal as a weight on top, just to get them out of the Tsar's sight.

'I thought you were getting used to that side of ruling a domain, when we were living in Koldunov,' said Mar'ya Morevna. 'You're getting as good at it as Strel'tsin.'

If these were meant to be words of encouragement, they fell distinctly flat. 'Let's leave Dmitriy Vasil'yevich out of this, shall we? I've had enough of him for one day.' Ivan took a long pull at the replenished cup, as though the sharp tang of the white Krimean wine was able to take the bad taste of hard work out of his mind as well as his mouth. 'Your High Steward was a great deal more obliging than mine. Strel'tsin believes that I can best learn by doing; Fedor Konstantinovich at least had the good grace to try teaching me how to do what I was supposed to be learning.'

The First Minister had been with them for the greater part of the day: five hours of administration that had felt much longer before breaking for a hasty luncheon, then this damned scrivener's work for the rest of the day. It was at such times that Ivan understood most of all that air of relief he had seen on his father's face, when Tsar Aleksandr had finally pushed his abdication through the Council's doubts and disapprovals.

It was also at those times that he failed most completely to understand the attractions that kingship had for all the adventurers in the old *byliniy* tales. Those stories never went beyond golden thrones and golden crowns and golden cups. They never explained how the thrones hurt your backside worse than any saddle, and the crowns hurt your head worse than any helmet, and the cups hurt your mouth and jarred against your teeth unless you were very careful indeed, and because it was difficult to get the embossed interiors completely clean, they always gave a new cupful of wine the distinctive and – after maybe a week – far from pleasant flavour of the last one.

At least Khorlov's Great Crown didn't need to be worn more than once, at the coronation, and though some of the lesser crowns were almost as heavy, they were worn only when the proper occasion demanded it. For the rest of the time, when he wore anything that might be called a crown at all, Ivan had persuaded Strel'tsin – in his rôle of High Steward and custodian of customs and traditions – that a new, younger tsar with new, younger ideas could make do very nicely with a row of small, worked-gold plaques set into the band of his most favourite, and most comfortable, fur-brimmed hat. There was a clasp of gold and pearls already at the front of the hatband in the rather fetching style affected by the *voivodes* of Wallachia and Transylvania. It held a spray of egret and peacock feathers that reared as high as the hat's crown of handsomely figured velvet, so that the whole effect looked magnificent enough in its own way – without leaving a groove on its wearer's forehead.

For all that, Strel'tsin – who didn't have to wear the damned thing – had sniffed at the way it looked, and made observations about how it looked more appropriate to a heathen Saracen emir than a tsar of Holy Mother Russia. Ivan had thought about what the Wallachians would have said about that, and muttered something under his breath, and offered to lay the matter open to discussion.

It was a decision he came to regret. What the First Minister and High Steward had been pleased to call *discussions* – but which to anyone else would have been screaming arguments, except that there had never been a voice raised on any side – had gone back and forth over that decision for more than a week. They were still fresh enough in Ivan's memory that he didn't care even to be reminded of them, much less to be compared favourably to Dmitriy Vasil'yevich Strel'tsin.

That was another thing the stories didn't mention about being a tsar or a prince or a king: getting your own way was seldom as simple as saying 'do this' and watching it be done. It usually involved pen and ink and parchment. And discussion. Ivan had discovered that no matter how Strel'tsin pronounced that word, it was invariably spelt 'argument'.

As if keeping a leash on his annoyance with the realm's First Minister wasn't enough, there was the arbitration in pointless disputes between the *boyaryy* and lesser nobility with which he had to contend. In the old days, the two or more parties would simply have arranged alliances and then indulged in a vicious little private war, until enough peasant levies had been slaughtered to satisfy the injured dignity of either side. Ivan's grandfather Tsar Andrey had put a stop to that, reasoning rightly that if enough of the *boyaryy* got into altercation at the same time, there wouldn't be enough peasants left alive to bring in the harvest. It was a just, wise and well-reasoned law; but there were times, when one representative or another had been droning rights and precedents for an hour at a time, when he felt inclined to throw old Andrey's ruling out of the nearest window, give each man a sword, and let them fight it out in open court.

'At least you *are* learning,' said Mar'ya Morevna, patting his hand reassuringly. She smiled wickedly and sipped at her own wine. 'Even if it's only how to keep your face from showing what you're thinking.'

Ivan looked at her thoughtfully and hunched his shoulders, then pulled at his still-youthful short beard. '*Gospozha Tsaritsa*, you should be more respectful to the Tsar your husband,' he said, speaking a fair imitation of Strel'tsin in one of his drier and more creaky moods. Mar'ya Morevna exploded in a splutter that was half laughter, half wine, and almost completely a risk to the newly finished court papers. Ivan mopped briskly with the small cloth he kept for wiping ink off his fingers and nodded in shrivelled approval. 'Yes, Lady, like that. Much better. Ah, how quickly you learn the elevated manners of this court . . .'

'If you want to act the fool,' said Mar'ya Morevna when she finally stopped coughing, 'then go and do it for the children.'

'I should really save it for the Kievans,' Ivan said, grinning, 'except that they'd probably just believe it proved everything they've ever been told about the Tsar of Khorlov.'

'They're still testing?'

'Pushing me as hard as ever. They – or rather, their Great Prince safe at home in his kremlin palace – want to find out how much they can provoke me before honour and policy force me to react.'

' "Honour and policy"? Strel'tsin's words, I suppose.'

'Yes. Did I mention "strictures of diplomacy"?'

Mar'ya Morevna sighed. 'You didn't have to.'

Ivan was walking a tightrope every time one of the other city-states sent their delegation of ambassadors to Khorlov, meeting them with his frequent annoyance hidden by the bland diplomatic mask of the Tsar. He had been warned about such behaviour, but warning and defence were two very different things. The practice of testing a new ruler's fortitude was common enough, especially if that ruler was young. Too severe a response was just as damning as too weak, since while the latter might encourage other Princes to take liberties with the interpretation of a border, the former would discourage them from friendly alliances. He had to prove steady and reliable, while all the time controlling a desire to see the smiling, mocking envoys kicked out of his throne-room, out of his kremlin and all the way back to where they came from.

There was a thud, a splash and a pause just long enough for an intake of breath. Then a shrill wail of dismay came from somewhere underneath the table, and Mar'ya Morevna groaned in despair. 'There was a second bottle of ink on the table when I brought the children in, wasn't there?'

Ivan looked, and smiled wearily. 'There was. But it isn't there now.' The wail became a howl of fury, and he peered briefly at its source. 'Don't worry, Kolya,' he told his son the Tsarevich Nikolai Ivanovich, who was interspersing the dignity of his screams with a vigorous blowing of black bubbles, 'it's not really poisonous. Ink made with mashed oak-galls always tastes like that.'

'You should use the Chin ink-sticks,' said Mar'ya Morevna reprovingly. 'Then this sort of thing wouldn't happen.'

'It wouldn't happen if you hadn't brought your daughter in here, and if she then hadn't tried to drown my son and heir,' said Ivan.

'Where does this *your* and *my* business come from all of a sudden?' Mar'ya Morevna demanded, ready to bristle with fury at him. Then she saw the slow smile creeping over her husband's face and decided merely to kill him instead. She picked up the little Prince and wiped at him in a not very hopeful way before giving up, since she was merely spreading the ink into an even layer.

'It ought to wash off,' said Ivan, 'eventually.' He reached for the wine-flagon and poured himself another drink, topped up Mar'ya Morevna's goblet – and then turned curiously as the door of the chamber was swung open. Any interest they might have had in this visitor died at the sight of yet another long, grey beard. It wasn't High Steward Strel'tsin this time, but Archbishop Levon Popovich, the Metropolitan Patriarch of Khorlov, and probably the last person in the realm that the Tsar wanted to see after a long and busy day.

Both he and Mar'ya Morevna managed to restrain themselves from groaning as they rose and bowed to the old prelate, but Ivan managed to catch his wife's eye and wink. In situations such as this, it was a signal long arranged; at the second wink, she would suddenly remember or discover that both of them had to be urgently elsewhere, and they would be able to make some sort of hurried escape. For the minute, Ivan supposed he might as well give Archbishop Levon the few minutes needed for him to drink that last cupful of wine.

'Good evening, Eminence,' he said as politely as impatience would allow. 'You are well tonight?'

The Archbishop signed them both with the life-giving cross, then sat down and helped himself to what was left of the wine without so much as a by-your-leave. 'Well enough, Majesty, Highness,' he replied. 'Well enough.' He didn't look it; not that he seemed sick or anything so obvious, but there was an air of unease about him, the look of a man with bad news and no good way to tell it.

The silence dragged on until Ivan and Mar'ya Morevna were both feeling as uncomfortable as the Archbishop looked, and until it was obvious that subtle mental prompts to get on with whatever he had to say were not going to work. 'Well, but not comfortable, Eminence,' said Mar'ya Morevna at last. 'Something is troubling you. What is it? Politics? Or religion?'

Levon Popovich gave her a look that suggested he knew well enough when he was being made game of, no matter how gently. 'Neither, Highness. Or perhaps both. It concerns the Tsar's Majesty, and the well-being of his domains, and also it concerns you.'

'Put that way, Eminence, it sounds more like a matter for the High Council in full session than a private conversation here.'

'I think not.'

'Meaning?' Ivan drummed a quick tattoo on the table with his fingers. 'We could go round and round all night with such vague intimations, my lord Archbishop, and I have other things to concern me, with equal demands on my time. Come to the point.'

The Archbishop set down his cup with a small, solid sound and stared at the swirls the movement had caused in the surface of the wine, as though hoping for some sort of inspiration. None was forthcoming, and at last he looked Ivan full in the face and said, 'The point, Majesty, is the Art Magic.'

This time Ivan did not bother stifling his grunt of annoyance. 'The old bugbear again? I would have thought my father had put you right on that. More than once, if I remember properly.'

'He spoke to me on the subject, Majesty. As did your wife and your High Steward. And as you correctly recall, on more than one occasion. But on no occasion did any of those lectures "put me right", as you are pleased to call it.'

He picked up the wine-cup and drank, as Ivan had done before him, like a man trying to wash a bad taste from his mouth. Whether that bad taste came from the topic under discussion, or from the way he was speaking to his Tsar, Ivan wasn't sure. Not yet, at least; but knowing the Patriarch of Khorlov as he did, he felt sure that he would not remain long in ignorance.

'And what would you have me do about it, that my father did not?'

'The laws concerning wizardry, sorcery, call it what you will – '

'The Art Magic,' said Mar'ya Morevna flatly.

' – Are unacceptably lax in Khorlov and its dominions,' the Archbishop continued, as if she had never spoken.

25

'Unacceptably . . . Who says so?' There was a crack of the knout in Ivan's voice by now, but Levon Popovich either did not or preferred not to hear it, since it was not such a tone as temporal monarchs normally used to address their Archbishops.

'I do, Majesty.'

'You said nothing of this at the Council meeting when my father gave me the crown of Khorlov and those same dominions, and that was more than a year ago. Why so slow, Eminence?'

'It did not concern me then, since you had been practising the,' he glanced sidelong at Mar'ya Morevna, 'the Art Magic for some years with no harm either to yourself or others.'

'No harm? *No harm?*' Mar'ya Morevna flared up, losing all her patience and most of her manners. 'Glory to God, Eminence, if that's all you can say about Prince Ivan's employment of the Art, then you had best go read some of the chronicles that mention it. He saved this realm more than once, and probably your intolerant stiff neck as well!'

'The use of sorcery, *gospozha Tsaritsa*, is only just acceptable in a youthful and headstrong prince, but quite without precedent in a tsar.'

'Only because the precedent has not been set,' snapped Ivan. 'Consider that done, as of my coronation. Consider too the good that the Art has done for all the lands of the Rus – and I haven't heard you level any criticism at *them*, Eminence.'

'What is done in Kiev is on the head of the Prince of Kiev,' said Archbishop Levon. 'I am the Patriarch of Khorlov, and my concern is with Khorlov.'

'Your concern is with me.'

'Then Majesty, my concern is with your children as well.' He gazed thoughtfully at the two infants, who were being quiet for once and playing some game of their own invention with the quill-pens they had shattered beyond repair. 'Are they not being taught the, the Art?'

'Yes, Eminence, they are. As they learn to talk, and while they learn their letters.' Levon Popovich looked aghast at this frank admission, and Ivan guessed he had been expecting a far more reluctant response.

'Eminence,' said Mar'ya Morevna, trying to be reasonable after her earlier outburst, 'take heed of what has already been said. If

26

he knows enough of the least part of the Art Magic, the lowest peasant in Russia can create a little fire without resorting to flint and tinder; just enough to light a candle in the dark, or a stove to keep him warm. But most peasants do nothing of the sort. It involves too much effort, and an untrained, unfocused mind would simply find it too much trouble. Besides,' she forced her mouth to form a smile, though smiling at this wearisome priest was the last thing that she wanted to do, 'what would the poor *muzhik* do if he started the fire burning on the wrong side of his skin? So he uses flint and tinder after all, and lifts a burden with his arms rather than the power of his mind. But the potential is there.'

'It's that potential which has been so good for Russia, Eminence,' said Ivan. 'It has kept the Tatars at bay, except for their damned raids. They fear us, not so much as warrior adversaries but with the fear of superstition.'

'Majesty, all this is very well, and probably true in its context.' Mar'ya Morevna drew a sharp breath to say exactly what she thought of that malicious comment, but swallowed the words and sat back in her chair as Ivan waved her to silence. 'Sorcery, however, is intrinsically evil, and while good may have come from it, it is also well known that the devil can quote scripture for his own ends.'

'You would not have said that to my father.'

'I did, Majesty, and as frequently as courtesy permitted. But your father the old Tsar – who is I believe presently spending the evening of his years in the company of those other sorcerors, your brothers-in-law – was a man well advanced in years, with his own idiosyncratic notions of right and wrong.'

'A fine and well-turned speech, Eminence,' said Ivan in the low voice that betokened real anger. 'Plenty of long words. If you are claiming that my father's judgements were in error because of his age – '

'I did not say so, Majesty.'

'Just as well for you, a man far older than he is. I say to you, Eminence, that if you had ever shown the slightest talent for the Art yourself, you would not be complaining about me. And what you would not tell my father to his face, you will not say to me behind his back. Thank you, Eminence. You may go.'

'But Majesty – '

'Go. *Now!*' The Archbishop went, and rather faster than he had come in. Ivan slumped back in his chair, blew out a gusty breath and regardless of the paperwork already there, swung his boots up onto the table. 'I think,' he said to Mar'ya Morevna, 'that I might just have made myself an enemy.'

'I doubt it. But you may well have gained yourself a little more respect.'

'Maybe.' Ivan yawned, more from nervous reaction than from the weariness that had been creeping over him. 'If this is the life of a Tsar, beloved, then I could easily wish for something to break the monotony. An adventure. Or is that the sort of thing only permitted to princes, like magic?'

'Again, I doubt it.' Mar'ya Morevna made the sign of the life-giving cross quickly, and a little deflecting hand gesture after it that had nothing to do with religion. 'But avert, my dear. Be careful how you ask for things in such vague terms as that. Like the wishes in the old tales, you can easily get much more than you expect.'

'What I expect right now,' said Ivan, halfway through another yawn, 'is some sleep. The Kievans tomorrow, remember?' He stood up and stretched, then looked quizzically at Mar'ya Morevna. 'Was I ever "youthful and headstrong"?'

'The Archbishop was much more polite than me,' she said with a quick smile. 'What he really meant was "young and stupid". Which you were. Now, my beloved Tsar, sorceror, diplomat and doting parent, let's get you and this pair of reprobates to bed before you're all too asleep to care . . .'

28

Chapter Two

The Principality of Ryazan';
November, AD 1237

'We can't be any more ready than this,' said Mar'ya Morevna, snuggling deeper into the thick fur robe covering her armour as an errant breeze chilled the metal. She looked from side to side from her vantage point at the top of the hill, and nodded in satisfaction. 'So now we wait.'

Mar'ya Morevna spoke with a resignation that should have sounded odd in someone commonly called the fairest Princess in all the Russias. It sounded less odd when that same Princess was the wife of a Tsar, married for four years eventful enough that they often seemed like more, and the mother of twin children. It did not sound odd at all if one knew that she was not only a sorceress of note, but a renowned commander of armies.

One of those armies was drawn up in battle array before her, secure behind a barricade of ponderous wagons and a bristling fence of sharpened stakes that had been driven into the snowy ground at just the proper angle to pierce the chest of an oncoming horse. Wagons and stakes; such a barricade might have seemed hasty and makeshift, but there was nothing makeshift about this, or about the wagons.

They were fastened one to another with great chains of forged iron, and their sides, with loopholes through which archers could shoot, were built of timbers almost as thick as those of a kremlin wall. The *gulyagorod*, the 'walking city', had developed over time as defence against a mounted enemy, and it had proven its worth time and again, when the Polovtsy and the Pechenegs and the Kipchaqs and the Tatars came raiding into the lands of the Rus.

The right and left wings of the host were in extended order, out to either side and concealed in ambush by the thickly wooded hills. As much, at least, as seven thousand men in battle formation could be called concealed. Though the centre was exposed, an obvious target, the men in the woods were well hidden. That was the important point. Without knowing of their presence, an attacker would concentrate his assault on the *gulyagorod* fort, and thus be caught in the jaws of a closing trap.

Tsar Ivan breathed out a pale plume of breath that joined the accumulated frost already bleaching his beard white, and glanced dourly at his wife from under the peak of his helmet. 'Waiting,' he said. 'My favourite part of any battle.'

Mar'ya Morevna gazed at him for a moment, then raised one eyebrow. 'Any battle?' she echoed, teasing just ever so slightly. The world-weary tone of his voice amused her, for Ivan had seen precisely one battle before in all his life, and that had been the famous victory over the Teutonic Knights on the frozen river Nemen, not quite three years ago. Not that he or she – or anyone but Prince Aleksandr Nevskiy – had really been there, of course. At least if one believed the official chronicle – the one that had been written by Prince Aleksandr Nevskiy's official chronicler.

There was something to be said for bringing a court archivist on campaign, so long as you were absolutely sure that he was going to be recording a victory and not a defeat. Mar'ya Morevna thought about that, and then smiled inwardly. Nevskiy was thoroughly unlikable. No, she corrected herself, he was a detestable creature whose personal and political habits needed watching from a safe distance; but his chronicler's presence at that battle on the river, suggesting success instead of failure, was as close to a compliment as he was likely to offer any of the other Princes whose presence had been overlooked.

There would be no such overlooking today. Khorlov's own archivist was somewhere back with the baggage train, and if he didn't present himself for duty very soon, Mar'ya Morevna was going to have words about the man's continued employment. It was not as if he would have much to do. Except for Ivan and herself, there were no other persons of note. In the depths of winter, with nothing worth stealing beyond the walls of their kremlins and no way in which a mere raiding-party could breach those walls, not one of the Great Princes of the Rus had bothered to stir from beside his palace fire.

That had never been Mar'ya Morevna's way, and nor was it Ivan's. The harvest was in and safe, but those who gathered it, the peasants, were far from safe. Most of them lived in villages, not kremlins – and a Tatar raid that would never dare attack a kremlin could stamp a village flat before the snug, safe Prince and his snug, safe army could do anything to help. If that happened often enough, there would be no peasants left to sow the next harvest, never mind gather it. Better by far to bring a kremlin of armoured wagons out to meet the Tatars, and persuade them by force of arms to take their depredations somewhere else.

Mar'ya Morevna watched as her husband studied the disposition of the army for a few seconds more, frowning slightly as she had seen him do when playing chess, moving the pieces around inside his head to check possible moves against possible consequences. He was doing the same now, except that this time the pieces were human, and the moves and consequences were worse than simply losing a game. 'Last time, I saw only the aftermath,' he said. 'Just what did you do?'

'To Manguyu Temir? Besides kill him? I'd have thought that was enough.'

'Funny. You know what I mean. Tactics, strategies – which did you use? Or was it magic after all?'

'Only the magic of defeating superior numbers in open battle, and you don't need to be told now what that feels like.' Mar'ya Morevna looked thoughtful. 'And it wasn't that much of an open battle, really. We drew the Tatars onto a prepared position like this one, and when they started to hammer against the walls of the *gulyagorod*, we closed the wings of the host around them and shot them off their horses from three sides. And we kept shooting them, because they kept coming, until there were no more left.'

'Obliging of them.'

'It was all that their khan knew to do. Manguyu Temir wasn't one of the Great Khan's better generals, Vanya. Not like Sübötäi, the greatest of Chinghis-Khan's "Four Hounds". He was little more than a brigand commanding brigands.'

Ivan laughed at that. 'Did you see Manguyu Temir?' he said. 'Meet him, even?'

'No. Why?'

'Because I did, at a banquet almost five years ago. In Khorlov.' Mar'ya Morevna raised her eyebrows, but Ivan shrugged. 'It was a political thing,' he said dismissively, 'and he was better invited to it

31

than ignored. At least that way we knew where he was. But I remember that my father said exactly the same thing about him. That he was a brigand. But this present gang . . . I wonder about them. Brigands don't normally raid in winter.'

The point was well made, so that Mar'ya Morevna wondered why she hadn't considered it before. A raid was a raid, and she had given little thought to its background, just as someone confronted by a wasp didn't pause to think before swatting. But it was true enough. Tatars – and the various other tribes of nomadic bandits – usually came raiding between late spring and early autumn, choosing their time carefully so that their horses and the livestock they hoped to drive away wouldn't be wallowing in the mire created by thaw or rain at either end of summer, or wasting their time during the icy season when everything worth stealing was locked away from harm. Why indeed?

Her mind jumped to the last enemy who had attacked the Rus lands in winter. 'The Teutonic Knights could have made some agreement with the Tatars, after what I did to Grand Master von Salza.' Ivan looked dubious, and after a moment she nodded agreement. 'No indeed. Why wait? Even though he wouldn't dare come back himself, an arrangement like this could have been made at any time . . .'

When Hermann von Salza and the Knights of the Teutonic Order failed in their attempt to take possession of the rich border country, von Salza had been taken prisoner. Before releasing the German knight, Mar'ya Morevna had laid *dyusha-razryvyat'* on him, a soul-rending enchantment that would strike the Grand Master painfully dead if ever he should set foot in Russia again.

That should have kept him, and the Teutonic Knights, out of the Rus lands for the rest of von Salza's life, because the Order, still busily conquering – though they called it crusading – along the Baltic coast, required their leaders to lead, and from the front. Any leader who deputised such a responsibility, never mind one who handed it over to such dubious outsiders as the heathen Tatars, would soon find himself replaced as Grand Master by whichever ambitious deputy acted first. He would be lucky to avoid an accusation of heresy for working with the enemies of Christendom. There had – so far – been no further incursions under von Salza. But rumour had him ailing and likely soon to be replaced, and there was no reason for the soon-to-be Grand Master Konrad von Thuringia to hire Tatars for his dirty work, when he could do it all himself.

'This is nothing to do with the *Nyemetsi*,' said Ivan. He sounded almost regretful to accord the German knights even that much back-handed innocence. 'It's the damned Tatars, trying to catch us off guard. I said so when we first heard about the raid.'

'I still wonder how much of what we heard was true, and how much of it was just exaggeration.'

'About the Kipchaqs and the Volga Bulgars?' Ivan snorted. 'What I heard sounded too much like men trying to justify why they ran away.' He turned his head and spat into the snow, more for punctuation than anything else. 'They resisted, the resistance didn't work, so they took to their heels and made up tales of an overwhelming enemy so that they wouldn't look too much like cowards.'

Mar'ya Morevna looked at him sideways, her expression something that might have been disdain had it not been filtered through a crooked smile. 'My husband the hero,' she said, 'armed with a hero's hard words. To be Tsar for exactly one year and nine months, and to be already so practised and cynical. Well, my hero, no matter what happened, here we are, here we stay – and as I said before, here we wait. But we might as well be comfortable while we do it.' She muttered under her breath and made an elaborate gesture with her fingers that still managed to be graceful despite the padding of her heavy gauntlets.

Ivan felt a glow of warmth spread through him, as though someone had been warming his blood over a fire before running it back into his veins. It was comfortable indeed, but he still grimaced at the prospect of waiting. No matter what he might say, he hated waiting, here, outside the Council Chamber, inside a barrel floating on the Azov Sea. He had always hated it. There was usually something nasty at the end of it all.

They waited, and time passed, and nothing happened. An hour went by, and the army held its formation while the Russian winter gnawed even the Russian soldiers who had grown up enduring such cold as a dog will gnaw a bone, slowly wearing them away. As a second hour crawled to its weary conclusion, Ivan and Mar'ya

33

Morevna could see that the formations were beginning to lose their integrity. Even the thickest mantling of furs, and a lifetime of acquaintance with such weather, was no preparation for this. Standing with shield and spear at the ready in the closed ranks of an army expecting imminent attack, even the smallest movement of the air chilled the metal of weapons and armour, penetrating fur and mail together with blades of ice so that men grew weak as they bled heat instead of blood.

'What are those damned scouts doing?' snapped Mar'ya Morevna, staring at the empty horizon where white ground met grey sky. More than an hour ago, and then again twenty minutes after that, the silhouettes of first two and then five horsemen had skylined briefly, paused, presumably stared hard, then wheeled and ridden away. The silhouettes had been unmistakable, stocky men on stocky ponies. Tatar silhouettes, without doubt the outriders of the raiding party whose main body was somewhere beyond that grey-white line where earth and sky came together. She had instantly sent a party of Kipchaq mercenaries out to shadow the outriders and keep an eye on what they did and where they went. Since then there had been no further sign of either the hunters or the hunted, and though Mar'ya Morevna hadn't said so aloud, she was no longer quite sure which might be which. 'Our last report said that the Tatars were no more than half an hour away, and we've seen their outriders twice since then. They know we're here, so why aren't they advancing? If they're not, I want to know it. And why not, too. The bait's tempting enough.'

'Maybe they're waiting for the cold to cut us up, before they come in to finish the job,' said Ivan. 'It's already doing a fair enough job. Look at that.' He pointed to where another soldier, by no means the first, had fallen over in the snow, and was now being helped out of the battle-line and back towards the baggage-train and the braziers of charcoal that had been set up amongst the wagons.

Mar'ya Morevna opened her mouth to say something, then shut it again with a snap that told Ivan her unvoiced opinion had not been a favourable one. But she was having second thoughts. She had fought against the Tatars before, it was true; but that had been in summertime, where waiting for a few hours before the onset would have made little difference to the reception awaiting them.

34

A raid in winter was different, and different enough that no Rus commander had any experience of Tatar tactics in cold weather.

'You may just be right,' she said, unbuckling her helmet and taking refuge instead within the deep hood of her fur robe. Mar'ya Morevna did not suffer fools gladly, but she was a good enough general that she was willing to take advice, and even criticism if it was well-founded. 'Boris Petrovich, to me!'

Guard-Captain Fedorov saluted, then responded to the summons at a jog-trot which suggested he was more than glad to have a reason to move. He, and the other captains and commanders, had been standing a little distance off, with an air of enforced idleness that sat uncomfortably on their mailed shoulders. They had been eyeing the brazier that had been hauled up here to keep their liege lords warm, but since those same lords had been ignoring it, none of them wanted to be the first to weaken and move nearer the heat.

Mar'ya Morevna issued rapid orders, speaking with brisk eagerness as though ordering others to action was enough to keep her warm. 'Detach a troop of light horse. Send them out to beyond the skirmish-line where we last saw the Tatars – they'll know enough to proceed with caution from that point onwards, or at least they'd better. When they make contact, any contact at all, they're to break off and get back here. They are not to engage, on pain of my extreme displeasure – '

'And on pain of pain,' said Ivan; but the small, hard smile that was only a stretching of his lips leached any humour from the words. 'In the meanwhile, pull every fourth man out of the line and send him back to the wagons for hot soup, bread and a stoup of wine for himself and the others.' He looked at Federov and raised his eyebrows a fraction. 'We do have all those things ready, don't we, Captain?'

'Yes, Majesty,' said Captain Fedorov. 'The soup is in kettles on the braziers, all the rest is with the baggage train.'

'Good. Do it. If there's still no sign of the Tatars after they've eaten, bring them back to the braziers by squads, at whatever interval seems good to you and your serjeants. We won't weaken the formations any more by keeping the men warm than we will by letting them drop at their posts.'

'By your command. Majesty, Highness.' Fedorov saluted them

both and jogged away again in a rattle of armour and a spatter of snow.

'Smartly done, Vanya,' said Mar'ya Morevna. 'You may be only a tsar, but you've got the potential to be a good officer.' She grinned briefly. 'I may well make one of you yet. Now, what are *you* going to eat?'

Ivan gave her another of those humourless smiles, but this time it simply made him look wretched. 'Eat? As if I could. This is worse than waiting for the Teutonic Knights.' He took a deep breath and held it, like a man about to jump into deep water, then let the breath out slowly. The exercise failed to make him look any better, and Ivan knew it. He unhitched his own helmet and dropped it with a metallic crunch into the snow, pulled up his hood, then stared at Mar'ya Morevna from the refuge of its shadows. 'How long did it take before you got used to the waiting? How many battles?'

'Not enough,' said Mar'ya Morevna gently. 'I'm still not used to it. Just better than you at hiding that I'm not.' She peeled off one glove and touched his face, frowned, shivered, and made haste to pull the big fur-lined glove back on again. 'The charm is wearing thin. You're beginning to get cold. Be advised by me, and take some hot soup at least.'

Ivan's mouth quirked in distaste at the prospect. 'There's no guarantee it would stay down,' he said. 'I'll be advised by me, and have some hot wine instead.'

'I had the strangest feeling you might say that,' said Mar'ya Morevna, plainly trying to keep the disapproval out of her voice. 'Don't you think that something other than wine – or ale, or mead, or vodka – might make a pleasant change?'

'Not now.' Whether Ivan was referring to her suggestion, or the beginning of a plea he was hearing more and more frequently, the answer was the same. 'After the battle. But not now.'

He watched his wife sigh and turn away, relieved that she hadn't persisted with her disapproval. What if he drank a little too heavily, or a little too often? The Great Khan Ögotäi was well known for enjoying a cup or three. And anyway, Prince Vladimir of Kiev had said it for all Russians three hundred years and more ago, when he had rejected the Moslem religion because of its strictures on wine. 'Drinking,' he had said, 'is the joy of the Rus.'

Joy maybe, and sometimes even a necessary buffer against the harder realities of life, but Ivan knew better than to quote the old Prince's words to Mar'ya Morevna.

Then all thought of wine, or arguments concerning it, fled from his mind as the thin screech of a badly-blown trumpet blatted from the distant horizon. Ivan swung about and shaded his eyes in an attempt to see better. The troop of cavalry newly dispatched by Captain Fedorov had barely passed the wooden ramparts of the *gulyagorod*, and now they were reining back in confusion, uncertain whether to continue or return. 'One of theirs?' he said, aware that Mar'ya Morevna was standing at his side again.

'One of ours. That's not a Tatar war-horn. It sounds like our scouts have finally decided to come back and tell us what the hell is going on out there.'

She was right. For their own safety's sake, since the Kipchaqs and their ponies were just as stocky as any Tatar, the scouts carried Russian trumpets whose note was distinct and quite different from the deeper Tatar horns. Ivan felt momentarily foolish – he should have known the difference – then dismissed it. There was more at stake than the sound of a trumpet blown by a tone-deaf nomad mercenary.

'Eight went out,' he said, 'and I count eight coming back. So either they missed the Tatars altogether – or they've led them straight back here.' Mar'ya Morevna said nothing at first; then she breathed another sigh, this one of relief.

'No. They're alone. I can't see any movement beyond them, and anyway they aren't riding anything like fast enough for a hot pursuit.'

'They aren't exactly cantering either,' Ivan pointed out.

'Maybe they heard about the soup ration,' said Mar'ya Morevna drily. 'Do you want to stand here and speculate, or go down there and find out?'

'Stand here,' said Ivan. His wife gave him a quizzical glance. 'I am Tsar of Khorlov; they're no more than my paid servants. Let them come to me.'

'Well and indeed. Now why didn't *I* think of that?'

'If I said it was because you're not the Tsar, would you be insulted?'

'I might hit you, if that's any answer.' Then she grinned and, regardless of the amused and interested captains, who had finally given in and now huddled around the brazier close enough that their furs were in danger of singeing, put her arms around her husband's neck and kissed him full on the lips. 'That, my loved one, was for keeping your sense of humour at a time when jests are few on the ground.' She kissed him again. 'That was for trying to get used to the waiting.' The third kiss was more leisurely, and for all that the deeply hooded robes granted them a remarkable degree of privacy, it lasted long enough to make the captains politely turn away. 'And that,' said Mar'ya Morevna softly in the fur-rimmed darkness, 'was to keep us warm.'

The chiefmost of the Kipchaq scouts, being a nomad barbarian ignorant of any sort of civilised good manners, was sitting astride his shaggy little pony and staring at them both when Ivan and Mar'ya Morevna finally disentangled each other from that last kiss. Ivan emerged blinking from between the hoods, feeling intimately tousled and emphatically aroused, met the scout's incurious stare – and for all his dismissal of the Kipchaqs as just servants, coloured to the roots of his hair. If the man had said anything out of place, anything at all, there might have been violence; but the ignorance that had put him at risk was the Kipchaq's saviour. For all he knew, such behaviour was customary between Rus commanders on the eve of battle, and might well have been acceptable even if they weren't husband and wife.

'What's to report, Torghul?' said Mar'ya Morevna quickly. One glance at Ivan's face told her that the Tsar would need a few seconds to get his thoughts back in some sort of order – at least where the battle was concerned. Ivan nodded gratefully. She was right to usurp his authority of course, at least in this matter. It would be a minute or two before he could talk to the man without wondering what was going through the mind behind that flat-featured, droopy-moustached face; and besides, the Kipchaqs had been in her service before they had transferred their allegiance to the twin realms of Khorlov and Koldunov.

'Mongol ride that way, many many,' said the Kipchaq, waving his arm back eastward in the direction from which he had come. It took Ivan only an instant to substitute the unfamiliar name for the familiar. 'I, Torghul, see Mongol. All Kipchaq see, but I, only I alone am wise to count, ten times I count, count many horse, many

38

camel, many Mongol, a score of scores, ten times. Then Mongol see Kipchaq, chase Kipchaq. All Kipchaq go, swift to come away, but I, Torghul, more brave, less swift, I see no Mongol follow from first chase. So I, Torghul' – this time he thumped himself on the chest for emphasis – 'only I alone go back. And I see Mongol ride again, *that* way as always.' He stood in his stirrups and gestured again, not just towards where the Tatars were, but in a long sweep that encompassed almost half the horizon from east to west by southwest, around to where they were going.

'Ryazan',' said Mar'ya Morevna, and thumped her clenched fist against her thigh. 'Damn them, they're heading for Ryazan'! They're trying to sack the city!'

'And this is winter,' Ivan said grimly. 'Nobody expects a Tatar raid in winter. The gates will be open, the guards half-asleep . . . Never mind trying, the bastards might just do it! Unless we take them in flank, now.'

Mar'ya Morevna thanked Torghul, gave him silver – since it had become a custom that the nomad scouts were paid for their work on the spot – and dismissed him, then looked at Ivan sharply. 'Vanya, we're in a prepared position here. The whole purpose was to draw the Tatars into a trap. Now you're proposing we throw all that aside?'

'You heard the man. A score of scores, ten times. They have four thousand men, we have almost ten.'

'They have four thousand horses, we have three hundred. All the rest are foot. That's why we brought the *gulyagorod* all this way, why we set up this trap in the first place. To negate the advantage of mobility with the advantage of surprise.'

'So why are they ignoring a threat on their flank? Because they know we won't come after them? If that's the case, then I say let's go, and now. The advantage of surprise, remember?'

'Now you're starting to sound like one of your own *bogatyriy*,' said Mar'ya Morevna, and she didn't mean it as a compliment. 'Brave as badgers, every one of them, but solid oak between the ears and no more notion of tactics than a, than a – '

' – A bull at a gate?'

'I was going to say, a French knight who thinks his honour is at stake, but there's not much difference. Well, maybe there is. The bull knows to stop when it hurts.'

'And?'

'And the army stays right where it is. At least we know the Tatars haven't been waiting for us to freeze, and we know that they're outnumbered, even if not yet outmanoeuvred. But if they're using the route I think they are, we may be able to move the trap around the prey rather than have to entice it in when it won't be enticed.'

'That rather depends on how well you know this area.'

'Remember my map?' Ivan nodded; it was hard to forget a piece of cartography that could draw, correct and then re-draw itself as a landscape was described. Useful enough, but unsettling until one got used to it – and Ivan hadn't, not quite yet. 'I studied that map before we left Khorlov, so trust me. I know the Principality of Ryazan' well enough to suspect they're using the rivers.'

'Rivers. . . ?' echoed Ivan, not seeing the connection for an instant. Then it hit him. 'Of course! A city of any size will have a river running close by, or even through it, and with the ice as thick as it must be now, the Tatars might as well have a paved road laid down for them. And it's a road that goes around the hills and through the forests.'

'There. I was right. I'll teach you to be an officer and a tactician one of these fine days.'

'Hah. But what I can't understand is why they haven't tried a winter raid before, if everything is as convenient as all that? Tell me that, teacher.'

Mar'ya Morevna shrugged elaborately, as though it was expected of her. 'I would if I could. But I can't. Maybe it never occurred to them until now. Maybe there's some new small khan with new big ideas. Maybe Tatars don't need to keep warm in the winter as much as they used to. Take your pick.' She stalked towards the gaggle of captains, nodding acknowledgement of various salutes, and threw back her hood before settling her helmet – kept comfortably warm beside the brazier – back onto her carefully-braided hair. 'But before I come to any theoretical conclusions, I'm going to see for myself.'

'So am I,' said Ivan, reaching for his own helmet. The prospect of spying on a Tatar war-band was no less unnerving than standing and waiting for them had been, but with one vital difference: he would be *doing* something. No sooner had the words left his mouth than a bulky figure in furs and armour left his place beside the brazier and placed himself politely but firmly between Ivan and where the horses stood blanketed among the sheltering trees. Ivan finished the awkward task of buckling his helmet's chin-strap without taking off his gloves – kept warm by the heat of the glowing charcoal or not, he knew better than to touch bare metal with bare skin in the middle of winter – then smiled quickly at Petr Mikhailovich Akimov. 'Coming with us, Captain?'

'I may, Majesty. You, however, may not.' Akimov was to Khorlov and to Tsar Ivan what Fedorov was to Mar'ya Morevna: Captain of the Kremlin Guard, personal bodyguard, aide, adjutant, confidant and friend. He was also, Ivan noted as he moved sideways and Akimov followed suit, an obstruction.

'Would you like to explain that, Captain? While you help me into the saddle?' He sidestepped, and was blocked again.

'Majesty, there is no need for you to go on this, this sightseeing expedition, and no especial purpose to be gained by your presence.' Captain Akimov folded his arms with the sort of finality that was meant to indicate the matter was closed. 'Therefore you may not go.'

'May not?'

Akimov looked uncomfortable, but the big Cossack's jaw set in a stubborn clench that Ivan recognised only too easily. 'Then must not, Majesty.'

Ivan stared at his Captain-of-Guards and frowned, but for though his temper was fraying slightly he felt certain that losing it at Akimov would be to shoot at the wrong target. He suspected he knew the right target, but shooting at that one would have to wait until he and the rest of the army returned to Khorlov. '*Must* is not a word addressed by any Captain to his Tsar,' he said. 'By whose authority do you use it?'

'First Minister Strel'tsin, Majesty.' So the suspicion had been right. 'He told me that . . . that you are the Tsar of Khorlov, and may not place yourself at hazard for adventure's sake as though you were some private person.'

'May not, again. If it comes to that, then what about the Prince I was two years ago? The Prince who was heir to the throne and just as irreplaceable? Don't be ridiculous, man. Nobody – not Dmitriy Vasil'yevich Strel'tsin, not even my own father – spoke such words

41

to me before I went to travel in the Summer Country, or went to stand with the men of Khorlov when they faced the Teutonic Knights. And nobody will do it now. Get out of my way!' He barged past Akimov, and this time the Guard-Captain did not attempt to block his path. Ivan took a couple of strides further through the snow, then hesitated and looked back over his shoulder. 'Or better still, get yourself onto a horse.'

It was easy to follow the tracks left by the Kipchaq scouts. Torghul and his companions had not exercised much woodcraft in their flight from the Tatars, and whatever he had said, there was little evidence that Torghul or anyone else had been riding much more slowly than the rest. Ivan knew from his own experience that it was hard enough to travel at any speed on horseback through deep snow and between trees whose branches were heavily laden with yet more snow, and well-nigh impossible to do so and not leave a track plain enough for a blind man. Even had they not already known where the army was drawn up, the Tatars would have had no difficulty tracking the Kipchaqs – unless they didn't want or need to.

That too made perfect sense. If, as Mar'ya Morevna suspected, they were attempting a surprise assault on the city of Ryazan', then any turning aside from their line of march, any delay at all, would increase the risk of their being spotted, of the city being warned, and of the gates being shut and the ramparts manned and bristling by the time they reached their target.

If there was no possibility of an attack on the attackers, Ivan had already determined what he wanted to do: pull the army back under cover of the *gulyagorod*'s chained and armoured wagons until they were at a safe distance from the Tatars, then return to Khorlov as soon as Mar'ya Morevna could open a spell-Gate. At the same time he intended to send couriers not just to Ryazan', but to all the cities that might be at risk; and there were so many of those. If the Tatars were foiled in their assault on Ryazan', for whatever reason, they could break out with all the frightening speed of those tough little horses and be pouring through the unwarned, unbolted gates of Suzdal, or Rostov, or even Moscow – though whether even a Tatar would want to waste time on such an insignificant pest hole was a matter of debate.

'So what do *you* think?' asked Ivan as they trudged through the churned snow. Mar'ya Morevna looked at him, then grunted something that drifted away from her mouth as a grey swirl of breath when she saw that the question hadn't been addressed to her.

'I think that my hoofs are frozen off at the fetlocks, little master,' said Ivan's huge black horse, in that voice which was so like the bass register on a cathedral organ. Sivka shook his mane and snorted smoky disgust. 'Further, I think that this is a fearful time of year for making war, and a habit that I could wish you would break, since last time Khorlov went to war it was wintertime as well, and I think that you above anyone else would prefer to be back somewhere warm and comfortable.'

Ivan cuffed the stallion amiably on the neck, a blow that thumped against the massive slabs of muscle with as much effect as if he had hit Khorlov's kremlin wall. 'I ask an opinion, and I get a lecture. Do you spend time with Strel'tsin when I'm not watching?'

'He brings me apples,' said the horse, 'and we talk about things.'

Ivan heard Mar'ya Morevna snigger into her gloved hand and shot her a quick glare that was, as usual, entirely wasted. Sivka, and Chyornyy his brother, had both come from the horse-herds of the witch Baba Yaga. That in the view of many served to make them magical enough, but they also spoke the speech of men with more intelligence than some supposedly educated people that Ivan had met, and when pressed for speed could gallop into the worlds beyond the wide white world of Mother Russia, and emerge at their destination without the tiresome waste of time involved in actually covering the distance between two points on the map. They were also, and Sivka especially, eager and quick to learn from any and every source, whether it be swearing from the stable lads, court gossip from the grooms, or a greatly expanded prolix vocabulary from Dmitriy Vasil'yevich Strel'tsin.

There was another advantage, and that was something Sivka had told him, with some pride thrumming in the deep voice: only humans lied. The big black horse spoke only truth, not because he lacked the wit to make up a falsehood, far from it, but because he disdained to descend to the level of deceitful men. Of course, those truths could be embarrassing. Reining Sivka a little slower so that the others of the party – Mar'ya Morevna, the two Guard-Captains and a dozen mounted men-at-arms and *bogatyr'* heroes – could draw out of earshot, Ivan leaned forward in his saddle and said, 'What sort of things does the First Minister talk about?'

'The world,' said Sivka, his tone suggesting that none of Strel'tsin's choices of conversation held any great interest for him. 'The Tsardom. The Tsar . . .' The horse flicked one ear and turned his head to see Ivan's face a little better, then produced the whickering sound that passed for laughter. 'Not to worry, little master. You are a good tsar, or so he says.'

'I sometimes wondered.'

'So did he.'

'That isn't so – ' Ivan stopped, conscious of a strange sound so low and indistinct that he could not have said when it first became audible, but so all-pervading that the air throbbed with it. Up ahead, in the lee of a small stand of pine trees, Mar'ya Morevna and the rest of the scouting party were dismounting, tethering their horses and transferring cased bows and quivered arrows from their saddles to the proper loops and hooks that adorned their sword-belts. All of a sudden the views and opinions of Dmitriy Vasil'yevich Strel'tsin were no longer as important as they had seemed five seconds ago.

Captain Fedorov trudged over to him through snow that, up here where the trees had not grown close enough to screen the ground, lay almost hip-deep in the places where the Kipchaq horses had not trodden it down. 'Best that we walk from here, Majesty,' he said. Ivan nodded, thinking privately that 'wade' would be more accurate than 'walk'. Even so, Torghul and his Kipchaqs had come to the same conclusion, for the tracks that led onward from this same group of trees were those of men, not horses. He kneed Sivka forward to join the others, slipped from his saddle and began checking the state of his own weapons. Bow and arrows, shield and sword and dagger; it took less time than he might have wished, with that murmurous rumble of a multitude of hoofs dinning in his ears. Once noticed, the sound was unmistakable to anyone who had ever heard a mass of horsemen on the move before. There was a booming quality to the noise, a reverberation from the crust of ice that in warmer weather was the

River Okya. It thundered under the advancing Tatars as though they rode across the skin of a gigantic drum.

'Shall we go and see what we came to see?' said Tsar Ivan quietly, feeling not at all ready to do anything remotely brave. He glanced at his wife, at his captains, and at the warriors of his retinue, and found it no great comfort to observe that every one of them, even the senior captains Fedorov and Akimov, looked no more eager than did he. He eased his heavy war-sword a little way from its scabbard, making sure that he could draw it in a hurry if need be, then drew a deep breath that he hoped did not look *too* deep and set off up the hill.

It was not a long walk, even though it was hard work for people wearing furs and armour and boots better suited to a pair of stirrups than the treacherous footing of a frozen layer of pine needles underneath three feet and more of snow. Regardless of that snow, and the chill which struck through metal armour and into their very bones, they completed the last distance to the crest of the ridge flat on their bellies, using their shields as a crude form of sledge. Once there Ivan raised himself up, cautiously and somewhat hunched so that if any of the Tatars chanced to look upward, they would not see anything so distinctive as a human head visible on a sharply-defined skyline. He peered over, stared, snarled a single passionate oath and then flopped back, swearing softly and steadily between his teeth.

Mar'ya Morevna followed suit – almost exactly, even to the foul language. Ivan rolled sideways after a few minutes and lay there, heedless of the snow, disregarding the sound of the Tatars down in the river valley, just gazing at her face. 'I didn't listen to your Kipchaq carefully enough,' he said finally. 'What was it he said: "ten times I count, a score of scores, ten times"? I thought he meant four thousand men, counted ten times over to make sure. I was wrong.' He completed the roll until he lay on his back, staring up at the dull grey sky. '*Slava Bogu!* How I was wrong!' Slowly and sincerely, Ivan made the sign of the life-giving cross on his chest, then squirmed over again and looked once more down into the valley. 'Was Torghul right, do you think? Forty thousand? Or more?'

'More. It has to be more. The Okya's wide enough here, bank to bank, that we could see four thousand men all at a single glance. Whereas . . .'

Whereas the surface of the frozen river was invisible beneath the river that covered it, a river made up of men, and horses, and camels, and the great domed wagon-tents, cart-*yurtu*, drawn by yokes of oxen. A mist hung over the Tatar host, formed of breath and body heat and a haze of infinitesimal particles of ice and snow churned up by those hundreds of thousands of hoofs. Had the sun been able to break through the clouds, men and horses together would have glittered, for there were more weapons and more armoured mounts and riders down there than seemed possible in all the world. What was most terrible of all was the way that they rode in their blocks of ten, and one hundred, and one thousand, all in perfect discipline and perfect silence. There was the bellowing of oxen and the blared complaints of camels, the occasional shrill neigh of a horse, but no horns, no drums, no singing such as a Rus army might have found necessary accompaniment on the march. Just that unending rumble on the ice, a sound less like something made by men than by some unstoppable force of nature.

'This,' said Guard-Captain Akimov, 'is no raid. Look.'

'I don't need to look again,' mumbled Ivan, still shocked by the thought that he might in ignorance have brought ten thousand men up here, and the far worse thought of what would have happened to them. 'The numbers alone are enough to tell me that.'

'Your pardon, Majesty, but you do,' said Akimov. 'Both of you.'

They looked, and Mar'ya Morevna said something venomous in a language that was definitely not Slavonic. The words left her mouth on a curl of exhaled air that looked much more like smoke than seemed reasonable. Ivan was beyond swearing. One of the biggest cart-*yurtu* was making its laborious way along the ice right under where they lay, but it was not the ostentatious drapes of gold-worked silk on its felt dome that struck him speechless. It was the standard that swayed above it. A tall spear-shaft decorated with cross-pieces from which hung nine white plumes, it looked unimpressive by comparison with some of the embroidered banners used by the Rus Princes; but Ivan, and Mar'ya Morevna, and all of the others who saw it, knew what that banner was, and what it meant.

It was the *tuk*, the yak-tail standard that signified either the presence or the vested authority of the Great Khan, and it told those who watched, as clear as lettering, that this was without question an invasion.

'No raid indeed,' said Mar'ya Morevna grimly. She looked once more, briefly, with the reluctant fascination of someone unable to tear their gaze from some horrible sight, then pushed herself back from the crest of the hill. 'There's nothing we can do here, except get away to spread the warning. Understood?' That last comment was directed at the *bogatyri*, who were already looking restive at the prospect of retreat without action, and more restive still that the command should come not from their Tsar, but from a woman.

'Do as you are bid,' snapped Ivan. 'My wife's words are my words. Heed them.' He watched as the warriors shambled back down towards their horses, moving with an ill grace that had little to do this time with the deep snow. 'Damn them,' he said, but without heat. There was no point in criticising a dog for barking, or a *bogatyr*' hero for wanting to be heroic. 'Never mind that we don't have enough soldiers. If only we had the Firebird with us now, we could teach those shaggy swine down there to stay off the ice in a way they wouldn't forget.' He looked at his wife speculatively. 'Could you. . . ?'

'Maybe – and maybe not.' Mar'ya Morevna sounded dubious. 'We would need to destroy a major part of the host; destroy it so utterly that even the Tatars would be forced to fall back in disarray. And I doubt that even the Firebird could do that much. It might be better not to stir up this hornet's nest until we're more sure of what the hornets plan to do. They're riding towards Ryazan', there's no doubt about that. I'll open the Gate and we'll turn the army back towards Khorlov. You wanted to send couriers when we got back. Do you want to wait even that long? We could dispatch someone to warn Prince Roman Ingvarevich right now.'

'I had more than an ordinary courier in mind. Otherwise he may not listen.'

Mar'ya Morevna nodded. 'I think I know who you mean. But listen or not, we'll warn him anyway. Send one of the Kipchaqs now, and Volk Volkovich when we return to Khorlov. What Ingvarevich does after that is his own affair. And Vanya?'

'Yes?'

47

'When we get home, we'll keep the kremlin defences of Khorlov at readiness for a while, just to be safe. Oh, Vanya – remember in the summer, when you wished for an adventure? If this is it, then I think you may have more of an adventure than you want. And I think . . .' Mar'ya Morevna stared into space, then shook her head and began to move back down the slope.

'You think . . . what?'

'I've just seen what may be our whole world turned upside down. I don't know what I think any more. And that's what scares me most of all . . .'

Chapter Three

The Princely City of Ryazan';
December, AD 1237

Prince Roman Ingvarevich might have been Prince of Ryazan' and its dominions, held in fief from whichever of the Great Princes of Vladimir had granted them to him, but to Volk Volkovich he was just an irritant, no more or less than one of the fleas that plagued him in hot summer weather. The only drawback was that being a Prince, even though a puny one owing allegiance to those same lords of Vladimir, he could not be scratched in the way such fleas deserved. Instead he had to be respected, honoured, praised even; his opinions heard with something that approximated interest; even his stupidities – and there were many of those – ignored or at least set aside for later consideration.

The Grey Wolf was well aware that even the briefest appearance in his true shape would have gained him a great deal more attention than Prince Roman had granted him so far. He was also aware that Tsar Ivan of Khorlov had asked him not to do any such thing, purely as a favour between friends. Had Ivan *ordered* him, Volk Volkovich would have had few scruples about disobeying those orders if disobedience was more convenient than compliance, but the amiably phrased request had put rather a different complexion on things.

Volk Volkovich the Grey Wolf had been in Ivan's service for a year and a day, no longer. After that term of service was done, it had pleased him to stay in Khorlov, at least whenever the mood moved him. The young Tsarevich, as he had been then, was one of the few humans that Volk Volkovich liked – at least as anything other than a potential meal. Mar'ya Morevna was another, but the rest he considered no more than meat that walked about.

Service and companionship with Ivan Aleksandrovich of Khorlov had been entertaining, exciting, and could even – had the Grey Wolf been inclined that way – have been profitable. The young Tsar also appreciated and managed to tolerate the fact that his comrade was not a man who could take wolf's shape, but a wolf in the form of a man, and a Russian wolf at that, with all of a wolf's lack of any scruples that any mere man or woman could understand. Though he tried, sometimes very obviously, Ivan could not understand either; but at least he had the good grace to admit it, rather than trying to force human strictures of conscience or morality onto a creature that was very definitely not human.

Volk Volkovich had been called *oboroten'*, 'werewolf', by people who, since they knew the truth about him, should have known better. There were few enough of those in any case; Ivan's father Aleksandr the old Tsar, the High Stewards and Guard-Captains of both Khorlov and Koldunov, all of them knew that regardless of what form he took, the Grey Wolf was always more than he seemed. No-one else had ever seen him in the shape of anything other than an enormous wolf, and Tsar Ivan had let it be known that he preferred matters to remain that way.

'Let it be our little secret,' he had said, 'especially when you travel on the Tsardom's business.' Ivan had been smiling thinly as he said it, in a cool, confidential way that was anything but an indication of amusement. The Grey Wolf had grinned right back at him, because Tsar Ivan had stolen that smile from the Grey Wolf's own mother.

Volk Volkovich had kept their little secret, at least whenever there were unauthorised eyes about. It was a weapon as useful in its way as a dagger concealed in one boot, and much less likely to be discovered and thereby cause suspicion. In his rôle as courier for the Tsar, the Grey Wolf did not carry any hidden weapons at all. There was already little enough trust between Khorlov and the other domains of Russia, and never less than with the Great Princes of Vladimir and their subordinates. Even the lords of Kiev and Novgorod had demonstrated a certain warming of their attitude when Ivan took the crown, but not Yuriy and Yaroslav Vsevolodovich, who shared the throne of Vladimir.

Those two brothers, and their heir apparent Aleksandr Yaroslavich Nevskiy, had taken mortal offence at Ivan's suspicions concerning their dealings with the Tatars. He had never said or intimated anything aloud that could be reported back by the inevitable spies that every ruler had in every other ruler's kremlin, but his attitude alone had been enough to raise their collective hackles like cats in the presence of a dog. The city and domains of Vladimir claimed just as much resistance to the occasional Tatar incursions as did everyone else: yet it was strange how no harm ever befell them.

Fifteen years ago, while Chinghis-Khan's army was returning from its four-year raid into Afghanistan and Khwarizmid Persia, the Great Khan had granted permission for his generals Jebe and Sübötäi to make a sweep west and north that took them through the Crimea and Ukraine. Vladimir, right in the path of the approaching host, had been signally undamaged. Since that time, the city had never been assaulted by raiders, its villages had gone unscathed when others burned, and its cattle remained in their pastures whilst the herds belonging to other princes were driven away into the wilderness of the high steppe. But times change, and Khans change, and secret agreements made without witnesses become no longer as convenient as once they were. If the present route of the Tatar army on the Okya river was an indication, whatever pact the lords of Vladimir had made with the Great Khan Ögotäi was at an end.

The problem was convincing Roman Ingvarevich to believe it.

Roman Ingvarevich, Prince of Ryazan', leaned forward to better give the impression of looking down on the tall, tanned man in the grey furs who stood before him. He appeared not to like the fact that the man's eyes were almost on a level with his own, even though the Prince's chair was raised on a daïs higher than most Rus noblemen required. Or perhaps it was just that he didn't like the eyes themselves. They were emerald green, those eyes, brilliant as gemstones or as if they were illuminated from some source within, and though they were an unnatural colour when set in a man's face, the Prince had the look of someone trying to remember where he had seen such eyes before.

'Your eyes are strange, Volk Volkovich,' he said at last, giving way to curiosity.

'From my mother's side of the family, Highness,' said the Grey Wolf, bowing his head a little to conceal his smile. 'Breeding will always show, or so they say. But they serve me well enough.'

'And have you seen this Tatar horde, Volk Volkovich? Seen them with these eyes that serve you so well?'

51

'No, Highness.' The Grey Wolf drew himself up even straighter than before, disliking this petty Prince with an intensity he would normally have considered wasted energy. Dislike was all he could indulge at present, and it was difficult to keep the expression off a face unschooled in the diplomatic niceties. 'As I already told you,' – *three times now* – 'I am reporting what was described to me by the Tsar of Khorlov. *He* saw them, with *his* own eyes; as did his wife, his Captain-of-Guards, his Kipchaq scouts . . . One of whom was sent to you directly, if my memory serves me right.'

'Ah yes, the Kipchaq. You must understand, Volk Volkovich, that when a noble prince receives a wild-sounding message from an equally wild-looking messenger – a messenger, moreover, who did not possess any seal or signet of authority from his claimed lord – no ruler of any wit would give credence to such a tale without further verification.'

'Highness, he was sent direct from what might have been a battlefield. Of course he had no seal or signet; no ruler of the Rus carries such things on a campaign. So you ignored him?'

'Oh no, no. We would never be so rash, since inside even the most unlikely story one may find a kernel of truth.' Prince Roman Ingvarevich made a little gesture of regret, partly a shrug and partly a pout of his full lower lip. 'Of course, such kernels must be properly extracted . . .'

Volk Volkovich blinked, even his ruthless wolf's mind caught off guard by such an admission. 'Highness, do you mean to tell me – ' he began, then thought better of what he had been about to say. 'Where is the Kipchaq?'

Again the shrug and pout. 'Kipchaqs are a stubborn people, Volk Volkovich. This one more than most. By the time he told us what we wanted to know, there was no alternative left to us but to kill him. So we did.'

'Why?'

'We have already given our reasons. Do not presume too far on your status.'

'The Kipchaq was a messenger from Tsar Ivan of Khorlov, and he was sent in friendship to warn you of the Tatars!' snapped Volk Volkovich, shocked at himself for displaying so human an emotion as righteous indignation. Playing the part of an envoy was all very well, and moderately easy so long as his shape remained human, but to become so involved in it was rather a surprise. Especially when this stupid creature on the throne might be provoked into repeating – or at least attempting to repeat – what he had already done to the previous courier. 'By what right did you torture him and kill him?'

'The right of a prince who was justly suspicious of the motives of a realm that has never before displayed much . . . *friendship* to ours,' said Roman Ingvarevich. 'But rest assured, your Kipchaq gave his life in a worthy cause. Had there been more point in letting him live after the, ah, questioning, and after his answers had been confirmed as truth after all, then most certainly he would have gone free.'

'Highness, could you not have checked his message first, then tortured him afterwards if it proved false?' The Grey Wolf was sweet reason personified, trying to correct any problems that his outburst might have created for Ivan or himself. It was, he reflected, the verbal equivalent of showing your throat to the pack leader; he wouldn't tear it out, but being given the opportunity to do so was enough to calm him down. Not that the Grey Wolf had ever run with a pack in his life, but the instinctive reactions were more a part of him than ears or eyes or teeth.

'You may be the Tsar's courier, Volk Volkovich, but you are very innocent for all that.' The Grey Wolf closed his teeth on the snigger that threatened to burst past them at such magnanimous praise – and such a remarkable misreading of character.

'How so, Highness?'

'The Kipchaqs have been allies of the Rus for no more than twenty years, and that only because they learned we would pay them to act as scouts, as messengers, as . . . as mercenaries.' Roman Ingvarevich poured disgust into his voice as a man might pour honey onto a wheaten cake. 'Bound to their duty by silver, rather than by honour like an honest Russian *bogatyr*'. But those same Kipchaqs were enemies for more than two hundred years, and those who have not accepted payment are still enemies. Do you understand what we are saying, Volk Volkovich?'

'That you can't trust Kipchaqs, no matter whom they claim to serve?'

'Yes, exactly so. Were we to send out our household guard to investigate this supposed message sent in supposed friendship from a tsar whose father was well known to be no friend of ours? A message that without proof of its source or provenance was nothing more than unsubstantiated rumour? We think not. It might have been the bait to a trap. Such things have happened before, Volk Volkovich. The Kipchaqs are too close to the Tatars, both by race and by past alliance, for any prince to give much credence to their unsupported word.'

'Highness, there are Kipchaq riders in the army of Ryazan'. I saw them – indeed, they escorted me into the kremlin.'

'We employ them. We do not depend on them. A wolf can run with the hounds; that does not make him any less a wolf.'

Volk Volkovich the Grey Wolf choked his laughter into a fit of coughing. 'Oh, most assuredly, Highness,' he said when he was able, and when he was sure that he had his mirth back under control. 'There never was a word more truly spoken!' He cleared his throat and wiped his eyes, trying to put various thoughts to the back of his mind for fear they would make him burst out laughing all over again. Of all the proverbs that the Prince of Ryazan' could have trotted out, few were less appropriate or more apt. 'But you said, you confirmed the Kipchaq's message as truth?'

'We did, by sending out scouts towards the River Okya. You merely confirm the first message and what we have already learned.'

'That the Tatars are on their way here, even as we stand exchanging pleasantries?'

'We have warned you already to curb that impudent tongue, Volk Volkovich. You should be aware by now that the office of courier is not a refuge from our displeasure.'

As it is in more civilised places, thought the Grey Wolf. *Unlike Ryazan', concerned with its own importance because there is so very little of it*. He bowed, extending his right hand towards the floor in the proper fashion, and allowed the bow to be a degree lower than was proper so that respect became insolence. As he had expected, Roman Ingvarevich didn't notice, so accustomed was he to the elaborate flattery that puffed his minuscule station as an ally and very subordinate landlord of the Great Princes of Vladimir.

'Your pardon, Highness,' said Volk Volkovich. 'I spoke from my concern for Tsar Ivan's wish to offer aid and – '

'There will be no need for the Tsar of Khorlov to trouble himself on our account. The envoys sent to our – , to the city of Vladimir, will return at the head of an army long before the Tatars are close enough to threaten our walls.'

'Highness, you requested military assistance all the way from Vladimir?' Prince Roman looked evasive, then angry, but said nothing. 'But surely you can see from Tsar Ivan's letter that his lady wife can bring aid from Khorlov by way of a Gate, almost in the minute of your asking for it.'

'We have said already that there is no cause for your liege lord to trouble himself,' said Roman Ingvarevich testily. 'And we have no desire that any such trouble should involve the sorceress he is pleased to name as his wife.'

'That was uncalled-for, Highness, and I will do you the courtesy of forgetting that I heard it spoken,' said the Grey Wolf, and the faintest trace of a snarl that crept into his voice was enough to warn Roman Ingvarevich against taking offence at the criticism. Instead he scowled in silence for a few moments, then gestured towards the door of the throne-room.

'You may leave the Presence. Now.'

'And when I enter the presence of my lord the Tsar, I shall say only that you have asked for help from your overlords, as is right and proper for a vassal. Tsar Ivan will understand.'

'*Go!*'

The Grey Wolf bowed again, smiled a bitter, fanged smile at his own feet, then straightened up and went.

He went not merely from the palace and the kremlin, but from the city altogether. For three days, Khorlov's ambassador was nowhere to be found; and during those same three days, rumours about an approaching Tatar army were replaced by frightening stories from the steppes. Stories about a gigantic wolf that had appeared from nowhere to slaughter sheep and goats and cattle, rending open the pens where they had been herded at the start of winter to spread their gore and entrails far and wide.

On the fourth day, Volk Volkovich was back in his lodgings, able to look at the citizens of Ryazan' again without that hot green glitter creeping into his eyes, as it had done during his walk from the kremlin palace four days past. The tale of his meeting with their Prince had travelled before him, and in the course of that short walk from the kremlin gates to the shabby tavern where he slept, the Grey Wolf had been shown the true face of Prince Roman Ingvarevich's people. He had been sworn at, spat on, and even the children who knew nothing of politics had needed no encouragement from their parents – though some got it in plenty – to pelt the tall, grey-clad figure with bones and filth.

By the time he closed the tavern door behind him and leaned against it so that he could better resist the temptation to go back outside, Volk Volkovich knew that he wanted, needed, *had* to kill something. Staying in man's shape in those city streets, among those foul-mouthed, foul-minded people, had been one of the hardest things that he had ever done. He had wanted to howl, to close his fangs on meat, to wash the dirt from his grey furs with the blood of those who had put it there.

Instead he had gone out of the city and up to the snow-clad pastures, and there he had worked the frenzy of slaughter from his heart and mind until both were cool and calm again. And on the afternoon of the day that he returned, the first Tatars were seen by the Prince and people of Ryazan'.

The Grey Wolf was lolling in the shadows of the gate, watching. No-one paid him any heed, except perhaps to remark on the size of someone's dog, because the Grey Wolf was back in the shape he preferred best. Interpreting Tsar Ivan's instructions about shape-shifting in his own way, he had simply made certain that no-one actually *saw* the change take place. After that, and having made sure that his wolf-shape was smaller than usual, it was easy.

Every Rus from the youngest child to the oldest dodderer knew what a wolf looked like. But they also knew that wolves haunted the deep forests or the treeless steppes, like the one who had wreaked such destruction in the past few days. Wolves did not, ever, loaf on the shady side of a city square with their tongues hanging out, wagging their tails in a hopeful sort of way at passersby. He even barked when the alarm bell over the gate began a frantic clangour, although anyone who was watching closely might have seen that this dog was barking with the same awkward care as a man speaking a foreign language. Only a passing child noticed, and he was ignored, that at least once the barking dog cleared its throat and actually said, 'woof!'

Volk Volkovich the Grey Wolf was getting bold.

If the guards on the ramparts had been warned to look out for a horde of warriors darkening the snow from one horizon to the other, they were disappointed. Only three riders came trotting slowly towards Ryazan', black and distinct against the snow, their spears reversed and wrapped from butt to hand-grip with green pine branches, waving overhead in token of parley. But they were Tatars. These were no half-glimpsed shapes seen flitting along the skyline on their little horses, but envoys who rode boldly up to the city gates, demanding entrance in the name of the Great Khan. They spoke neither Uighur nor Türko-Mongol, the two languages that might have been expected – regardless of the fact that no-one on the city wall would have understood them until an interpreter was summoned, but then that was the Tatar way. Nor did they speak in any of the Slavonic Rus dialects. The words were Farsee, the lowest form of common trade-talk, and though it was a certain way of ensuring that their meaning was clear, it gave another and most insulting meaning to everything they said thereafter.

The envoys were two men and a woman, and save for white garments worn by the woman and the drooping moustaches worn by the men, there was little to choose between the three. Except for their green-garlanded spears, none of them was armed. There were no cased, stubby bows of wood and horn and sinew that were as thick through the limb as a child's arm; no quivers packed with iron-tipped arrows tempered in brine to better toughen them for punching through armour; no swords, either straight or curved; and above all, no armour. They wore only the conical, wide-brimmed Tatar sheepskin cap and two cross-wrapped coats laid fur-to-fur against the cold.

Volk Volkovich sat more upright and watched as they were invited into the city of Ryazan', his head on one side and his tongue lolling for all the world like any other brainless hunting dog. The envoys, he noted suspiciously, were all Mongols rather than Tatars, and he wondered if Prince Roman Ingvarevich knew or cared about the difference. Volk Volkovich knew. For all that the Rus used it as a convenient label on all nomadic raiders, *Tatars* were but one tribe of the many who had been absorbed into Chinghis-Khan Temüchin's empire. That these three were of the Khan's race rather than some subordinate people made the hackles start to rise along his spine. Someone, some cold intelligence beyond the distant hills, was playing a game with live pieces. Volk Volkovich the Grey Wolf had never thought, during his dealings with Tsarevich and then Tsar Ivan, that he would ever find human kind more savage than wolf-kind. He was learning otherwise.

The envoys looked around at Ryazan' and its breathlessly staring people without the interest that might have been expected had they been spies. Stocky in themselves, and made broad by those dense-furred coats, they had the flat, wide-cheekboned Mongol features and those slitted eyes that looked so sinister – but which the Grey Wolf knew from personal experience came more from squinting into a winter gale on the steppes, where every gust of wind was like a handful of razor-blades in the face.

His sharp ears heard the clatter of boots against the slabs of tree trunk that did duty for paving in Ryazan', along the single paved street in the city that led from the gate to the kremlin palace. Volk Volkovich swung his head around, just in time for the wolf's eyes that were so much keener than a man's to catch a glimpse of Prince Roman Ingvarevich's face. An instant later, when the Prince reached full view of the people by the gate, he was all smiles and amiable curiosity; but the set of his features when he was still out of their sight had been very, very different. Accompanied by a troop of soldiers, Roman Ingvarevich was flanked by his First Minister and his Captain-of-Guards, and he had been talking hurriedly to both those worthies as he strode down from the kremlin. There had been too much noise and babble for even the Grey Wolf to sort out the sense of what was being said, but his brief acquaintance with the Prince, and the grim looks of approval that his words had prompted in his two officials, did not bode well for the Tatars.

Prince Roman Ingvarevich of Ryazan' stopped well away from the three riders and planted his hands on his hips, eyeing them disdainfully for long enough that his honour-guard could take position all around the square and, significantly, across the gateway. The gates creaked, then slowly swung shut, their bars and bolts slamming into place with a heavy rattle and boom of metal against wood. One of the Tatars turned to watch, seeming unconcerned by what he must have guessed was an ominous precaution. The Grey Wolf watched him in turn, feeling again that shiver of apprehension. The man could not be blind to what was happening, and yet did nothing. That, in turn, had to mean he and his companions were expecting something of the sort. However far Roman Ingvarevich might go, they were prepared for it, and uncaring of the consequences.

'What is it that you want with us?' snapped the Prince of Ryazan', refusing to use Farsee and speaking instead in High Slavonic. Nor did he trouble with any of the usual preliminary courtesies that he had employed even to Volk Volkovich, that despised courier from the equally despised Tsardom of Khorlov.

The Tatars gazed impassively down at him, then at his Guard-Captain, his Minister, his soldiers and all the other people gathered around. It was the woman who spoke at last, and that in itself was as much an insult to Roman Ingvarevich as her own failure to use a preamble of flowery compliments – or her continued use of Farsee when the very fact of her reply made it apparent that she understood Slavonic well enough.

'Submission and tribute,' she said. There was a ripple of disbelief around the square, among the people who knew what had just been said. Among them was Volk Volkovich, who groaned inwardly and laid his head down on his paws, grateful more than ever that he wasn't a human and specifically a citizen of Ryazan'. He wasn't surprised; all of this had so far followed what he knew already of Tatar 'diplomacy', but knowing and actually being there to see were two very different things. Especially when the diplomacy was being exercised on someone like Prince Roman Ingvarevich.

That Prince went white, then red, at being addressed so by a Tatar and a woman, but managed to keep his voice more or less calm. 'And just who are you to speak to us so boldly?' he said, seeming to bite each word off and spit it out like bad meat.

'I am shaman to clan Korjagun.' There was pride in the Tatar's voice, whether from being a priest or because her clan had some importance mattered little to the Prince, since now he had a third reason to be insulted.

'A sorceress!' Roman Ingvarevich stared her up and down, curling his lower lip in a sneer, then turned to his citizens. 'They send a sorceress, and a pagan sorceress at that, to treat with

59

Christians!' He laughed derisively, and the guards and people dutifully joined in.

'What *I* am is nothing,' said the Tatar woman, holding up a small metal plaque that hung on a chain around her neck, a *paiza* or tablet of authority incised with the curling Uighur script. Even in the flat winter light, its polished surface gleamed dull gold. 'But I speak with the voice of the Orlok Sübötäi, who speaks with the voice of the Ilkhan Batu, who speaks with the voice of the Khakhan Ögotäi, Khan of all Khans of the Mongols, who speaks with the voice of Tängri, God of the Eternal Blue Sky. Hear their words.'

Prince Roman Ingvarevich had the look of a man who wanted to utter a sarcastic remark, but the sonorous roll of all those names, at least some of which he recognised and if at all sensible, feared, was enough to make him control his tongue. 'We will hear them,' he said.

'The Rus will make submission, and give tribute to the Khan of all Khans. The tribute shall be like the tithe you give willingly to your Church: one-tenth of all things, be they horses, or slaves, or grain, or beasts, or women. Your Church promises you Paradise in the next world; the Khan promises you life in this one. Choose: bow down, or be destroyed.'

'And those are the terms?' said Roman Ingvarevich, sounding as though he could not believe the evidence of his own ears.

'They are not terms. Terms may be negotiated. These may not.'

'And your Khan sent you to tell us this?'

'Yes.'

'Three of you, alone, into our city, to tell us this?'

'Yes.'

'He must care little for your safety.' There was an unpleasant smile beginning to take shape on the Prince's full mouth, a smile that Volk Volkovich fancied had been seen before by his unfortunate Kipchaq predecessor. The Tatars might have seen such expressions many times on the faces of their own ruthless comrades, but they seemed indifferent to its menace.

'We are the Khan's hounds,' said one of the two men, speaking for the first time and using good Russian to do it. 'When he tells us, *Come*, we come; when he tells us *Go*, we go; and when he tells us to leap into the fire, we do as we are bidden.'

There was a long silence after that; the Grey Wolf guessed that it was mostly disbelief from listeners who could never imagine themselves doing any such thing at any lord's command. They knew little about the Tatars.

'We are the Khan's arrows,' said the other man, also speaking Russian, and as well as any of the various Rus who listened to him, 'that he may let fly on a venture and not fear to lose, if that loss serves his purpose.'

'If your Khan has no more concern about your loss than that,' said Roman Ingvarevich, his voice taking on an ugly, husky tone, 'then why should I disappoint him?'

For the first time since Volk Volkovich had heard him speak, he forgot or no longer chose to use the plural of his princely dignity – and what *that* might mean, the Grey Wolf could only wonder. It was apparent from the man's words that he had completely failed to hear the threat or promise in what the Tatar had just told him. Whatever he did now, except submit, would be fatally wrong.

And being the sort of prince he was, Roman Ingvarevich did just that.

'Seize them!' he yelled, as everyone including the Grey Wolf – and probably the Tatar emissaries too – had been expecting since this conversation first began. Spear-butts swung and thudded, and the three riders were spilled from their saddles to sprawl at the Prince's scarlet-booted feet. His soldiers leapt on them, lifted them, looped cords around their wrists and ankles, then jerked the knots brutally tight and let them drop back into the snow. Roman Ingvarevich of Ryazan' looked down at them and smiled. 'Now that,' he said, 'is a better position to adopt when you dare to speak to me. Have you anything else to say? Any other wise observations? Threats? Pleas for mercy, perhaps?'

If you're expecting that, dear Prince, thought Volk Volkovich, scrambling to his feet and backing further into the shadows, *then best not hold your breath while you wait*. The Prince had just doomed himself and his entire city to whatever the Tatar army had been intending for it all along, except in the unlikely event of a surrender. The reason was obvious, made plain from the first by his treatment of the Kipchaq that Tsar Ivan had sent to warn him. Prince Roman Ingvarevich was totally ignorant of the numbers he faced, because he did not believe that what he had been told could possibly be the truth. Tsar Ivan himself teased his Kipchaq mercenaries for their practice of routinely doubling numbers encountered, or dangers faced, or hazards surmounted, all for the sake of justifying their desire for more than the silver he had already paid them. But he believed them more often than not, rather than automatically dismissing every word as a lie just because of their race. The Grey Wolf would not have been surprised to learn that the Prince of Ryazan' habitually halved, and then halved again, whatever he was told by a Kipchaq. He might, just might, live long enough to realise what a fatal mistake that had been, and yield up the city before Sübötäi or Burundai or Batu brought their boot down and ground every living thing within its walls out of existence.

Or then again – Volk Volkovich eyed the preparations that were being made – he might not.

A prince acting in the heat of passion after an insult might have made excuses afterwards for having his guards hack off the heads of whoever had insulted him. The Tatars, themselves notorious cutters-off of heads, might have understood and forgiven – assuming that the prince in question grovelled properly before the Khan and banged his forehead against the earth in the approved fashion.

What they were unlikely to forgive was the removal of their emissaries' heads not with the quick sweep of sword or axe, but slowly, under the teeth of a double-handed saw from the city's lumberyard.

A block of timber was brought and the two male Tatars were flung across it from opposite sides, with a broad plank laid flat from shoulder to shoulder across their necks to give the saw something to bite into before its blade reached flesh. Then at a gesture from Prince Roman Ingvarevich, two guardsmen grasped the handles of the saw, and fell to with a will until blood steamed in the cold air and sticky gobbets of meat mingled with the drifts of fresh pine sawdust, and the heads rolled free at last. The messy execution had fewer witnesses at the end than at the beginning, for citizens at first fascinated and later nauseated fled in ever-increasing numbers once the saw-blade passed through the plank and began to tear into the two human necks instead.

Even the Grey Wolf, though his mouth was watering as the

scent of freshly-butchered meat filled his nostrils, regarded the proceeding as a pointless shambles. He had never taken so long over killing even armoured men, and while he could understand the Prince's desire to strike terror into his enemies, such a desire made sense only if the terror would do some good. Volk Volkovich doubted that it would; no Rus could teach anything about inspiring dread to a host whose warriors, sixteen years past, had methodically, efficiently and systematically slaughtered the seven hundred thousand people who had crowded for safety behind the walls of the Persian city of Merv, simply to encourage the next city along their line of march to surrender more readily.

Prince Roman Ingvarevich looked on with an irritable air of vague dissatisfaction, vexed that from first to last the Tatars had made no sound. There was little point in creating original methods of putting people to death, when those on whom they were inflicted had the bad grace not to suffer.

'And the woman, Highness?' said his Captain-of-Guards. The Prince broke out of some private dream and glanced at her, hoping perhaps for more reaction to the beheadings than he had seen in the men under the blade. He was disappointed.

'Do your men want her?'

'No, Highness.' The man spoke with rather more emphasis than was truly needed, so that Volk Volkovich, listening with pricked grey ears from well out of sight, lolled his tongue and grinned nastily. It seemed that there were limits even to what the brutal and licentious soldiery would put up with. And perhaps, now that they had followed their Prince's orders and the deed was done, they were beginning to feel the first tiny prickles of apprehension that this might be seen – by someone their minds dared not specify – as more than was strictly necessary for justice.

'Then put her where she belongs.' The Captain looked blank for long enough to become a target for his Prince's unfocused frustration. '*Bolvan!* Idiot! On the horse!' The sound of the back-handed slap was louder than any other noise in the square since the soggy rasping of saw-teeth fell silent. 'Do I – do we have to explain every attempt at wit before we get some sort of response?'

The Guard-Captain shook his head, not in response to a question which in truth needed no answer, but to shift the stars that were floating across his vision. Cheated of pain from one source, Roman Ingvarevich had done his best to create it elsewhere; there had been the full weight of his arm and shoulder behind that blow, and for all his affected daintiness, the Prince of Ryazan' was no scented exquisite. The Captain's head was still ringing when he forced his mouth to say, 'Shall we tie her in place?'

'Yes. And tie that carrion to their horses as well. Then get them out of our city, and out of our sight.' Roman Ingvarevich turned away, nursing his knuckles – not even a prince can box the ears of a man in a helmet and mail hood without suffering the consequences – then swung back with a grin tugging his lips back from his teeth. It was such a grin as men might have called wolfish; though not in the Grey Wolf's hearing, if they valued their lives.

'No,' he said. 'Take off her boots, put her in the saddle, then *stitch* her feet onto the stirrups.'

It was done eventually, using coarse twine forced through holes made with a bradawl, and though it took three men to hold the horse's head, the Tatar woman herself put up no more resistance or sound than her two companions had done under the saw. Their headless corpses were slung unceremoniously over their horses' backs and strapped in place with stirrup leathers, and the severed heads were each tied to a loosely-flopping wrist with a braid of its late wearer's own long hair.

Volk Volkovich the Grey Wolf arose, yawned, stretched, and watched as the three horses and their grisly burdens were whipped away from the gates of Ryazan'. He was half-inclined to be just one more big dog of the many lurking around the Tatar camp when they arrived, unnoticed for the same reason that he had gone unseen here. Equally, he considered that Tsar Ivan would welcome a report of the past half-hour's proceedings. But there was one place he was now quite certain he did not want to remain, and that was within this city's walls. Especially after the Tatars arrived . . .

For all that he suspected it was closer than the Prince of Ryazan' believed, Volk Volkovich did not go looking for the Tatar *bok*, the encampment that would be large enough to look like a city made of tents. Nor did he take even the little time that would have been required to make his report back to Tsar Ivan Aleksandrovich in Khorlov. But he did get out of Ryazan', and that quickly.

Though the Grey Wolf had never seen a Tatar horde in action, he had read and been told enough before setting out on this dangerous duty to know how easily the fast-moving nomad horsemen could throw a circle of steel around their quarry, whether that was man or beast – or city under siege. They practised such manoeuvres in the hunting field, where the common soldiers could hone their skills with spear and bow, and the commanders of tens, of hundreds and of thousands could learn the art of tactical command.

The greatest hunt of all, the *nergei*, took place each year in autumn, to lay up stocks of dried and smoked meat for another long, cold winter on the open steppe. It would begin with an advance on a broad front that like a battlefield could be sometimes miles across, while the game was driven before them into a suitable killing ground that might have been chosen perhaps weeks beforehand. When that point was reached, the outer wings of the formation would curve around like pincers not on the prey, but beyond it. With wild animals, or with a city, that encirclement would close tight; when the object of the operation was an enemy army, the wings would remain open, craftily providing an escape route for panicked men who might otherwise gain the courage of despair and fight to the finish. Once the enemy broke and ran, what might have been a hard-won victory became just another leisurely hunt that might last for days on end . . .

He also knew that retaining his proper shape of wolf, or at least of wolfish dog, was not a guarantee of safety when – not if – the city fell. That dry stick Dmitriy Vasil'yevich Strel'tsin had personally warned him of it, driving home the message with a vigorous tapping on the page of one of his precious illuminated Persian chronicles. Chinghis-Khan's favourite grandson had been killed during the taking of the town of Bham'yan in Afghanistan, and in retaliation the Khan had obliterated the city so completely that when he was done with it, the site could have been ploughed, and sown, and given how well it had been fertilised with blood, brought forth an excellent crop of grain. By his command, no head was left on any body either human or animal. Nothing remained intact: neither the livestock nor the poultry, not even the dogs and cats which had survived being hunted by starving citizens during the siege. All, living or dead, were beheaded, and their heads added to the appalling, crow-haunted pyramid raised outside the flattened city as a memorial to that one young man.

The envoys Prince Roman Ingvarevich had killed might not have been the relatives of anyone important, although given the woman shaman's prideful announcement of the name of clan Korjagun, there was always that risk. But they had been Mongols, rather than some lesser and subordinate tribe. That was bad enough, but the manner of their dying and the insulting mutilations inflicted on the woman who was after all a priest, would have been enough to inspire the notion of pitiless reprisals even in a Rus commander's breast. How much more likely, then, that a Mongol khan would deal most savagely with the slayers of his kin.

The Grey Wolf intended to be there, to see and to report back what he saw to Tsar Ivan and thence to the other Princes of the Rus; but not, if possible, to be any more involved than that. Involvement in a massacre, even one of the strictly controlled and disciplined massacres conducted by the Tatars, was likely to prove unhealthy for even the most innocent bystander. And when he entered Prince Ivan's service, two years and more ago, the Grey Wolf had promised his mother that he would always be careful of his health . . .

For all that, he remained in wolf's shape. It made survival on the wild winter steppe that much easier. If they caught him, it might grant him no more safety from the Tatars than had he stayed in Ryazan', but first and most important, they had to catch him. He could run faster, see and hear better, smell what could be neither heard nor seen – and could rip the throat from any threat before it could even react to his presence. Even so, anyone who chanced to see him might have thought twice about being a threat. There was something unsettling about this wolf – and that he was a wolf rather than a dog was obvious, once he was back on the steppe or in the forests of pine or birch. A wolf within the confines of a city might be presumed to be a dog, but not the huge, loping grey shape that he had become. Volk Volkovich had returned not merely to his proper shape but to his proper size, which was big enough for him to have carried Prince Ivan on his back like a horse more than once. Even in Russia, few wolves were so big – and most of those were his relatives, of one degree or another – and even in Russia, no wolves whatsoever wore a backpack.

There was a perfectly good reason for the pack. When Volk Volkovich made his change from wolf to man, the man was naked save for a long mantle of grey wolf-fur. For most situations that was less than adequate. Hence the pack: it contained a shirt, a pair of under-drawers, the foot-wrappings that the Rus wore instead of stocking-hose, a tunic, trews and long, soft boots. All were the same soft grey as the fur of cloak or pelt, and by dint of much necessary practice during his service with Ivan of Khorlov, the Grey Wolf could transform himself from wolf to well-dressed man – or back again – in a matter of something less than three minutes. That had saved his life or his secrecy on more than one occasion, for adventuring with the Prince of Khorlov and his wife Mar'ya Morevna had been anything but dull.

It would do him no good right now; a wild wolf in the woods would have a better chance of watching undisturbed than either a man or a domestic animal associated in any way with the Principality of Ryazan'. Volk Volkovich wondered briefly whether he should find some way to dye himself blue, as he had done last year to great advantage when dealing with the Mongol clan Borjigun, Chinghis-Khan Temüchin's own people. His size and his – carefully-applied – colour had made them certain that he was an incarnation of their ancestral deity the Sky-Blue Wolf, and superstitious good manners had prevented them from wondering why their ancestor would not address them in their own language, but conversed instead in a debased and rather nasty form of Farsee. Or indeed how it was that, despite the legends stating that the Sky-Blue Wolf was female, she had through the passage of years become not apparently but rather obviously male.

The Grey Wolf sighed gustily; that was then, and much less vital and less dangerous than now. He began to dig a hole between the gnarled and tangled roots of the tallest pine tree he could see, and was forced to give up only when he reached soil frozen so hard that even his claws could make no impression in it. He shrugged off the pack and buried it there, marking the place and its environs not as a real wolf might, by pissing on the tree, but in his mind's eye. There might come a time when he might need that human clothing at a moment's notice, and he had no desire to waste the seconds he might not have to spare in running from tree to tree like a dog in a garden. Scraping the loose dirt back into place and stamping it down, the Grey Wolf rose up on his hind legs and shook the lower branches of the tree to bring down loose snow over the patch of raw, freshly-turned earth. He had no desire that some wandering Tatar should discover the pack; the colour of the garments it contained was muted, certainly, but at the same time they were well enough made, and of sufficiently fine material, that such a dull grey would be unusual and therefore distinctive. That was the sort of attention a spy could well do without.

His few preparations made, Volk Volkovich became completely what he had always been before he encountered Prince Ivan Aleksandrovich, and discovered the amusement to be gained from interacting with the petty politics of men. A great grey Russian wolf swung his long, fanged muzzle from side to side, testing the scents that hung in the cold, still air; then howled mournfully down the wind so that his fellows should know of his presence in their domain, trotted slowly over the crest of the hill, and vanished from sight among the dark, snow-laden trees.

The Tatar siege-lines closed around Ryazan' like a noose encircling an unwary throat. Nothing went into the city, and most assuredly nothing came out. The citizens and the Tatars just sat there, staring at each other over the cleared and empty ground that lay for more than a bowshot around the walls. Once in a while an optimistic flight of arrows might be exchanged, more as a relief from boredom than anything else, but for the most part it was as if one side or the other was waiting for some event that might break this stalemate before the action could properly begin. A sortie might have succeeded in breaking through for long enough that someone, perhaps Prince Roman Ingvarevich and a chosen few of his supporters, might have made good their escape; but the frightened townspeople were unwilling to leave the shelter of their wooden walls, and the Tatars seemed content to remain among their hunched felt tents, watching and waiting. There was nothing that a cavalry army, no matter how large, could do against a fortified city locked, bolted and ready for them. The only tactic possible was an escalade and pitched assault, but Ryazan' had the look of a place that would eat many, many lives before it was taken.

So they watched, and waited, and bided their time. If the folk of

Ryazan' were waiting for some response from Great Prince Yuriy of Vladimir, their suzerain lord pledged to their defence, they waited in vain. He had received the warning from Ryazan' of the coming of the Tatars on the same day as the news of the fall of the small town of Moscow, swallowed up without so much as a hesitation in the Tatar advance, and had gathered his armies in response. But then, either guided by the more craven among his council and *druzina* retinue or deeming his own princely neck of more importance than the survival of a vassal city – or of his own city, if it came to that – instead of coming to the rescue of Ryazan', or even staying to defend Vladimir, he retreated to a new headquarters on the River Sit and left Ryazan' to its fate.

That fate was not long in coming, for on the second day, the slow, creaking ox- and yak-drawn wagons of the Tatar siege train arrived. The engineers, not just Tatar and Mongol but lean Arabs of the annihilated Khwarizmid domains and small slant-eyed Chin men from the silk lands of far Kithai, unloaded their burdens, and made ready to ravage the city that lay before them as defenceless as a bride on her wedding night.

For half of the first day, the Grey Wolf watched these preparations with mild curiosity from the nest he had trampled for himself in the deep, drifted snow among the trees halfway up a convenient hill. Thereafter and by accident, he had an opportunity for closer observation. It was not his fault: he had taken care to bury his pack beneath a tree that was tall and massive enough to be more trouble to fell than it was worth in firewood. He hadn't considered the possibility that the Tatars might have more than kindling in mind.

The tall man on the small horse who came ambling through the snow-deep woods had not been looking for anything in particular. At least, so it seemed at first. But he was not carrying the bow that might have suggested he was hunting for something tastier than route-march rations. His appearance had come as something of a surprise even to the Grey Wolf's senses; snow had been falling since before dawn, descending in soft, sodden white whirls, and the rider had appeared out of the middle of one of them as though the snow had given him solid shape. There was a short-handled axe in his hand, and every now and then he would pass a tree, study it closely, then chop a pale blaze of bark from its trunk to mark it for . . .

What?

Volk Volkovich raised his nose and stared at the man on the horse, quite unseen under the layer of snow that lay unmelting on top of his own dense pelt. The dark patches of fur that in his wolf-shape did duty as eyebrows drew together in a frown as he watched the erratic to-and-fro wandering of the Tatar, and first one, then both triangular ears flicked up and forward at the repeated *chunk* of the axe. Green eyes that glowed inwardly with a light of their own watched the man as he worked his way through the tall timber, studying first one and then another before leaning over and swinging that broad-bladed axe. There was one tree in particular that the Grey Wolf was watching, and the Tatar horseman was drawing dangerously close to it.

Chunk went the axe-blade, and then again, twice in rapid succession. He was marking out tall, straight trees – regardless of whether they were pine or spruce or birch or whatever – and ignoring all the others. The tree where Volk Volkovich had buried his gear was just such a one: tall, straight and unmistakable. He had chosen it for just that reason, and now someone seemed likely to choose it again, for reasons of their own.

Angry, irritated or simply wary, the Grey Wolf eased himself from his bed of body-warmed snow and padded silently in the Tatar's wake.

A few minutes later the man suddenly reined his horse to a dead stop and twisted in his saddle to look behind him. The Grey Wolf, still mostly white from the blanket that had covered him while he dozed, froze in his tracks and became a part of the landscape. Only his eyes were alive, and more brilliantly, wickedly alive than usual. Whether he chose to run down his prey, or watch it and then let it go, the wolf in him was hunting.

And the prey knew he – or at least *something* – was there.

Without the thud of his horse's hoofs and the intermittent metallic clank of his axe-blade against wood, the snow-silence closed in around the Tatar and his mount like a stifling blanket. It was a silence where any sound, whether it was heartbeat, or breathing, or an imagined noise from somewhere unseen, would strike like a hammer in the stillness. One tree-branch, a scrawny old arm protruding from the blaze-mutilated body of its trunk, shifted ever so slightly so that the heavy sleeve of snow which clad it inches thick slid free and fell to the ground. The sound was no more than a slither and a muffled thump, but the Tatar all but jumped out of his own covering of furs and leather. He stood up in his stirrups and peered around him, while the axe gripped in his hand shifted its angle slightly, no longer a woodsman's tool but a horseman's weapon.

Volk Volkovich pressed lower against the drifted snow, and held his breath so that he would not be betrayed by the faint plumes of vapour from his nostrils. Not that any mere man could see them; men were so short-sighted, even those who, like the Tatars, boasted of the sharpness of their eyes. It was the horse that concerned him. Horses had to see a threat and run from it; men, scant generations removed from the hairy monkeys that his dire-wolf ancestors crunched up as snacks, still thought instinctively that climbing trees was their best defence. In boots, and gloves, and heavy coats. . . ? The Grey Wolf snorted a silent laugh, and squirmed closer. Able to climb or not, at least it meant they didn't think they had to see so far, or so well, or so quickly . . .

The Tatar called something into the woods, but his voice rang flat in the muffled stillness. The Farsee words soaked into the snow and choked to death within a hundred paces. If any of his companions were out there, they didn't hear him. Certainly they didn't reply. Volk Volkovich grinned with all his teeth, and went belly-flat in a drift of snow on the far side of a tree, and peered with one eye around the trunk, and watched.

The man's horse had seen nothing, heard nothing, and more importantly, smelt nothing, and its placid unconcern decided the Tatar at last. He shuffled back down into his saddle and continued about whatever task had brought him up out of the siege-camp, muttering to himself. The Grey Wolf had no need to understand the words to know what they were: morose griping about being jumpy in a strange place, what would your friends say, don't be so stupid, get on with this and get it over with and then you can get back to being beside a warm fire. Familiar words, grumbled low in the throat. He had heard them all before, and even sheared some of them in half at the source when he had to.

Chunk again, and another tree grew that handspan of white against the darkness of its trunk. The Tatar was definitely marking a particular shape of tree for a particular purpose, and the Grey Wolf wrinkled his brows as he tried to think of what they might be. Then that concern faded as something far more immediate took its place. For all his silent mocking of the short-sightedness of men, he had taken care over burying his pack in case just such a half-blind human should stumble across it; and this one was far from blind. The man stopped his horse again, without the nervous urgency of the last time, and peered down at the snow tumbled between the twisted roots of a very particular old tree.

The Grey Wolf went flat again, then flatter still, and swallowed to silence the deep growl that flowed up from the barrel of his chest.

The Tatar unhitched his spear from where it was thrust under the girths of his saddle, and poked curiously at the snow. The long iron point went through the snow, and then on into the ground, much more easily than would have been possible in mid-winter – unless someone or something had been digging there. Burying valuables in the face of a threatened attack was common enough that the man must have thought he had found such a treasure-trove, for he slid down from his horse's back and set about poking in the dirt with his sword-point as though there had never been a moment in the woods when he felt frightened.

Volk Volkovich the Grey Wolf curled back black lips from ragged white teeth and snarled softly. This time he wasn't quite so silent, and its sullen rumble echoed through the trees and made a noise that might have been mistaken for distant thunder.

The Tatar straightened up momentarily, but instead of looking into the woods he glanced up at the sky, sketched a salute with his sword and mumbled some rapid prayer to Tängri before returning to his digging. The loose soil crumbled away with surprising speed, so that it was only a few minutes before he rammed the sword into the ground and knelt to grub rapidly around the leather pack that seemed almost to float up and into view. If he was disappointed that it contained only clothing, the expression didn't show.

He didn't have time for fear – or even surprise, or any of the more appropriate emotions – when a gigantic grey shape blocked out the sky as it sprang straight for his throat. The man was a Tatar and a warrior worthy of the Great Khan's host: there was no scream of terror, no throwing up of hands in futile defence, only

72

a wild grab for his sword that all but put the Grey Wolf off his aim.

But not quite.

The sound of fanged jaws slamming shut was horribly similar to the sound the Tatar's axe had made, shearing chunks from trees.

The Grey Wolk clenched down and shook his head savagely, like a real dog worrying a rat or a toy dog killing a length of cloth. The juddering vibration scissored his huge carnassial teeth together until they grated on backbone, and the hands scrabbling wildly at his muzzle thrashed briefly with a quicker frenzy, then went limp and sagged away.

He sneezed blood, ran a long, pink tongue over the ragged spikes of his teeth, and glanced from side to side. By sheerest good fortune and thanks to that last stupid lunge for the discarded sword, he had hit the Tatar right over the patch of disturbed earth, and any fluids that had not flowed down his own gullet had soaked invisibly into the ground. After a sensible wait while the steaming damp patch cooled and froze, another shaking of snow would cover the evidence. Or at least, most of the evidence.

The Tatar pony had moved a wary few paces away, and was watching him as he made the shift from beast to man. Otherwise it hadn't moved. Volk Volkovich grinned at his own good luck, and the grin lasted all the way through the change. A Tatar mount had most likely seen and heard and smelt more death and destruction than one Russian wolf could provide in the course of a month, and even his smell was sufficiently unlike that of an ordinary wolf that the stumpy little horse was relatively unconcerned. He reached out and patted its nose, then shivered violently; but despite the cold that slapped at him the minute his skin was bare of fur, he didn't waste time in dressing since horses were hard to scandalise at the best of times, but easy to scare. Instead he gripped the animal's reins and walked it far enough away that what he intended to do next wouldn't provoke a panicked gallop into the next principality. Once the horse was securely tethered to a tree, and hobbled with the convenient coils of rope that he found near the top of one of the laden saddlebags, the Grey Wolf turned his attention back to its late rider.

The man was much of a size with himself, tall and lean but very broad in the shoulders from much use of the heavy Tatar bow. He wasn't really a Tatar at all – Volk Volkovich had fallen into that lazy Rus term of reference from habit and convenience – but a Türk of some sort from the high steppes. Stripping the corpse of its conveniently blood-free clothes, and noting idly that for some reason Türks kept themselves a good deal cleaner than their Mongol overlords, he stared at the drooping moustache and long braids of hair while an idea began to form inside his head.

Then he shifted back to the shape of the Grey Wolf, licked his lips, and fed full to bursting for the first time in a long, long while.

Volk Volkovich found out what the Tatar had been looking for within the next few hours, when a coffle of slaves came trudging through the woods to fell every tree that had been marked. By then he was riding a dead man's horse, carrying his weapons and wearing not only his clothing but his moustache and hair-braids as well. He had considered snipping them away skin and scalp and all, in the manner of the ancient Scythian people, but then decided against it. Untreated leather behaved strangely, and the last thing a spy could want would be for his disguise to fall off somewhere obvious and inconvenient. Instead, the carefully knife-shaved moustache was gummed onto his upper lip with pine resin, and the braids were plaited painfully but permanently into his own hair. It didn't matter much that the Grey Wolf's hair was grey regardless of its wearer's shape, and that the braids were black; he had seen enough men going badger-coloured that the difference was of small account. Anyway, the long-flapped Tatar cap was on top of everything, and anyone impudent enough to knock his hat off was someone impudent enough to kill.

The trees went crashing down one after another and were dragged away, sometimes by the slaves and sometimes by teams of horses or the complicated-looking two-humped camels that he had seen in the Tatar baggage train. The purpose of all that timber was not apparent while it was just newly felled, but once the Arabs and the Kithaiyan engineers got at it, the function became all too clear.

Siege engines did not have to be constructed of clean, planed, polished lengths of wood; raw trees with the bark still on were quite sufficient. All that mattered was length, and girth, and how hard and frequently they could shoot. Volk Volkovich mulled those phrases over in his mind as he constructed the preliminary wording of his report to Tsar Ivan, and decided that sardonic comparisons to the act of sex would not be well received. Even if successful penetration *was* the whole point of both procedures, Ivan would have found nothing remotely amusing about the rape of Ryazan'; it was too intimately close to the real thing.

The first engines that were constructed were simple traction siege-slings, long beams that were sometimes entire trimmed trees, set to pivot between a pair of braced uprights. A leather sling was fitted to the longer end, and ropes hung from the other. When those ropes were dragged violently downwards by a gang of slaves – of which the Tatars had an unlimited quantity – the farther end of the beam swung upwards hard and fast, and the sling whipped out in a long arc until it snapped open and released its missile.

They built twenty of those in the first afternoon alone, and put them to work hurling sawn-off sections of tree-trunk at Ryazan'. Even though Volk Volkovich was in human shape and no longer had enough hackles to be worth raising, they rose anyway. There was something terrifying about the leisurely curving flight of a chunk of timber, especially when you knew it weighed half as much as a man. And that was only the first day.

By the second day, the engineers had fussed and nagged for long enough that they had finally started to build their greater engines. Some of them were laying out positions with rod and measuring chain, others were supervising the bolting together of monstrous wooden boxes whose function was for the moment obscure; and a third group, assisted by the shamans from half a dozen tribes – including one woman who limped on feet that were thickly wrapped in bandages – were mixing grains and powders and thick black oils, and pouring the results of their mixing into pottery jars. Strangest of all were the hordes of men, and this time not just slaves, who had started digging with a frightening diligence that paid no heed to the iron-hard ground that turned all but the most persistent pick or shovel. They heaped the spoil into enormous piles of frost-crusted earth and stones that were too small to be of use as missiles for the great catapults.

The purpose of those heaps of rubbish became plain once the wooden boxes were complete. Crudely constructed of split logs held together by a framework of iron strips, their function was simply to hold vast quantities of anything remotely heavy: soil, stones, chunks of wood, anything at all. But they held that massive weight at the end of yet more sling-armed beams, and this time, once they were propped between their uprights, the missiles those slings could throw were not just half a man's weight. The huge counterpoise catapults flung rocks of two and even three hundred pounds that had been prised out of the ground, and most awesome of all, they did so in virtual silence. There was the squeal and creak of timber and cordage as the counterweight was released, and the gigantic muted rushing sound as the sling unfurled, but to Volk Volkovich it always seemed eerie that so much power should be expended for so little apparent effort.

When they began to sling what had been put in the pottery jars, he, a creature of magic and a companion to those familiar with the darker Arts, heartily wished himself elsewhere. Whatever those substances might have been when separate, once mixed together they were a terrifying compound that produced a monstrous bellowing sound as it left the catapults, and spewed a blazing trail of fire and smoke to mark its passage through the air. As each jar burst against its target – which was anywhere at all within the walls of Ryazan' – they exploded with a slamming detonation and a splash of yellow flame that erupted outward like ripples in a still pond. Volk Volkovich had watched half a dozen of them being shot into the city, and he could see nowhere that they had been extinguished – until there was nothing left for them to burn.

He went to and fro along the siege-lines with absolute impunity, speaking Farsee when any other soldier spoke to him, and for the rest of the time being a huge, harsh, gruff figure from one of the Blue Türk tribes, the sort of man who went untroubled without good reason to disturb what passed for his tranquillity. And as for the man he was pretending to be . . .

No-one noticed the difference.

In a raiding party, he might have been spotted within the first day; but in this host, the Golden Horde of that Batu Khan who was the eldest son of Chinghis-Khan's own eldest son, he found that he could go completely unnoticed. There were so many men and women of so many clans and tribes and races, that the absence of one or the presence of another went completely unremarked outside a small and immediate circle of companions.

Volk Volkovich soon learned to behave as a Tatar among the Tatars; that is, as one to whom the great God Tängri has gifted all the world, if that one is willing to wrest it from those who think their lands belong to them. It was a disturbing philosophy, and one which got into the brain and the blood so that he tended to snap at slaves and those of lesser race without even thinking that he had to play a part. Within three days, the part had begun to play him, and so well that accepting it was easy and rejecting it was hard.

The bombardment went on for five days, by both day and night. Once the great counterpoise catapults had been aligned, their engineers no longer needed to observe the fall of shot – although with the jars of Chinese fire, a man half-blind could have seen where they burst and burned. All they had to do was have their assigned slaves wind the engines back to the chosen setting, then load and loose. The magic of weight and speed and distance did the rest.

Prince Roman Ingvarevich's city of Ryazan' became a crawling lake of fire, hemmed in by its own walls as it blazed from end to end. It seemed to the Grey Wolf that there would be very little left to pillage once the horde finally broke through the walls, and he suggested it to one of the Chin-speaking Uighurs who was supervising the loading of yet another pottery jar of fire-compound. The man rightly paid him no heed while the missile was being loaded; a momentary lapse of concentration might have had the fire-pot dropped and smashed upon the ground, and Volk Volkovich fancied that its contents would be unselective about what it burned once it got loose. Only when the catapult had creaked and slung, and another long trail of oily black smoke had joined the scores already crisscrossing the grey sky, did the Uighur turn to stare at him as though he had lost his wits.

'Where were you when the orders were given out?' the man rasped in Farsee. 'Sleeping, uu? No,' he gave Volk Volkovich an odd, amused look, 'maybe not sleeping.'

'What makes you so sure of that, brother?'

The Uighur grinned. 'You still have a head on those broad shoulders. Now *my* commander would have lopped it off if you had so much as yawned while he was speaking, but maybe yours is more well-disposed to his men, uu?'

'I was,' said the Grey Wolf with all the dignity at his disposal, 'riding patrol with the others of my *arban*. And my commander. What were you doing that you didn't know it?'

'Hui! Working with these damned engineers, probably.'

'At least they know their business.'

'They still have heads, don't they?'

'Huu. Maybe they know their business too well.' Volk Volkovich glanced towards Ryazan' in time to see another fire-pot burst, its new gout of flame quickly lost amid the rest. Then he shrugged, dismissing such lesser mortals. 'I ask again, brother: what about our plunder?'

'Since you were too busy to hear the orders, brother, you had best know that there will be no plunder, not this time.'

'None?'

'None. When the assault breaches the walls, there will be no looting, no slaves, no hostages. Kill all and destroy all, says the *Sain* Khan. Would one called *Splendid* give such a command without good reason?'

'The Khan's reasons are the Khan's reasons,' said the Grey Wolf sagely, 'and who are we to question them? Thank you, brother, and good shooting.'

He wandered off, a man with nothing to do until the engineers were done with playing their artillery against the doomed city. Ryazan' was doomed indeed, though it had nothing to do with what Prince Roman Ingvarevich had done to the Tatar envoys. Had he merely sent them on their way laden with presents, but still with his refusal to submit to the Khan, the result would have been no different. Batu Khan had determined to practise what had proven so successful in the campaign against Islam; to offer the chance of surrender to the first city encountered, and if that chance was refused, then destroy it utterly and slaughter the inhabitants. The news would weaken the resolve of the next city, or the next, or the next, and as many would be obliterated as was necessary. There was far richer plunder to be had from a place completely undamaged by siege, and sooner or later, the citizens of such places would throw open their doors to the Golden Horde, and be glad to be alive to do so.

The assault went in that same afternoon, under an intensification of the bombardment so ferocious that Volk Volkovich saw several missiles collide in midair. When one or both of them were the Chinese fire-pots, the resultant explosion was spectacular indeed. He managed to keep clear of the escalade, not merely for his own safety's sake – the people of Ryazan' were somehow still able to shoot back – but also because he simply didn't want to see what was going to happen when the city fell at last. That he, the Grey Wolf, could be sickened by what men might do was ridiculous; but it was also true.

Some eighteen of the largest engines had shifted their point of aim under cover of the frenzy of that last barrage, and now a salvo of stones came lumbering ponderously down through the smoke-fouled air. Ryazan's wooden walls went crashing down in five separate places, so suddenly that the Rus defenders had not fully realised their defences had been breached before an entire *tuman* of ten thousand horsemen were pouring into the city streets. Anyone worth raping was raped in a perfunctory way, then wrenched forward by the hair to stretch their necks out under a descending blade. Others were herded at spear-point into the fires that still guttered all over the city, fires that sprang up anew when fuelled by human fat. The riders hunted men and women, priests and nuns and children up and down the spattered, smoking streets, trampling them with their horses or cutting them down with sword and axe and spear; not with any wild excitement, no more than any butcher hard at work, but merely harvesting as they had been told to do, as if they were men with scythes in a field of standing grain.

And one of them caught Prince Roman Ingvarevich alive.

Volk Volkovich saw the Prince a little later, and found that once again, he had to look up at him. Far up, this time, thirty feet above the ground and silhouetted against the sky; but even though he still lived, after a fashion, there was no recognition in the man's eyes. He would never recognise anything again, for whatever might have remained of his mind was concentrated entirely on the slender stake driving slowly upward through his guts.

Roman Ingvarevich had been given to Tängri of the Eternal Blue Sky, as a punishment for the insult he had visited on Tängri's priest. The shamans had gone into the woods and returned with a tall birch tree, slim and straight as a spear-shaft. They had trimmed it of its branches, whittled points at top and bottom, then greased one end carefully with sheep fat and rammed it into the

Prince of Ryazan'. After that they had hoisted the squirming, screeching burden up into Tängri's sky before ramming the other end into the ground. And there they left him, to the mercy of the crows, and the ravens, and his own weight. The Grey Wolf looked up once more, his face carefully disinterested, and turned his horse away, reflecting grimly that Roman Ingvarevich had several hours left to him in which to regret he was not heavier.

An instant later, Volk Volkovich regretted that he himself had not been more careful, or less proud, or even that his own fur was not so fine. He had reburied all of his other clothing, but he had been unable to force himself to put aside the splendid cloak that was his own pelt when in wolf's shape. And it was that cloak which had caught the eye of the drunken Mongol who came reeling towards him. The man had evidently been busy obeying his khan's commands, for he was smeared to the eyebrows with blood and other, far less pleasant, fluids. There was a stoneware vodka flask in one hand, and a notched sabre in the other, and a reek like that of an abbatoir hanging around him. It would have been an affront to the nostrils even of a human; to the Grey Wolf it was an outrage. In wolf-form or in man-form, whenever he killed, he washed; no wild beast would go through life smelling of his last kill, not if he wanted to make another one.

The Mongol shoved his flapped sheepskin cap more or less straight on his head, and gestured once again at the cloak. He said something that, not being Farsee, Volk Volkovich didn't understand; but the sense of the question was plain enough. He, Volk Volkovich, had looted a fine fur cloak, which was against orders, but the Mongol was willing to forget it and not report such a grievous breach of discipline if the cloak became his.

Volk Volkovich the Grey Wolf would as soon have given the man one of his eyes. That cloak was not just a garment; it was a part of him. And it was something that he could not have risked explaining, even had they a language in common and the Mongol warrior been stone-cold sober. 'No,' he said in Farsee, and shook his head.

The Mongol stopped smiling, glowered at him for a moment, then swigged more vodka and rattled out several sentences that were no longer a friendly suggestion about the ownership of the cloak. The way his sword stopped wavering about and became much more purposeful made even more sense than the words. Volk Volkovich grunted one of those noncommittal noises he had heard throughout the *bok* siege-camp, swung down from the horse's back and then, as though taken with second thoughts, gestured at the vodka flask.

'Where did you get that, brother?' he said. As he had begun to suspect, the Mongol understood Farsee well enough, and probably spoke it as well, except that he was not taking the trouble to do so right at the minute. The man's sullen face lightened as quickly as anger had shadowed it at the first sign of refusal, and he pointed towards the wrecked city.

Volk Volkovich glanced up at its impaled Prince, and shrugged. He was in a fouler frame of mind than he would have believed possible, and the awareness was stealing over him that there might be something in his own much vaunted claim to be not merely a wolf, but a *Russian* wolf. It was strange that the last time such a killing mood had come over him, Roman Ingvarevich and the people of his city had been responsible; now it was because the death of that Prince and those people and the destruction of their city had achieved some sort of backhanded revenge. Except that this level of vengeance was excessive, even for a Russian wolf.

He followed the Mongol into what remained of Ryazan', and into a wine shop. At least, he followed the man to the doorway of the shop and then stopped on the threshold with his nostrils twitching. The smoke-scarred interior was dark enough that not even he could make out more than a few vague details, and for that much he was grateful. He knew this shop, from his brief sojourn in the city as Tsar Ivan's envoy. There had been a family living here, and they had still been alive when the Golden Horde poured through the breached walls. They had even been alive for a little while after that, but from the smells assailing his sensitive nose, the Grey Wolf guessed that such a little while had still been far too long. There had been a family . . . A father, mother and two small daughters, and the father had been killed first. The others – but his nose had already told him much more than he wanted to know about what had happened to them before they died.

The Mongol came out of the shadows with an armful of bottles, grinning.

Then he screamed, briefly, at the horrific fanged thing with phosphor-yellow eyes, a thing which had been a man but was a man no longer, just before it lunged forward to tear the grin from his face and the face from his skull. The Grey Wolf spat foul-tasting meat onto the floor of the shop, wiped a dribble of blood from his chin, and leaned against the doorpost to watch his victim die.

He ached; his whole body ached. What had happened had not been a shape change, not quite; it had been some sort of horrible warping that allowed both sides of his nature to flow together. It had never happened before, but then he had never been so angry before. All the wolfish ruthlessness and the studied human cynicism had vanished in one hot red flare like the bursting of a Chinese fire-pot, and suddenly there was a wolf's muzzle, and a wolf's fangs, extruding from what was still mostly a human face. That had hurt. His limbs had tried to twist themselves into the animal configuration without changing from human shape, and the nails of both fingers and toes had become ragged claws bursting out through the leather of gloves and boots. That had hurt too. Biting off the Mongol's face had hurt most of all, for those wolf-teeth had been powered by the muscles of a human jaw poorly equipped for such savage work.

Volk Volkovich scrubbed at his own face with both hands, trying to rub some sort of proper feeling back into the outraged muscles. *So what if it hurt?* he thought. *Not enough has ever really hurt me, not so that I cared about anyone else.* The Mongol bubbled briefly, kicked, squirmed and died at last. The Grey Wolf stared down at the corpse, his face impassive. *And anyway, it felt much more right than using a sword would have done.*

He wrapped his cloak more closely about his shoulders and strode from the wine shop, taking the first steps on the long road back to Khorlov.

Chapter Four

**The Independent Tsardom of Khorlov;
January, AD 1241**

Tsar Ivan Aleksandrovich looked at the ciphered scroll and its goose-quill container, which half an hour before had arrived in Khorlov strapped to a homing pigeon's leg, then reached out to poke at it gingerly with the butt-end of a wooden pen. His expression was that of a man confronted by a venomous insect, rather than a scrap of parchment.

'More bad news?' Mar'ya Morevna had seen that expression, or variants of it, too many times in the past few years. Ivan dropped the pen with a clatter and watched it spin slowly on the tabletop, a compass needle with nothing left to point at.

'The worst,' he said quietly. 'Kiev has fallen.'

'*Slava Bogu!* That's impossible!' Dmitriy Vasil'yevich Strel'tsin made his pronouncement sound like the voice of God, and looked as though he was defying anyone to take issue with such certainty.

The young Tsar looked at his First Minister and shook his head. 'If denial could shape reality, I could believe you,' he said. 'But nothing in five years has stopped the Golden Horde, and I doubt that your claims can start now. They took Kiev last month, and kept on going as if the place was of no importance.'

'Kept on going?' Strel'tsin looked at his Tsar in disbelief. 'Where to, for God's sake? Will they *never* stop?'

Mar'ya Morevna pushed her chair back from the table and stood up, needing to make some movement however pointless rather than sit still listening to nonsense any more. For all his venerable years and accumulated wisdom, Strel'tsin could always be relied upon for stupid comments. 'They'll stop whenever they please, my dear First Minister,' she snapped. 'And as for where they might be going now, let me inform you that there is more to the wide white world than Mother Russia. I suspect the Tatars want all of it, or as much as they can take – and right now, whether you like the concept or not, they have Russia.'

'They don't have Khorlov,' Strel'tsin persisted.

Ivan groaned audibly. 'Dmitriy Vasil'yevich,' he said, 'that may just be because Khorlov isn't big enough to warrant their attention. Not when they have their gaze set on all of Europe. And let me be honest with you: I'm grateful. Tatar attention appears to be something very few people have survived.'

Ryazan' had been first, and though Ivan was not susceptible to nightmares brought on by even the most lurid second-hand descriptions – hardly surprising, given what personal adventures had befallen him – the Grey Wolf's report of siege and sack had given the young Tsar bad dreams and restless nights for almost a week afterwards. Moscow had been next, an unimportant little place swatted in passing for no other apparent reason than that it was there, and close enough, and the Golden Horde was passing by during an idle moment.

Vladimir had gone the same way as Ryazan' – the execution of the emissaries who came demanding surrender, followed by a brief siege of four days and then the obliteration of the city and everybody in it who was of no use as a slave. Rostov; Suzdal; Yaroslavl; Torzhok; Kozelsk, Pereyslavl; Glukhov; Khorobor; Chernigov; and now Kiev. All of those strong places with their high walls and fortified kremlin palaces; and the many others, large, small and insignificant. The list seemed endless, and it did not even begin to include the small towns and villages that were simply stamped out of existence without even the dignity of a formal assault.

Khorlov had as yet seen nothing of the invaders; and if the book-men and historical chroniclers were to be believed, there was no such thing as an invasion in any case. The vital word *conquest* was never used in their written records. A reader unaware of the truth of the situation, or unadvised by an eyewitness such as the Grey Wolf, might well have been led to believe that nothing worse had happened to all those cities than the armed robbery of a successful raid. Of course, that same reader might well have wondered at the continual success of the raiders, or the equally continual failure of the Rus Princes to do anything about their depredations – but such questions were not encouraged, indeed were dismissed, and often downright ignored.

What the chroniclers' refusal to answer or adopt could not conceal was the arrogant presence of Tatar couriers. These solitary men, mounted on fast horses and lightly armed as if they had nothing to fear, were riding to and fro across the face of Moist-Mother-Earth as if they owned it. Which was of course untrue.

Wasn't it. . . ?

Those who had thought so were mostly dead now, their cities in ruins, their people either slaves or corpses, and their treasure in the possession of the most successful robbers that the world had ever seen.

'If the Tatars come to Khorlov, Majesty, what will *you* do?' asked Strel'tsin.

The old man seemed slightly chastened, even though Ivan knew from past experience of the Chief Councillor's moods that it was always no more than a temporary change in manner. Tsar Ivan glanced at Mar'ya Morevna, who nodded in silent approval, then poured himself a fresh cup of wine and sipped it in slow deliberation while gazing calmly at the First Minister. He hoped that Strel'tsin hadn't heard the cup clink against his teeth as he drank, for now that the question had been asked, Ivan's intended response was making his hands shake.

'*When* the Tatars come to Khorlov, I will submit,' he said.

Dmitriy Vasil'yevich stared at his Tsar, then emitted a strangled sound of disbelief that could never have been described as a word. He controlled himself with an effort; although from the look on his face he would have preferred to have torn his beard in a formal display of indignation, Ivan suspected it would have had little of formality left in it. 'Majesty, you dare not – ' Ivan's eyebrows went up and Strel'tsin stuttered to a halt. 'I, er, that is, the Council would never permit it.'

'The Council has already been summoned to attend me,' said Ivan. 'Not that I intend to give them any choice in the matter.'

Strel'tsin took a deep breath. It did little to help his colour, which had gone pale except for two feverish spots of red below his eyes. 'Tsar Aleksandr would not have done this,' he said finally, knowing that Ivan could not deny such a statement without insult to his own father. Ivan did not give him even that much satisfaction.

'I know it,' he said. 'And so did he. That was why he abdicated in my favour. So that when the time came, Khorlov would have a tsar who could make such a decision.'

'He *knew*?'

'My father has the Sight, Dmitriy Vasil'yevich. You know that as well as I do, even though conveniently you appear to have forgotten the fact.'

'I remember well enough – '

'So much for convenience.'

' – But he would never have used it to justify the action of a coward!'

'Old man,' said Mar'ya Morevna, 'guard your tongue. You may be First Minister of this realm, its High Steward, Court Sorcerer, Castellan of Khorlov and sundry other things, but all those hats are worn by just one head, and heads can be removed.'

Shocked, Strel'tsin stared at Mar'ya Morevna, then turned to Ivan in the hope that he might take his wife to task for overstepping her authority outside her own domains. 'Majesty, surely . . .'

'Surely not,' said Ivan coldly. 'You presume too much on your age and long service, Dmitriy Vasil'yevich. Be more careful. I would not be faced with this decision if those so quick to voice opinions had been as quick to hear them.'

'After Ryazan' was destroyed,' said Mar'ya Morevna, 'we sent warnings to all the Princes of the Rus who rode with Khorlov against the Teutonic Knights.'

Ivan nodded gloomily. 'My father said that they might have better memories of that battle, and of me, than of other past dealings with this Tsardom. Except that they wouldn't listen! They – or their First Ministers – were too busy looking for the catch, the trick, the advantage for Khorlov and the loss to themselves. We could have made Russia a single mouthful big enough to make the Tatars choke on it, and instead we let them chew us up one bite at a time! So don't use the word "coward" to me. I may not be able to restore Kiev and all the other places that have been destroyed, but at least if I have the courage to put my self-esteem aside, I can prevent my own city from suffering the same fate.'

He stood up abruptly, drained his wine-cup to the dregs, and slammed it back against the table's surface hard enough for the little pigeon-borne scroll to leap off it. 'The Council will be waiting,' he said, and bent to lift the parchment from the floor and tuck it into the pocket of his belt. 'Your choice is a simple one, Dmitriy Vasil'yevich; either you support me, or oppose me. The time for standing to one side is past and gone.'

'Failing to support the Tsar's decision is treason,' said Strel'tsin. He spoke quickly, to forestall Mar'ya Morevna from saying the same thing, and bowed slightly in her direction. For all the hard words exchanged over the table, he was smiling, a small, dry curving of the lips but a smile nevertheless. 'And I have never yet failed to support the decisions of any Tsar of Khorlov' – Ivan opened his mouth to protest such an outrageous lie – 'when those decisions were wise, and worthy of support.'

Ivan shut his mouth again. He could not dispute the truth.

Tsar Ivan stared at his High Council, turning that scrap of parchment over and over between his fingers, and waited for a pause in the babble of conversation. Then realised after a few minutes that if he was going to wait for that, he would wait a very long time. Instead he got to his feet and gestured to Guard-Captain Akimov.

'*The Tsar! Silence for the Tsar!*' roared the Cossack in that same voice which Ivan had once heard carry clearly halfway across an engaged battlefront. It slapped through the Council Chamber and produced a sudden quiet not so much because that had been requested as because none of the councillors were capable of competing with that extraordinary bellow.

'Better,' said Ivan, and straightened his fur-trimmed crown to give his trembling hands something to do. 'Lords and gentlemen, I have called this meeting for reasons of safety and security.' If there had been discreet speculation beforehand, the Tsar's use of such ominous words sent a ripple of dismay through every councillor, young or old.

'The Tatars,' he continued, 'have passed through Russia like a storm sent by God as retribution for our sins – whatever those may be, to warrant such a severe punishment from so loving and merciful a deity.'

There was a flurry of moving hands as the Council in a body made the sign of the life-giving cross, though Ivan wasn't sure whether it was a reaction to his opinion of the Tatar invaders, or his faintly blasphemous view of God. *Perhaps Archbishop Levon Popovich was right*, he thought grimly, *perhaps working with the Art Magic does have an effect on your faith. Or perhaps encounters with good Christian people like the Teutonic Knights and their pets from the Holy Order of the Inquisition have more effect than that.* He gave them another chance to recover their composure before he went on; and took that opportunity to sit down himself, so that the slight tremor of his fingers was less apparent.

'Spies and other trusted agents have kept a close watch on their progress across Moist-Mother-Earth. I can tell you now that with the exception of a few garrisons, the bulk of their host has passed beyond the borders of Russia, heading westward towards the lands of Hungary, Wallachia, Poland and the Holy Roman Empire. The cities of Buda-Pest, Krakov, Vienna and many others lie before them.'

Ivan paused, listening to the undercurrent of murmuring and heard what he had expected. Not one man in the Council Chamber cared a whit about what was happening or might happen further west. The foremost hope voiced was the Tatars would find the lands of Europe so much more to their taste that they would settle there for good. The Tsar of Khorlov closed his eyes briefly to shut in a spasm of disgust with his own people.

'Councillors, it is my belief that they will find these western countries a far harder nut to crack than they found us.' There was a small hum of denial, but Ivan shook his head. 'The Princes of the Rus have become so used to feud and private war, or at the very least so used to distrusting one another in anticipation of such wars, that even in the face of Armageddon and the Judgement Day itself, I doubt that we could act together. The Kings and Dukes of Europe may have squabbled with each other just as much, but unlike us, they have also banded together in the common cause of their Crusades. What they have done once, they may do again – though whether it will be of any use against the Tatars, I can't say. But their cities and kremlins are walled with stone, not wood, and their lands are mountainous and thick with forests, a terrain less suited to the Tatar way of making war than our wide steppes.'

He paused again, and looked at his hands. Now that he was coming to the crunch, they had stopped shaking and were as steady as those of any man with a clear conscience. Ivan interlaced his fingers and flexed them outward until a couple of knuckles popped with a noise that was surprisingly loud in the intrigued silence of the chamber. The councillors were aware that he had called them here for more than a summary of what – he hoped – they all knew already; but Ivan knew the High Council of Khorlov well enough not to trust any optimistic assumptions. They all held their positions more by rank and inheritance than by ability, and though Ivan intended to change that situation, now was not the time. Thus for the most part the older *boyaryy* were comfortable, indolent and disinclined to change, while the younger *bogatyri* were warriors who viewed war with the starry eyes of ignorance. Too few of them had been with Ivan in the battle on the ice, and for all the fondness of Rus Princes for making small war on one another, Khorlov's Tsars had managed to avoid involvement in such pointless and unprofitable activity for long enough that most of these blindly courageous blockheads had never drawn their swords in action.

'The Tatars are gone, and we in Khorlov have not seen them pass us by. Be grateful for that respite, my lords and gentlemen. They will be back. If they are defeated in the west, they will fall back to regroup on the Russian steppes as they have done for the past three years. Even if their downfall is so complete that they return whence they came, to Sibir'ya and the high steppes of Asia, they will pass through Russia on the way. But if they conquer in the west, they will *still* need the steppes of Russia to raise their horses; and they have conquered all the lands of the Rus already.'

As Ivan had expected, there was a rumbling of disapproval at that. He had guessed right: the High Council of Khorlov, advisors to the Tsar on affairs of government and policy, either did not know or did not care to know what had been happening to other cities and domains. It had not happened to them, therefore it did not matter.

It had not happened to them *yet*.

'Last month they laid siege to Kiev,' he said. 'The siege lasted five days, before the city fell on the feast of St Nikolai. Now do you begin to understand me?' Ivan watched the effect of such blunt words with a detached, cool interest. For a few minutes it was like loosing a fox in a henhouse, and then one of the gabbling poultry thought to ask a sensible question at long last.

'Majesty, if the Tatars come to Khorlov, what can we do?'

In what sense do you mean 'we'? Ivan didn't voice the doubt aloud. He had prepared his speech for this moment with an actor's care, but now that the moment had arrived, like many actors he found that the lines had fled from memory. 'If by that you mean resist, then we – the Tsar and the Council and the people of Khorlov – can do nothing. Kiev tried to resist. Ryazan'; Vladimir – all the others. And what are they now, except names? Those cities are gone. Destroyed. Wiped from the face of the earth. I will not see that happen to Khorlov. So even though together we can do nothing, there is something that I as Tsar alone can do. When the Tatar envoys come to the gates with their demand to bow down and submit or be destroyed, I – '

His hands were shaking again, and he clenched them so tightly that his fingernails cut crescent welts into the palms, pressing them so hard against the arms of the chair that they might have been tied in place.

' – I will put my pride in the dust, and I will bow down to the Khan, and I will submit.'

As he walked from the kremlin to the Council Chamber, Ivan had tried to imagine what the uproar would sound like when it came. None of those imagined noises were adequate to describe the pandemonium that greeted his announcement, a cacophony of denials, refusals, jeering and formless howls of outrage beyond even Captain Akimov's ability to shout down. There were few words clear enough – or any louder than the rest – that they could be distinguished from the general clamour, but Ivan heard some of them; words no ruler wants to hear from those who are nominally his loyal supporters.

'Abdicate. . . ! Renegade. . . ! Coward. . . ! Traitor. . . !'

Warned in advance that there might be trouble at this Council meeting, Akimov had quadrupled the usual guard of honour; and on his own authority, had made sure that they were equipped not for parade, but for battle. It meant that by the time the shouting had begun to die down, the Tsar of Khorlov was flanked by two troops of armoured men, with a third ranged across the doors of the Council Chamber. The place became relatively quiet after that.

Ivan studied the rows of choleric faces, glistening with the sweat of righteous wrath, and found himself despairing of seeing even one that might understand an appeal to reason. There was such a thing as being a High Councillor for too long. It was becoming all too obvious why some Princes flew into those notable passions, had all their advisors slaughtered, and then appointed completely new ones. Such behaviour, while reprehensible, was not too far removed from the Tatar approach to military diplomacy: the example of their predecessors would serve to keep the replacements in order, for fear of the same treatment. Just so long as they didn't make a habit of it, those Princes were the ones with relatively stable reigns. It was the softhearted rulers who usually had trouble, because their nobility knew that taking liberties would not be punished as it deserved.

Looking from side to side, Ivan saw that all the doors had been secured; every single councillor was here; and Guard-Captain Akimov's men carried the only weapons . . . Then he stamped that overly appealing line of thought into the back of his mind before it could take the form of a quick rattle of commands that, from the look on his face, Akimov would not hesitate to obey. If he was going to act like a Tatar, then he might as well join forces with them rather than merely capitulate, and that would justify the cries of 'Traitor' more than anything else could do. It would have to be reason after all, though talking something like sense into heads that plainly had no room for it was not a task he relished.

The High Councillors of Khorlov conceded the point at last, though Ivan's throat was dry and hoarse by the time he was done with them. They had agreed to all his reasoning, and most of all that resistance was not just futile but suicidal, as witnessed by the ruins of so many cities. Those same ruins, and the death or flight of the Princes who had once ruled them, precluded any scornful fingers being pointed at Khorlov in later times. And men in chains could plan a future way to rid themselves of their fetters as dead men never could.

It had taken almost five hours, and in all that time – he was proud of it – he had not once resorted to the simple declaration of his rank and title as a reason for obedience. Dmitriy Vasil'yevich Strel'tsin had been equally proud, though Ivan was sure that his success here had condemned Tsarevich Nikolai to the same wearisome tuition in rhetoric and oratory that he had suffered as a boy. If it worked, then it worked, and the Prince would probably thank him for it later; although now he came to think along those lines, thanks to his own father had been the last thing in Ivan's mind when the lessons had begun.

What had made Ivan's task more delicate than almost anything else was the realisation that any consent had to be unanimous, otherwise there would always be at least one loudly righteous Council member who could make the others question their decision at any time he chose. But there had at last been no protests, no objections, and if the final murmur of compliance had been less than enthusiastic, at least it had been consistent.

Mar'ya Morevna had come into the chamber at some time during that five hours of debate, slipping quietly into an unoccupied chair near the door, and had brought the children with her. They had slept for most of the time, but Ivan had been grateful for her presence both then, and now that everything was settled, because as the day dragged on, an expression of friendly support had come to count for more than those of stern or scholarly approval worn by Akimov and Strel'tsin. But it was done at last, and hopefully Khorlov was safe. He had made it plain that if the Tatars did not offer their usual terms, then he would be the first to make them pay in blood for every span of ground they gained; but if that land could be bought more cheaply, then he for one would not scrutinise the bill too closely. That had provoked a weak laugh, but at least it could be recognised as such.

The young *bogatyr'* who stood up near the back of the chamber was not one Ivan recognised. Certainly he was not one of the warrior heroes who had fought the Teutonic Knights, every one of whom now made up the core of the new Tsar's *druzina* retinue. Now that the discussion was over and everyone was shifting about in their chairs to force movement back into arms and legs and specifically backsides that had been immobile for far too long, it would hardly have seemed worthy of note – except that this young man was moving too deliberately to be merely stretching his limbs, and those who had been sitting near him were visibly attempting to pull him back. He wasn't heading for the privy, then; anyway, he was going in the wrong direction. And if he was leaving the Council Chamber for any other reason, then he was gravely out of order to the point of open discourtesy. The Tsar left such meetings first, and only after they had been formally concluded.

'You, sir! Where are you going?' First Minister Strel'tsin was also on his feet and pointing with one finger so that there could be no mistake about the subject of his question. Even so the *bogatyr'*, already halfway to the door, turned around and gestured to himself as though he was not alone. There was something faintly insulting about the way he did so, and Strel'tsin seethed with all the affronted dignity of his rank. 'Yes, *gospodin*, you. This meeting is not over yet.'

'It is,' said the warrior. 'For me at least.'

Ivan stood up with a single smooth movement that betrayed nothing of his own stiff joints and stared at the *bogatyr'* through narrowed eyes. The man was no older than himself, and that meant he was a deal too young for such dramatic posturing, and quite possibly too young to have a place on the Council at all, unless . . .

'Your name, sir,' he said.

The young man looked at him, and the contempt in his eyes was a startling and rather shocking thing. 'Aleksey Mikhailovich Romanov,' the warrior replied, and then, as a deliberate after-thought, 'Majesty.'

Under Ivan's beard, a muscle twitched in his cheek. He had not heard such a tone of derision in a human voice since Hermann von Salza and Koshchey *Bessmyrtnyy* – even though Old Rattlebones scarcely counted as human. He could identify the young man now; the son of a *boyar* whose absence from the meeting on an excuse of some unspecified indisposition had been heartily welcomed, since Mikhail Petrovich Romanov was if anything more stiff-necked and honour-besotted than all the others put together. If he had been here, Ivan would still have been trying to insinuate some-thing remotely approaching common sense into the chunk of oak that did duty for his brain.

The son had agreed where his father would never have done, and now he knew the family, Ivan was surprised. Yet there was something not quite right about all this: first, the unexpected acceptance of a decision that had to be sticking in Aleksey Mikhailovich's throat just as much as it would have with his father; second, the blatant attempt to leave the meeting; and third, the subtle insults directed at the Tsar's person. That third case in particular could be dealt with easily enough, by any one of several penalties ranging from a fine, to loss of certain privileges of rank, to an actual stripping of property and titles.

And then it hit Ivan like a fist in the face. That was what he was supposed to do; and by so doing, forfeit the hard-won sympathies of the other council members for their young Tsar, the reasonable man wise beyond his years, forced by circumstances into an unpleasant decision. But not the Tsar whose response to criticism was to unleash the full weight of the law.

It wouldn't matter to any of them that he had not done so faced with their own provocations. It wouldn't matter that Aleksey Mikhailovich was going through the motions of an elaborate plan created by his own father, who didn't seem especially concerned about what might happen to his son. Ivan knew that none of it would matter, because those five hours had told him more about his own councillors than he had wanted to find out, and very little of it was to their credit.

And where was Aleksey going, anyway?

'I was going to do what any *bogatyr'* of honour would,' he said when the question was asked, speaking in a prim and self-important voice that sounded properly heroic but still managed to set Ivan's teeth on edge. 'It is my intent to find a Tatar and kill him, in vengeance for the dead of Mother Russia.' He stared defiantly at the Tsar for several seconds, then conceded the last word as though reluctantly parting with a high and thoroughly undeserved tribute. 'Majesty.'

Guard-Captain Akimov muttered under his breath and took a step forward with one hand going to the hilt of his sword, but Ivan hastily signalled him back, aware that allowing the realm's Captain-of-Guards to do no more than his duty was also enough to lose him all that hard-won favour. But it prompted the young *bogatyr'* to make his first mistake.

'Of course, if I had a stalwart body of paid soldiers to protect me,' said Aleksey Mikhailovich to the world at large, 'I would have no fear about making unpopular decisions either.'

'You have your soldiers, *boyar*'s son,' Ivan said. 'I've seen them. I've reviewed them. I've fought beside them in battle, which is more than you or your worthy father ever did. Is that what makes you so very righteous, Aleksey *bogatyr'*?'

He put his head on one side in the old way and gazed at the young warrior for a long moment before sinking the barb deep. 'What must it feel like, knowing that you have something still to prove, and not sure that you can? Yuriy of Vladimir left his city to be burned, so that he could meet the Tatars in open battle; but when it came to the push, he ran away, and when he died it was his own men who killed him for leading them to ruin.'

'I will know soon enough, Ivan Aleksandrovich,' Aleksey snapped, controlling himself with an effort. 'And better dead trying to be a hero, than alive knowing I am a coward.'

'How many will you take with you down that road? Just yourself – or the household retinue that may not think your glory is worth dying for?'

'If I die alone, then at least the Tatars will know that Khorlov had one man left among the sheep!' He wrenched himself away from yet another restraining hand, turned his back without the customary bow, and made for the door.

'Stand *still!*' Ivan hadn't guessed until that moment that he could match Akimov shout for shout. The guards at the doorway jumped to stop Aleksey from taking a single step further, grabbed him by the arms and swung him back to face his Tsar. 'Explain that!' said Ivan, although he had the horrible feeling that he knew the explanation already. He was right.

'I will wear my colours and carry my banner when I go into battle,' said the young *bogatyr'* with a pride that was sickening to hear, and left every word sitting like chilled lead in Ivan's stomach. This mad child had sat here for five hours, and had not listened to a single thing that had been said.

The voice from the doorway was not particularly loud, but it carried from one end of the chamber to the other, and it was as cold as ice. 'Let him go.'

The two soldiers holding Aleksey's arms knew that voice, and knew its tone, and released him without needing to be told a second time. The young man did not. He went through a ridiculous performance of straightening his garments and brushing imaginary dust off his crumpled sleeves before turning to leave – then stopped in his tracks.

The Tsaritsa Mar'ya Morevna stood in his way. Her twin children were by her side, and a sword was in her hands. She stared at Aleksey Mikhailovich with the same despising look of hatred he had directed at the Tsar her husband, then wrenched the weapon out of its scabbard and presented it to him hilt-foremost. 'Here,' she snapped, her voice hoarse with emotion. 'Take it.' The *bogatyr'* stared at the heavy pommel and cross-guard as though he had never seen a sword before, but made no move to accept the gift. 'Damn you, take it!'

Aleksey Mikhailovich closed his fingers on the grip, and as Mar'ya Morevna released the heavy blade, its point sagged forward as though taking aim at Princess Anastasya's head.

'That's right.' Mar'ya Morevna pushed the children forward. 'Kill them.'

'What?'

'I said *kill* them. That's what you were going to do, wasn't it?'

'No! Never!'

'I heard otherwise.'

'I don't make war on children! I didn't say anything like that. I was going to kill the Tatar . . .'

'A Tatar whose companions would kill you. And they would know from your accoutrements and banner where you came from. Well, what are you waiting for? Kill them both. You'll be saving them from rape, hero. Think of how much glory that will bring your name, since glory's all you care about.'

The sword clashed against the floor of the Council Chamber as Aleksey let it fall, then dropped to his knees in front of Mar'ya Morevna and bowed his head. 'Forgive me, Highness,' he whimpered. 'I . . . I didn't think.'

Mar'ya Morevna looked down at him with a strange expression that mingled sympathy and understanding in equal measure. All the hate was gone, as though it had never been there. 'The men of Russia seldom do, these past years,' she said softly, putting out one hand to ruffle his hair as she might have done to her own small son. 'And the women of Russia will long weep for it.'

Until their mother ushered them away, the two children stared curiously at the young *bogatyr'*. They had never seen a grown-up cry before.

Ivan released the breath he had been holding in a long hiss through his teeth, and indicated that Captain Akimov could lower his bow. If Aleksey Mikhailovich had been as mad as he had seemed, and tried to use the sword, the Cossack could probably have put an arrow into him before any harm was done. His hand was resting on his own sword-hilt; it was not unknown in the old times for a tsar to defend his decisions by right of combat, as the North People had done, and Ivan would have been defending more than a decision. The lives of everyone in his domains rested on not fighting the Tatars when they appeared, and if it was necessary to kill a member of his Council to make that point, he would do so. But it had to be in combat; an execution or worse, a simple disappearance of the sort that other Great Princes had arranged for their opponents, would not improve his already dubious standing.

Then he saw Mar'ya Morevna's clenched fist, and the hot blue sparks that drizzled from between her fingers, and wondered if either his sword or Akimov's arrow would have been needed at all. A mother defending her children had no need of due process of law, or of fearing loss of status, and he half-wished she had gone ahead and blown Romanov's head off. That young man and his ambitious father might yet prove troublesome. But not, at least, today.

The Independent Tsardom of Khorlov;
July, AD 1243

The bells of Khorlov's cathedral were striking for noon when the first spear-points glittered through a haze of dust and distance, and the nervous watchers on the ramparts got their first view of an enemy they had been expecting for almost two years. Why the Tatars had taken so long before turning their attention to Khorlov, not even Volk Volkovich the Grey Wolf had been able to learn, but they were here now. The bells stuttered to silence at once, halfway through the ringing of a complex change, and that elaborate tumble of notes from every bell in the cathedral tower became the single, sonorous tolling of the alarm tocsin.

The arrival of the Tatars was no surprise. Khorlov had been on a war footing for three days, ever since the first courier had reined his lathered horse to a skidding halt on the cobblestone paving outside the kremlin. Once the alarm had been raised, Tsar Ivan's first response had been to send out a screen of mounted scouts, Mar'ya Morevna's most trusted Kipchaq mercenaries for the most part, but all of them men who understood the Tatar way of making war from horseback. They had been reporting back assiduously ever since, and the first, most gratifying news had been about the small size of the approaching column.

At the same time, there were many more in that column than the customary two or three envoys who came with the usual demand for surrender. It was not beyond the bounds of possibility that another warlord like the late and unlamented Manguyu Temir had decided to turn some private profit. Ivan could not shake the uneasy suspicion that it was all just a little bit too easy. There was a doubt nagging at the back of his mind, a suggestion that had the Tatars meant real mischief, there would have been a deal less warning and fewer messengers left alive to bring the information back.

And then there was the band . . .

Though Ivan had said nothing one way or the other, Mar'ya Morevna had been openly sceptical – at least until the next two reports brought confirmation. This column of Tatars, though heavily armed and armoured, was nothing like the great host they had watched marching along the ice of the River Okya. It was far too small to pose a threat to a fortified city like Khorlov; and at least one-third of its men were in truth a mounted band.

One of the Kipchaqs, shaggier and more disreputable than the others, claimed that he had actually heard them playing, and claimed further that he had – at some risk to himself – sneaked close enough to be certain that what he was hearing was actually music, and not just the usual military signalling of kettledrum and trumpet.

Ivan was unsure how much he could believe. Certainly the band was real enough – while exaggeration was tolerated, downright invention was frowned upon – but without witnesses to corroborate the Kipchaq's familiar claim of courage above and beyond the call of duty, he was half-inclined to regard it as one more instance of a mercenary bragging in the hope of a bonus to his pay. The other half of that inclination persuaded him to cause the man to be paid some extra silver, in the hope of encouraging similar devotion among the other scouts. Assuming, of course, that it *was* devotion, and not just inventive lying.

'You,' said Mar'ya Morevna, when the Kipchaq had bowed himself out backwards and they were briefly alone, 'are getting soft.'

'I was exercising the Tsar's prerogative of rewarding virtue,' said Ivan, aware even as he spoke that the words sounded a touch stuffy. 'He might have been telling the truth about getting within bowshot to check what he'd seen.'

'And he might have been secure in the knowledge that since he was alone, you wouldn't know one way or the other.'

'Whatever.' Ivan shrugged. 'Truth or lie, it's not as if it cost the Exchequer a great deal of silver.' He leaned back in the great Chair of State that did duty as an informal throne, squirming slightly in yet another unsuccessful attempt to find some sitting position that was free of carvings poking him in the spine. Khorlov's throne was plated with gold and ornamented with enamel and precious stones, while the Chair of State was plain oak; other than that, there was very little to choose between them where discomfort was concerned. Ivan suspected that was quite deliberate, intended to enforce a regal posture. Certainly a relaxed slouch was impossible in either.

'Shall we go and watch our' – Mar'ya Morevna hesitated delicately on the choice of words – 'visitors?'

Ivan winced and sat bolt upright again. 'We might as well,' he said grimly, twisting to give the carved warriors marching across the seat-back a swift glare of disapproval. 'The only other choice is to sit in this thing until they're brought into the Presence.'

'You always complain about the formal thrones, and yet you never do anything about them,' said Mar'ya Morevna sweetly. 'Why not exercise another Tsar's prerogative and have somebody make you a cushion?'

'I couldn't do that,' said Ivan, shocked – and how much of that shock was genuine, and how much was feigned for good-humoured mockery, not even he could have said without pausing to think about it. 'The Tsars of Khorlov have always sat on – '

'Damnably uncomfortable chairs – '

' – Elaborately carved thrones.'

'So if a bruised backbone was good enough for your father and his father before him, then it's good enough for you. *Okh*, Vanya, I'm all for maintaining tradition, but do you ever listen to yourself? There are times when you sound so much like First Minister Strel'tsin that I find myself wondering where you keep the long grey beard.'

'Very amusing,' said Ivan, not amused at all. He hadn't forgotten the amount of trouble he had provoked over the Lesser Crown just after his coronation, and just now wasn't up to facing another round of discussions over whether or not the Tsar's chair could be cushioned without provoking the collapse of the realm. At least, not until the Tatars had been and gone. He would never have believed that there might come a time when the uninvited presence of the official and Church-recognised Scourge of God would be a welcome diversion from the affairs of state.

'You wanted to watch the visitors arrive?' he said, placing both hands on the arms of the Chair of State and levering himself gratefully away from the damned carvings. 'Then let's go do it.'

It seemed that the Tatars were in no great haste to reach Khorlov's gates, for even though Ivan and Mar'ya Morevna took their own leisurely time in walking from the Presence Chamber at the heart of the kremlin, by the time they reached the outer ramparts the riders were still far distant. The summer dust raised by their horses' hoofs hung on the still, hot air like a silken scarf in their wake, and the bright metal of armour and weapons twinkled through it as though that scarf had been scattered with sequins.

Ivan leaned on the wooden battlements of the kremlin and gazed out without much enthusiasm across grassland that had once been lush and green. Not any more. It had been a fierce summer, coming early to suck the steppe dry of moisture and then scorch it biscuit-brown, and he didn't relish the thought of the autumn rains. One good downpour would turn most of the land he ruled into a single vast mire, until the winter came and froze it solid. Ah, Russia. He stared at the distant sparks of steel. 'Two hundred men, the Kipchaq said. It seems like more.'

'It always looks like more,' said Mar'ya Morevna. 'But he told the truth. About their numbers and – ' She cocked her head as the rattle of *naccara* drums and the drone of deep-voiced trumpets blended with a high, melodic scream of shawms. ' – And about the band as well. They've been in Khwarizmid Persia, this lot. Reeds and kettledrums. Listen.'

'It sounds like a pig being roasted,' said Ivan, after a few seconds while the thin shrieking of reed instruments came floating faint but clear across the steppe. 'Several pigs. And not dead, either.'

'But you can hear it, can't you?'

'Unfortunately, yes.' The young Tsar grimaced and scrubbed his knuckles into his beard. It might have made him look wiser and more regal, but he had been clean-shaven for most of his life and the damned thing still itched in hot weather. If it wasn't for Mar'ya Morevna frequently insisting that he shave it off, he decided, he *would* shave it off. 'I presume there's some significance about that remark which is temporarily eluding me?'

'Yes,' said Mar'ya Morevna.

That was all. Ivan wished she wouldn't do things like that, wished she would understand that there were times when he wasn't up to thinking for himself and was more than willing to let ministers and stewards and councillors – yes, and wives too – do the thinking for him. Right now was one of those times. Dmitriy Vasil'yevich and his blasted paperwork since sunrise, the prospect of tuition in the drearier aspects of the Art Magic later in the afternoon, and now the Tatars on top of it all.

What Tsar Ivan of Khorlov really wanted to do was to spend an hour or so in the company of a flask of vodka and a bottle or three of white wine cooled in the ice stored underneath the kremlin palace, an hour in the bathhouse taking strong steam, and then the rest of the day behind locked doors with Mar'ya Morevna, making a determined attempt at fathering some more children. Not that the children mattered overmuch, two were enough for now – especially when the two they had could sometimes seem like a great many more – but it was the prospect of the attempt that Ivan found appealing.

'Well?' Mar'ya Morevna asked.

'Well what?' Ivan dragged himself out of what had been rapidly becoming a very pleasant daydream, and glowered at her. Mar'ya Morevna in the daydream had been just as demanding, but not in quite the same irascible way.

'Vanya, haven't you realised yet what I mean about the band?'

For a few seconds he hadn't an idea of what she was driving at, but then some wicked spark of intelligence came to Ivan's rescue.

'You mean, that we can hear the instruments? Military signals, surely. They carry well.' He smiled slowly. 'Was that all? I had started to think it might be something important.'

Mar'ya Morevna, Tsaritsa of Khorlov and fairest Princess in all the Russias, stared at her husband with an expression that managed to suggest that had there been anything worth throwing, she would have thrown it. Then she grinned crookedly at him. 'Important enough,' she said. 'If we could persuade our people to use the Tatars' own battle skills against them, we might stand a chance of defeating the bastards.'

Ivan did not return the grin. Instead he shook his head sombrely. 'If we could have persuaded,' he said, correcting the tense with heavy emphasis, 'we might have stood a chance. But we left it all too late. As usual.' Mar'ya Morevna opened her mouth to say something, but Ivan gestured her to silence. 'I'm not being a pessimist. I'm being realistic. Practical. The way you used to be.'

'Before these barbarians stamped our country flat.'

'Yes. But they did it. It's past, and it can't be changed. Ögotäi Khakhan might have succeeded anyway, but we should have made him pay far more dearly for the victory. Except that you know as well as I that not one of the lords of the Rus could agree with any of the others for long enough to do anything worthwhile. So let it be, Mar'yushka. There may be something you, or I or all of us, can do before all this is over, but now is not the time. Now is the time for making the best of things.'

'Like a woman being raped, you mean?' Mar'ya Morevna's voice went suddenly harsh. 'Just because you can't change it, you might as well enjoy it?'

'No. I didn't say enjoy. Enduring is something different. If you endure, and live, then maybe you can do something to make a difference afterwards. But you can't endure if you're dead, like everyone in Ryazan', or Vladimir, or Chernigov, or Kiev, or . . . Do I need to go on? If you're dead, there is no afterwards. I've been saying that for years. Only the places that offered no resistance have survived – and now we've started to blame each other for surviving. That must give much amusement to our new overlord Ilkhan Batu. Yes, and the entire Golden Horde.'

'I . . .' Mar'ya Morevna stared at him for several seconds, then lowered her eyes. 'Vanya, I'm sorry for what I said. I wasn't thinking. I was sounding just like those stupid *bogatyri* heroes who still just want to fight. No matter what they're told, no matter how many times they're told, as soon as they're confronted with an adventure they have to jump at it, and be damned to anyone they leave behind.'

'But I was the one who asked for this adventure in the first place, remember? All those years ago, when I was bored with being just a tsar . . . Now there's a joke.'

'You're still Tsar, so don't fret too much about your joke. Do you want to hear a better one? If they wanted to be really legendary heroes, and we could build them a big enough coffin, they could all play at being Svyatogor. I'd nail the lid down myself.'

According to the old *bylina* tale, Svyatogor the Giant had discovered a coffin which was the first piece of furniture, bed or chair or anything else, big enough to fit him comfortably. He had refused all warnings in the face of such a strange adventure, climbed into the coffin, put on the lid which promptly locked in place – and that had been the end of him. It had been a pointless end which had done nothing to aid his companions, and to Ivan, Mar'ya Morevna and many others of a practical turn of mind, was a demonstration of nothing more heroic than stupidity and stubbornness on an epic scale. Needless to say, as an example of perfect heroism even in the face of death, the *bogatyri* loved it.

Ivan laughed out loud at the image her words conjured up. 'You, sound like a *bogatyr*? I don't think so! Not now – and not then. I thought you were sounding like the great commander, the woman whose army smashed Manguyu Temir's horde. Like the woman I married. There's a difference.'

'Is there?'

'Yes.' Ivan paused, then quirked one eyebrow at his wife. 'I couldn't marry a *bogatyr* on the longest day I lived. Archbishop Levon wouldn't let me.' He smiled very slightly, the moment of unpleasantness between them past and already forgotten, and lightly touched her face. 'Besides, I don't like my lovers to have hair on their faces.'

'Neither do I.' Mar'ya Morevna reached out and stroked disapproving fingers through the carefully-trimmed beard that covered her husband's chin. 'I've said so often enough, if you

103

remember. You do remember, don't you?' She closed finger and thumb and tweaked hard enough to make Ivan wince. 'Or weren't you paying attention?'

'Ouch! I was, I was!'

'So when are you going to shave it off?' Mar'ya Morevna examined her fingertips, then blew lightly and watched as a few golden strands of hair drifted free.

Ivan rubbed at the plucked place on his chin. 'Soon.'

'How soon?'

'When I don't need it any more.'

'You've been saying that for years, too. When exactly?'

'When that collection of old fools in the Council and the *druzina* have been convinced I'm old enough to be their Tsar. It seems a six year reign isn't enough for them.'

'Vanya, if you want to wait that long, you might as well just say you'll wait until you've outlived them all, and be done with it. You're the Tsar of Khorlov. You can do what you please!'

'Can I? Or didn't we already have this,' he hesitated on the word, 'this *discussion*?'

'That was about the throne.'

'Not the throne, Mar'yushka, the Chair of State.'

'No matter. Crown regalia is one thing – your choice whether or not to wear a beard is something else entirely! Well, isn't it?'

'Of course, the Tsars of Khorlov have always been bearded . . .'

'If you're teasing me, I don't think it's funny. And if you're not teasing me, it's even less funny. Ivan, this isn't just about your beard, or about the throne, or the chair, or the crown. You've been Tsar for six years, and in that six years you've been fair, and just, and passed good laws, and kept Khorlov from being destroyed by' – she gestured expressively towards the Tatars, still far away among their dust and their fierce music – 'by our visitors. Yet in the little things, the things that matter just to you – and to me – you still let the councillors from your father's time tell you what to do. Even how to look!'

'Nobody has ever told me to wear a beard!'

'No? But when your wife asks you to shave it off, you don't. It's not as if you like having a beard. I could understand that. But you don't. You wear it because you're expected to, just as you're expected to sit on carved chairs for hours at a time without cushions to make that sitting comfortable. Just as you were expected to wear the old, heavy crown.'

'Not any more.'

'So. That changed. Other things can change. You don't need to change the world, or the laws, or the traditions that have some point to them. But after six years it's time you started to tell, not ask. After so long, it's about whether you intend to rule Khorlov and the people in it – or let its old men rule you!'

Mar'ya Morevna often made her views known on all manner of subjects, but seldom on this one. For all that she had been the lord of her own wide domains before ever she met and married Ivan, she seemed to feel that it was not her place, or that of anyone else except ministers and stewards appointed for the purpose, to tell any Tsar how to govern his domain. Ivan knew her well enough to understand that it was not feminine reticence, but the courtesy due from one prince to another. Where Mar'ya Morevna was concerned, if reticence was nourishment, she would starve. She had given advice to Ivan, and to Tsar Aleksandr before him, but only when asked. Even though she had never raised her voice above the level of ordinary conversation, this intense and unsolicited outburst impressed itself on Ivan more than if she had screamed at him and slapped his face. He stared silently at her, with an expression glittering in his pale eyes that wasn't reflected sunlight. It might have been amusement, or resignation, or the beginning of anger, or a mingling of all three. Tsar or Prince, few things abraded Ivan's temper more thoroughly than the feeling of being pushed into a decision against his will. Then he blinked and the ominous glitter was gone, replaced by a much more wholesome squint as he peered out across the dry expanse of steppe at the approaching Tatars.

'How long before they reach the gates?'

Mar'ya Morevna narrowed her eyes, studied the specks wavering in a haze of heat, then at the noon sun overhead. 'If they keep to their present pace, twenty minutes. Maybe half an hour.' She looked at Ivan, and raised an eyebrow. 'Long enough to get rid of that beard, if you've made up your mind to do it.'

'Not long enough for a six-years-delayed razor burn to fade,' said Ivan, and smiled ruefully. 'The Tatars will think I'm a picture of pink-cheeked health.'

Mar'ya Morevna flexed her fingers so that their jewelled rings sparkled, and there were more sparks clinging to her fingers than light reflecting from faceted gemstones. 'I didn't say anything about razors.'

'If I spend the rest of the day smelling of burnt whiskers . . .'

'I doubt you'll even notice,' said Mar'ya Morevna, and gestured at Ivan as though to cup his face in her two hands.

Ivan did notice. His face stopped itching and began to tingle, and then a sensation like a splash of impossibly icy water, water so chill that it felt scalding hot, rushed from throat to cheekbones. Though there was no mirror to see what was happening, and probably nothing to see in any case, in his mind's eye the young Tsar could visualise his carefully trimmed beard and his lovingly cultivated sweep of golden moustache go flaring past his nose and ears in streamers of cold blue fire.

After a few sorely needed seconds of silence, during which he got his breath back and considered – then prudently abandoned – several scathing comments, Ivan ran the tips of his fingers warily over skin that had not been so smooth since before he had ever needed to shave at all. The skin stung as though it had been mildly sunburned, so that with every wince away from a tender place he felt, and probably looked, more like a man probing himself for unsuspected wounds than one examining the work of his barber. 'You might at least have given me enough time to say whether I preferred a razor,' he said accusingly. 'It was *my* beard, after all.'

'This way was quicker,' said Mar'ya Morevna. 'And I don't have much opportunity to work the smaller spells any more. Or the larger ones, if it comes to that.'

'Oh, indeed?' Ivan felt a little spasm jolt him in the stomach, a reaction that was close kin to the feeling he might get at any small accident barely avoided. He didn't know whether to smile or frown, and settled for neutral annoyance instead. 'So you could have scorched my eyebrows off for want of practice . . . Well, madam, I find that most reassuring!'

'Don't be silly.'

Motherhood has definitely done things to your vocabulary, thought Ivan, and this time the smile came easier to his mouth. *You would never have settled for something as weak as* silly *before.*

'You know I'm a better sorceress than that,' Mar'ya Morevna

continued, massaging one hand against the other to ease where the transmitted force of the spell had shocked her finger joints. 'And what if I *had* scorched your eyebrows off? I could always have conjured them back. Or maintained an illusion of eyebrows, anyway. At least until the Tatars left.'

'If that was intended to reassure me, my dear, then you need to try a good deal harder. I think I'll let the court barber use his razors next time. He might cut my throat by accident, but he won't make me look ridiculous.'

'I don't think you look ridiculous,' said Mar'ya Morevna. She gave him a look that was at once sleepily heavy-lidded and speculative, the sort of look that is commonly described as smouldering. Mar'ya Morevna smouldered very well. 'I think you look like the energetic young Prince who spent so long in my tent all those years ago. *Golubchik* Vanya, I should have taken your beard off when the thought first crossed my mind to do it, but I was so patient, so restrained, and now I don't need to be either any more . . .'

Her voice had dropped to a soft murmur like the purr of a big, lazy cat, and as the mouse under scrutiny, Tsar Ivan was more than willing to be played with.

'You – ' No purr there; Ivan discovered that his own voice had developed a slight tendency to squeak. Appropriate for a mouse, perhaps, but not a tsar. He cleared his throat and tried again. 'You do, at least until the Tatars are dealt with. If one of them *is* some sort of envoy from Batu Khan, he'll have to be formally received at the gates, and after that, given an equally formal banquet tonight.'

'Good. Formal banquets take time to prepare.' Mar'ya Morevna favoured her husband with another hot stare, then turned her head and gazed irritably at the Tatar horsemen. 'What's taking them so long to get here?'

'They've halted to make formal ablutions,' said a voice from the rampart stairway, so unexpectedly that the sound of it made both Ivan and Mar'ya Morevna jump. 'To go with all the other formality that's being prepared in Khorlov.'

Volk Volkovich the Grey Wolf stood there in man's shape, grinning a white grin in his brown, cruelly handsome face; and the human grin was not much improvement on the wolf's. Neither of them had heard him climb the stairs, and neither of them knew how long he had been there. From the gleam of wicked amusement in the wolf's eyes that never changed from his true wolf's shape, long enough to see and hear anything and everything that could be pleasant in private, but embarrassing before a witness.

'*Chyort voz'mi!*' snapped Ivan. 'Don't *do* that! Must you always sneak everywhere you go?'

'No,' said the Grey Wolf, sauntering up from the wooden stairs to the wooden walkway without so much as a creak from a plank or a click from his grey leather boots to betray his passage. 'I move quietly.'

Ivan couldn't help but smile at such monstrous self-assurance. He shook his head, and let the breath he had gathered for a swift lecture on the proprieties go hissing out between his teeth. Grumbling at the Grey Wolf about anything at all was slightly less productive than beating smoke with a stick, and he had long since given up wasting words on the effort.

'And you've been moving quietly around the Tatars, I presume?' said Mar'ya Morevna. 'Why didn't you report before now – or were you just too busy moving quietly around *us*?'

'Now, now, Tsaritsa,' said Volk Volkovich reprovingly, 'I'm more than just another Kipchaq. For one thing, I'm doing this for amusement and as a favour, not because I'm in anyone's service any more.' Mar'ya Morevna had the good grace to look abashed, if only very slightly, but it was enough for the Grey Wolf, whose good humour returned once more.

'Your, ah, ordinary spies bring ordinary information, and if I'd come running back with them, you wouldn't know anything more than what you know already. But from me, you've learned that the Tatars are showing enough respect for the Tsar of Khorlov that they've paused to wash the dust of their journey. Maybe even the top few layers of their personal grime as well – although I suspect they don't respect even the Great Khan that much.'

He pointedly ignored the second part of her question, and, remembering the chilly glitter in his eyes which had been answer enough, Mar'ya Morevna didn't bother repeating it.

'You wouldn't happen to know why they're here?' asked Ivan. 'We thought perhaps an envoy of some sort. But after all this time, for what? There are too many for just . . . just the usual.'

The Grey Wolf made himself comfortable, leaning back against the battlements with his long legs stretched out in front of him and crossed at the ankles. It looked completely natural, but to Ivan and Mar'ya Morevna, who knew his true form and nature, even that gesture had the studied air of a rôle being played for effect.

'Several times I was close enough to hear them talking,' he said, 'but they never spoke Farsee.' His voice managed to suggest by intonation alone just how disobliging that had been to the average hard-working spy. 'Indeed, they never spoke anything other than Uighur and some other one of those Türko-Mongol dialects that the tribes use to understand each other. Which I don't.' He saw or sensed some shift in Mar'ya Morevna's expression, and shrugged.

'Oh, I recognise the sound of the language, *gospozha Tsaritsa*, but even when I'm that close to a Tatar, I never trouble to make a close study of what he's saying to me.' He grinned, a slow, vicious display of teeth that seemed suddenly more raggedly pointed and less human than they had before. 'Mother always told me it's not good manners to talk with my mouth full.'

No matter how many times Volk Volkovich said things like that, Ivan had never grown used to them. It mattered very little that the Grey Wolf had long ceased to be a servant – his original offer of service had been only for a year and a day, and that had expired six years ago – because he had remained a friend ever since. Or a sort of friend, anyway. Ivan had often tried to work out his exact title; 'friend' sometimes seemed too, well, friendly for some of the attitudes that the Grey Wolf took roguish pleasure in displaying, but 'acquaintance' was too cold and distant. Ignorant of their Tsar's struggle with the niceties of definition, as they were ignorant of a great deal else, neither the Council nor the *druzina* knew Volk Volkovich as anything more than a somewhat sinister henchman who came and went much as he pleased. In that ignorance, thought Ivan, lay not only a certain amount of advantage, but a good deal of truth.

The shrill sound of children's voices drifted up from the courtyard, mingling with the clatter of feet on the stairway that were moving anything but quietly. Nikolai and Anastasya bounded onto the ramparts and flung themselves at their parents, babbling gratitude for being summoned to see the parade.

'Parade?' said Mar'ya Morevna, her arms full of a seven-year-old daughter who was struggling to see over the battlements, and quite possibly fall from them in an excess of enthusiasm.

'Summoned?' said Ivan, picking up Nikolai and tucking the boy under one arm for want of anything better to do with him.

Both of them looked at Volk Volkovich, who spread hands and shoulders wide in an eloquent shrug. 'If you had sent for them already, what of it?' he said. 'And if you hadn't, then I was merely pre-empting your decision.'

'Oh, *were* you?' There was a definite edge to Mar'ya Morevna's voice, even though the Grey Wolf pretended not to hear it.

Having met Volk Volkovich for the first time in his true form, she had seemed slightly uneasy about him ever since; especially since the twins were born and he had begun – without invitation or encouragement – to act like an indulgent uncle. Mar'ya Morevna had pointed out rather sharply to Ivan that every one of their uncles was a shape-shifter, but that this one, the one most frequently seen, was also the only one whose natural shape was a beast, rather than the more acceptable reverse. It had taken Ivan several weeks to cajole the reason for her concern out of his wife. In the process he had learned some disturbing things, and guessed at others which were truly harrowing. Chief of them was that 'uncles' sometimes had an unhealthy taste for the children they visited – Mar'ya Morevna would say no more than that, though Ivan suspected he could deduce the rest – and that an 'uncle' whose true shape was a wolf might display a similar taste for children in the worst and most literal way. There had never been any sign of it, of course, but as Mar'ya Morevna said, the first sign in this instance would already be too late.

It had been a strange feeling, this injection of such a very domestic unpleasantness into one which had already spilled beyond the borders of Russia. Ivan, toughened perhaps by having to say, and repeat, distasteful truths about policy to his councillors and retinue, had summoned up the courage to ask some equally unpalatable questions of the man – when he was a man – who best qualified as his friend.

There was one advantage. Like the black horse Sivka, Volk Volkovich the Grey Wolf disdained to indulge in the human vice of telling lies. It was true that at need he could and would stretch the truth out of all recognition, but to those who knew it, it remained still identifiable as truth. That there should be worries about the consequences of his nature was something the Grey Wolf had come to expect, it seemed. There was no twisting of truth this time, and fortunately no outrage or insult either, as there might have been with a human. He had simply promised that no harm should come to the children by him, either through action or *in*action – and he had grinned toothily at Ivan's realisation of just what had been offered, unasked. Not even the children of a tsar of all the Russias, if the Princes should ever tolerate the creation of such a creature, would be able to boast such a protector and guardian. It had served to make Mar'ya Morevna a little easier about his presence, though as her sharpness had just demonstrated, not completely. Not just yet.

'The Tsarevich was attending tuition in a class on Greek logic and thought,' said Volk Volkovich, and nodded slightly to Ivan as the Tsar winced. 'The Tsarevna was with the Mistress of the Kitchens, learning household accounts. I considered, *gospozha Tsaritsa*, that both these subjects could be continued later; watching the arrival of a deputation of foreign dignitaries happens only once. Not even you would ask them to go out and come back in, just for the sake of a spectacle.'

'Just how long were you in that class on logic?' Ivan asked idly, then waved his hand to dismiss the need for an answer. 'Never mind. They're here now. They can wait with the rest of us.'

'Wait for what?' asked Nikolai, still inverted and enjoying it immensely.

'For the Tatars to make up their minds about when they want to come closer to the city, Kolya,' said Mar'ya Morevna. 'They're washing, apparently. Ivan, put the child down.'

'Oh,' said Ivan, and did. Prince Nikolai immediately made a dash at his sister, who was peering out from underneath the swinging shutter of an embrasure, and gave her just the merest suggestion of a push. It was quite enough to produce the desired impressive squeal and totter, but before either parent could move to save her, Princess Anastasya had recovered, turned with the speed of what had to be long practice, and swung a vicious punch right at her brother's nose. If it had connected, there would have been blood spilled – but she misjudged her distance, because Kolya simply wasn't there. Without needing to dodge or duck, he was no more or less than the handspan further away which was all he needed to save himself.

'That boy is going to make a remarkable swordsman one of these days,' said Ivan with great satisfaction. 'Assuming his sister doesn't kill him first.'

He watched as Mar'ya Morevna and Volk Volkovich forced peace on the beginnings of yet another family feud by simply getting between the hail of blows, and observed that at least this time there was no complaining about the Grey Wolf's presence. Especially as he was taking most of the punches. But there was an odd expression on his wife's face that had nothing to do with that more commonplace concern, and it was made the more peculiar because Volk Volkovich was wearing it too. Ivan wondered, not for the first nor likely the last time, just what subtlety he had missed now.

The Grey Wolf and Mar'ya Morevna exchanged glances that had more in common than anything Ivan had seen for a long time, and both of them turned to him together. But whatever they were going to say was put aside by the same mutual agreement, forced to wait by the long, deep groan of a horn-blast from out on the steppe.

The Tatars were on their way at last.

Chapter Five

The Independent Tsardom of Khorlov;
July, AD 1243

Their delay might well have been as the Grey Wolf suggested, a pause to wash and brush and otherwise set things to rights after the long journey over the dusty summer steppes of Russia. It served equally well to give the people of Khorlov time to gather, which noble and common alike they did; to increase curiosity to fever pitch about this un-Tatar behaviour, which it did; and to give the musicians time to get their breath back, which they had very obviously done.

That fact was amply demonstrated as the column of men and beasts began to lumber up the long slope towards the city at the summit. It was difficult to describe the sound they produced as musical, at least to Rus ears, for it lacked most of what might normally have been called melody. Or pity, or mercy, or anything else remotely soft and gentle. But there was a savage power to it that was all Tatar. It was the music of a people who had conquered almost all of the known world in the space of thirty years.

The thudding rhythm of the *naccara* drums swelled and faded into rolls like the beat of surf on a rocky shore. That was the truest Tatar military music, since after the silent movement of flags and yak-tail standards, they were the principal signalling devices for each one-tenth unit of the hundred thousand strong *tuk* army, from the ten thousand men of the *tuman* division right down to the ten men of the *arban* patrol. The *naccara* resembled huge bronze kettles ornamented with pendant tassles and capped with drumheads of taut leather; they were slung to either side of stolid camels that were more capable of bearing their weight, and would be less unsettled by their noise than horses.

The consideration of weight was reasonable enough, but that of noise did not seem to extend to the use of the accompanying cymbals and trumpets, which blared and clashed indiscriminately from the saddles of horse or camel. Both of those instruments were larger and louder than seemed sensible, until it became obvious that their sole function was to impress. After that, the discs of polished brass large as a swordsman's shield that flashed in the sunlight as though newly burnished – as they probably had been – and the great horns as long as that swordsman was tall seemed all too right and proper.

With the scream of what Mar'ya Morevna had called shawms cutting a high counterpoint through the sonorous marching music, its accumulated raw noise slapped at Khorlov's walls like a physical force. It was loud enough that Ivan, standing in the city's gateway with his dignitaries and his guards in parade robes over their armour, hoped it might drown out any rumblings of rebellion that still featured in his Council's collective breast. For reasons best known to themselves, the Tatars were making a more overwhelming display before this city than they had troubled with at any other, and he would have liked to know why.

There were horses of all kinds, most of them the characteristic stocky ponies that watchers from Austria to the shores of the Nippon Sea had come to know, hate and fear. Among the others were tall Western destriers plundered from the shattered ranks of Poles, Silesians and Teutonic Knights after their crushing defeat at Liegnitz, and fine-limbed Arab steeds from Bokhara and Samarkand, in what was beginning to be called the Ilkhanate of Persia. And then there were the camels.

They in particular were a source of wonder and loudly remarked upon. Though horses of all shapes and sizes were commonplace to the people of the city whose Tsar rode a black stallion that was far from ordinary, these other strange, lumpy creatures with their hides shedding fur like an elderly carpet were new to all but the most well-travelled merchants. Even some of the latter, those who fared West instead of East, had not seen the shaggy, double-humped Bactrian of the deep Gobi desert.

During a pause in the music, Tsar Ivan overheard one man tell his companion how even the Saracen dromedary with its single hump and sneering face and whore's eyelashes was a relatively sensible creature, as all things became sensible to a man well drunk on *arak* after a hard session of haggling in the marketplace. But these Bactrians – well, at least the space between their humps

114

made a man less likely to fall off when he was well drunk on . . .
And so on.

Despite the presence of the Tatars, which he had been secretly
dreading for nearly three years now, Ivan grinned to himself and
wondered if there was some way in which a Tsar could find out
more of these travellers' tales without obviously confessing to a
lack of the omniscience he was supposed to possess. And if the
Saracen beast was described as sneering, then it must truly have a
supercilious expression to be more so than these. Or perhaps they
looked so superior simply because they belonged to the Tatars,
and had every right to look down on the people that their masters
had so thoroughly conquered.

Ivan's grin went sour at the thought. But another took its place
almost at once, and that had to do with the way the Tatars were
showing Khorlov courtesy of a sort. It was strengthened when a
tuk standard of six yak-tails went up above the most splendidly
attired and foremost rider, a token that the man beneath it had the
authority of Ilkhan Batu of the Golden Horde. In a circumstance
where the usual most senior representative was the *tuman-bashi*
commander of whatever army waited to crush potential resistance, the presence of that standard was significant indeed. If they
were being so mannerly as to present their threats and demands at
such an elevated level, then such respect could at least be
matched.

'Akimov,' said Ivan to the Captain-of-Guards, 'send one of
your men for bread and salt. Quickly.'

Petr Mikhailovich Akimov gave his Tsar a swift look of
curiosity. That didn't delay his salute, or the rapid departure of
one of the soldiers in the direction of the kremlin kitchen. Akimov
was a Cossack, a pragmatist and a loyal servant of the Crown of
Khorlov, whoever might be wearing it; if the Tsar had a notion
that the old offerings of hospitality were a good idea even to a
potential enemy, it was not his place to gainsay the command.

As he drew closer, it was apparent that even though his face was
hidden by the iron eyebrows and moustache embossed from the
visor of his helmet, the man riding under the standard was neither
Tatar nor Mongol like the warriors behind him, but a Türk.
Though his elaborate armour covered all but his hands and booted
lower legs, it could not conceal his height. That was yet another

115

mystery, for the Khan of the Golden Horde was a Mongol of the *altan uruk*, the Golden Clan descended in right line from Chinghis-Khan Temüchin himself, and as such was known not to entrust important or delicate tasks to those outside his own clan Borjigun, never mind those of different race. At least, that had been the case until now, as the six white yak-tails bore mute witness.

Ivan glanced sideways at Volk Volkovich, but received only an unhelpful shrug. The Grey Wolf had seen several Tatar envoys arrive at the gates of several Rus cities since Ryazan', and from his reports, all of them had followed the same routine of a contemptuously small group, and occasionally only a single rider, making outrageous demands on the ruler of the city. This was evidently as new to him as it was unfamiliar to Ivan. For all of that, it felt eerie to have so many of the old, traditional enemies of the Rus people approaching the city gate that lay open before them, rather than shut and bolted and spiked with steel.

As the music reached its shattering conclusion, the Türk horseman and his Mongol guards rode forward in silence until only some three spear-lengths separated them from the Russians at the gate. At least the man looked the part of a visiting official, unlike the scruffy individuals described by the Grey Wolf. His harness, matched by that worn by his horse, was of the usual lamellar construction, although each alternate row of leather-laced scales was covered by a handsome fabric of scarlet worked with tiny golden flowers, and a spray of peacock plumes rose both from between the horse's ears and from the top of its rider's visored helmet. The iron stare of that visor swept to and fro across the watchful Rus faces, as though the horseman was looking for something in particular and not finding what he sought.

Ivan took a step forward, and the fixed gaze of those metal features snapped around to study him. If hammered iron could have displayed surprise, he would have seen it at that moment, for it was as if the Türk had been taken unawares by the Tsar's appearance. Ivan wondered if he had been expecting someone older, or taller, or more richly clothed, because the Tsar of Khorlov was dressed no better than most of his councillors, and worse than some of the more ostentatious among them. Ivan did not believe in wearing his best garments for court paperwork; he had discovered long ago that the more expensive a coat of figured velvet might be, the more it had, like his children, an affinity for ink and other stains that was almost supernatural. Moreover, he was not wearing anything that the unfamiliar might recognise as a crown; only his comfortable fur-trimmed hat with the gold plaques set into the band.

With a scraping and rustling of mail against scales, the Türk removed his helmet, shook loose the three braids of his long hair and looked down at Ivan from a face that was hawk-angular, as though it had been carved from wood with an adze but not smoothed down afterward. Once freed from the confines of the helmet, his moustaches – for there were two of them indeed, separated from each other by most of the width of his upper lip – hung down on either side of his mouth almost to his breastbone. They were as thin as two streaks of ink painted on the air by a particularly narrow brush, and they framed a beard that had been placed on the point of his already sharp chin by the same overly meticulous artist.

'You are Ivan, son of Aleksandr, son of Andrey, crowned Tsar of Khorlov?' he said, speaking in excellent Russian with only the merest trace of an accent.

Ivan looked him up and down, not entirely sure whether that choice of phrasing was merely pedantic or if it contained some subtle form of insult. 'I am the Tsar of Khorlov, yes,' he replied finally. 'And you are. . . ?'

'Amragan *tarkhan*, son of Temür, of clan Barlas.' By rights a salute, a bow, or at least some indication of pride, should have accompanied such an announcement made in such a voice, but the *tarkhan* sat as still as though his armour was no more than a part of that worn by his immobile horse. 'I am envoy from the Ilkhan Batu of the Golden Horde.'

And that was all. No demand to bow down or be destroyed, no list of required tributes, no threats. Nothing but that bald announcement of name and status. Ivan blinked just once, then successfully stifled any other indications of confusion. All would doubtless be made clear in good time; though whose good time, his, God's or the Khan's, remained to be seen. He was uneasy, wondering about the delay. For three years now he had been steeling himself against the day when he would publicly lay his

117

honour in the dust and throw away the respect of his people in the hope of maybe saving all their lives. And now it seemed that all the fretting, all the acid griping of apprehension in his guts, had been a waste of time. Or at least held over until some later occasion.

He gestured at the guardsman who had arrived at last with the bread and salt. Because there had been no advance warning that one might be needed, there had been no guest-loaf in the kitchen, the proper large, round loaf of black bread baked with a recess to take a wooden dish of salt. Instead, the soldier had done the best he could, and was carrying an ordinary small rye loaf meant as a part of that night's dinner, with a hollow hastily carved from its centre and filled with a mound of brilliant white sea salt from the Tsar's own table. He went forward and held the bread up to Amragan *tarkhan*, who looked at it and then at Ivan, both times with the same quizzical expression on his hard features as though he too had been caught unawares by the way events were falling into place. Out of all the receptions he might have been expecting, this, the old rite of hospitality, was the most unlikely. He shrugged – or perhaps that was just a movement to settle the weight of his armour more comfortably on his broad shoulders – tore free a small chunk of the bread, sprinkled salt on top and crunched the mouthful up. Though his mouth twisted slightly, as was only reasonable from a man who had just eaten a good spoonful of raw salt, his face betrayed nothing else of what he was thinking. Then he kicked free of his stirrups and dismounted with an easy grace that was made only slightly ponderous by all the iron he wore.

'What I have to say may take some time,' he told Ivan. He did not bow, but then the Tsar had not been expecting it. 'I accept the hospitality of bread and salt, but while it is good to speak beneath Tängri's blue sky, out here are many ears and many eyes. Too many. Shall we go in?'

'Alone,' said Ivan, eyeing the escort of Mongols and Uighurs who were still sitting on their tough little horses, apparently disinterested in the proceedings – but who were in his opinion still far too close to the city gate. The Türk followed his gaze and grunted softly to himself, then shook his head.

'Not alone,' he said. 'That would be unseemly.'

'Other . . . envoys have approached Rus cities alone,' said Mar'ya Morevna. 'Why should you be any different?'

The *tarkhan* favoured her with a long, speculative look, and for the first time Ivan saw a small crack appear in the man's veneer of controlled good manners – though whether it was just irritation at being addressed so by a woman was more difficult to tell. Any man of the Tatars should be well used to that, at least: from what Ivan had heard of Mongol women, they entered freely into conversations with their menfolk, expressed opinions whether asked for or not, and generally comported themselves as equals. The envoy took Mar'ya Morevna's comment with better grace than a Russian who had never met her before might have done.

'Lady, if you have not observed already that this envoy's behaviour is somewhat different to the usual . . .' he said quietly, and left it at that.

'But for what reason?'

'As to that,' said Amragan *tarkhan*, 'I have already suggested somewhere populated by fewer flapping ears.'

The observation was almost completely accurate. Once convinced – for the moment at least – that they were not all to be slaughtered or enslaved, the common people of Khorlov were hanging onto every word spoken, straining to hear more than they should like a pack of dogs doing their best to get more than a fair share of meat. If their ears had been larger, they would have flapped in very truth.

Ivan looked back at the ranks of his own subjects, noting for possible future consideration that not just the commons but some of the nobility were displaying too much interest in matters that were none of their business. There was a sharpness about those faces, dogs keen not for anything so simple as meat, but for the sharp scent of scandal at the sight of a Rus lord being so amiable with this steel-tipped lash of the Scourge of God. He knew enough of the names already, names of the men who had been most troublesome over the past two years, most subject to second thoughts about their Tsar's decision regarding the Tatars. They were all there now: Rostislavl' and Vladislav, Gyorg'yevskiy, Fedorovich and Romanov.

Especially Romanov. Ivan had kept a particularly close eye on the Romanov father and son ever since that almost-ugly incident at the Council meeting in '41, and for the most part had done so personally rather than leave the matter in the hands of a

119

subordinate. Volk Volkovich had helped, of course, but none of Akimov's guard; all of them were men of too much loyalty and passion, and not enough sense. If any opportunity had presented itself to have the Romanovs legally put away – permanently – Ivan had long convinced himself to take it and never mind his scruples. As if aware of that decision, they had been on what passed for their best behaviour ever since. Aleksey Mikhailovich had absented himself from court on all but the most unavoidable occasions, and his father, though a councillor and expected to be in his place whenever that august body met, had been a model of quietness and rectitude.

He had, in Ivan's opinion, been far too quiet; but the Tsar had been unable to find a law allowing him to condemn the man for that. Not that he hadn't spent long hours with his High Steward and the old legal statute rolls, just to be quite sure . . .

He turned away from the stares of curiosity, and considered the escort riders who had come up to the gate with Amragan *tarkhan*. 'Very well then. For the sake of seemliness, not alone. Which of these,' Ivan stumbled for an instant on the word, 'gentlemen will accompany you?'

'Not soldiers,' said the *tarkhan*. 'I judge you a man of sense, one to whom the Khan's response to my murder carries more weight than any number of swords for a more immediate defence.'

Am I that *transparent?* thought Ivan, a little surprised even though the Türk was right. There was no point in fair talk at the gateway when what waited for the envoy inside was a knife in the back.

'What, then? Or who?'

Amragan *tarkhan* raised one mailed arm and closed his fist. There was a scuffle of activity among the Tatar horsemen as four of their number dismounted and came forward, and even one of the bandsmen left his place and joined them. Ivan stared.

'And just who are these?' he wondered aloud, indicating the gaggle of greasy and disreputable figures who now stood behind Amragan *tarkhan*, making him look all the more magnificent by their own shabby appearance.

'They are shamans. Priests, necessary for the religious well-being of my men,' said the Türk. He spoke smoothly, and perhaps a little too fast, so that both Ivan and Mar'ya Morevna favoured the 'priests' with a more careful second look.

'Priests, keeping company with a military and diplomatic envoy?'

'To bring us the solace of our religion in foreign lands. The Christians and the Moslems do so all the time.'

Ivan raised his eyebrows a notch, but decided to say nothing. At least not yet. From the little he knew of the Tatar faith – if such a formless and unconstructed collection of tribal superstitions could be called anything so organised – the Tatars, Uighurs, Mongols or whatever had no need for great numbers of priests to accompany them anywhere. Tängri the Eternal Blue Sky was above them wherever they went, and from Chinghis-Khan on down, they spoke to him personally. A man wishing to commune with the god or with the spirits would go to a high place, rare in their flat, treeless steppes and therefore imbued with great power. He would make a token of submission by laying his fur cap on the ground and his belt about his neck, and then he would make whatever prayers or supplications or sacrifices had brought him there. Priests were not necessary.

But as a defence against the *kelet*, the spirits of sickness or enmity – *or unfriendly magic*, said a voice of small but blinding clarity in the back of his mind – they were vital.

'Follow this man,' he said, indicating Guard-Captain Akimov. 'He will take you to the Council Chamber.'

'Not the Council Chamber,' said Mar'ya Morevna quickly. 'The Hall of Audience.'

'Highness? For so few?' The big Cossack was confused. The Hall was perhaps the biggest single open space under the roof of the entire kremlin, able at need to hold more than two thousand people, and Akimov knew well enough that even when the Tsar and his party joined the Tatars, all of them together would rattle around in that great reverberant emptiness like the last grains of wheat in a barrel.

'Yes.' Mar'ya Morevna's voice suggested that any further questioning of her orders would have to be well-justified later. 'Once there, you will see our, our guests to seats at the centre of the Hall. Under the principal vault.' Then she smiled as she made things clear at last. 'After that, open all the doors, post sentries outside them, and make sure that the ornamental fountains are running . . .'

Ivan, Akimov and Amragan *tarkhan* all looked at her with exactly the same expression of respect. In so large an open space, and with guards at every open door, no-one could creep close enough to eavesdrop on voices kept cautiously lowered, and any word that travelled further than was intended would be swallowed up by the hiss and splash from the fountains. Mar'ya Morevna had employed such subterfuges before when consulting with her own group of capable spies, and both she and Ivan had long known that the other Princes of the Rus had spies of their own in the kremlin at Khorlov. It might have appeared that such cautions were excessive when those other Princes were either dead or fled; but dead men can have successors, and those who run away are able to come back. If they chanced to learn anything about the meeting that was about to take place, it would not be through any lack of caution on her part.

Ivan watched as Amragan *tarkhan* and his aromatic entourage tramped off towards the kremlin, then quietly summoned Mar'ya Morevna, Volk Volkovich and First Minister Strel'tsin to attend him.

'Shamans,' said the Grey Wolf, and he managed to growl the word low in his throat. 'Call them doctors, or priests, or wizards, they can be any one of those, or all of them together. I've seen them before, too many times. They come usually as one of the first envoys, intended as a pagan affront to good Orthodox Christian sensibilities. A deliberate sacrifice, meant to provoke foolish violence, and so justify reprisals. As if the Tatars need to justify anything of the sort.'

Strel'tsin uttered his little snort that was almost an audible question mark. 'Then why weren't they with the *tarkhan* from the first?'

Volk Volkovich grinned and shot a pointed stare at the Metropolitan Patriarch, who was standing with a group of lesser clergy on the far side of the gateway and looking more than ever as if he had a bellyache. 'Maybe because they knew that neither you nor the Tsar would use such an excuse,' he said. 'Others perhaps, but not the men whose words have all the power in Khorlov.'

'Um.' Dmitriy Vasil'yevich looked thoughtful, digesting the information that someone in the city actually considered him other than tradition-bound and old-fashioned, never mind capable of sharing the opinions of a tsar fifty years his junior.

'More than that – they're his defence against us,' said Mar'ya Morevna. Ivan had seen that look on her face before, when she emerged dusty-fingered from a stack of ancient books with the scrap of information she had sought scribbled on a piece of parchment, and decided not to ruin her satisfaction by explaining how the same thought had occurred to him a few minutes before. Instead he remained silent and let her continue uninterrupted for the benefit of the other two. 'That's what's behind all of this. You'll see. The Tatars are afraid of Khorlov – because of Khorlov's sorcerers.' Her gaze slid to Archbishop Levon and rested there a moment, smugly satisfied. 'Remind me to tell the old prelate all about this sometime.'

'Not afraid, *gospozha Tsaritsa*,' the Grey Wolf corrected. 'The Tatars are afraid of nothing on the face of Moist-Mother-Earth. But they're wary. Careful of something they don't yet know how to deal with.'

Ivan looked down at his hands, then wiggled his fingers, interlaced them and cracked his knuckles thoughtfully. 'Whatever they are, I prefer them like this. Better wary and polite than arrogant and grasping. Or afraid. That would be worse still; when people are afraid of something, they have a tendency to resort to violence – and since we all know how the Tatars employ violence as a matter of policy . . .' He let the others think about that for a few seconds. 'At least with their envoy in his present mood, I think we might well be able to come to an accommodation with more honour in it than I was expecting. Something that might even keep the Council happy.'

'You mean conquering back all the lands the Tatars have seized in the past twenty years?' mocked Mar'ya Morevna gently. 'That's the only thing that would satisfy your councillors – and even then they would complain about why you hadn't done it sooner.'

'So why,' said Ivan Aleksandrovich, 'have you and your Tatars come to Khorlov, if not for the customary demands of tribute and surrender?' The shamans muttered amongst themselves at such forthright speech that threatened almost to spill into arrogance. *A tone and an attitude*, Ivan thought, *that you gentry are not accustomed to. And one which if nothing else so far, has at least told me that you all understand Russian.*

123

'Hear me,' said Amragan *tarkhan* formally. 'I speak with the voice of the Ilkhan Batu of the Golden Horde, who speaks with the voice of the Khakhan Ögatäi, Khan of all Khans of the Mongols, who speaks with the voice of the god Tängri of the Everlasting Blue Sky.'

'An interesting chain of command,' said Mar'ya Morevna. 'Since you're obviously on such close terms, how *is* God nowadays? Healthy and well, I trust?' She smiled, gazing at the Türkic envoy as though daring him to take exception to her words.

Surprisingly, Amragan did not. He returned the smile – or rather, his drooping moustaches moved in something that might have been a smile, had the lips beneath not stayed as thin as a razor cut.

'I cannot say, lady,' he said. 'For had you listened with greater care, you would know that I, *I*, speak with the voice of men.'

'And of angels?' Ivan wondered behind his raised hand, then waved that hand to dismiss the comment as though the words were no more than smoke on the air. Amragan *tarkhan* was not only possessed of sharper ears than the Russian had given him credit for, he was also not about to allow the matter be let go so easily.

'You are pleased to make play with the words of your holy book,' he said. Ivan kept surprise off his face. He had not expected a pagan Türk and a Tatar envoy to recognise the provenance of the phrase, and hastily revised his opinion of the man's education. 'That you are pleased with such jests does not concern me, save that it proves how much your religion is weaker than ours.'

'How so?'

'No man of the Great Horde or the White Horde or the Golden Horde would dare to make a joke from worship words.'

'Because your god Tängri doesn't have a sense of humour?'

'No. Because the Everlasting Blue Sky has a greater dignity than that. Besides which, the shaman priests would slay any man who used the words without respect.'

'Ah.' Ivan glanced at the five shamans, who glowered back at him with as much disapproval as the entire College of Cardinals and, despite the discomfort of the carvings, settled himself more firmly into the Chair of State. It was one of those times in such a mannered, artificial conversation when settling back was what one of the parties had to do, and the rôle had fallen to him. 'The

Romans do that too. They have a special band of holy fathers, the Inquisition, who do nothing else.'

'Then the Romans are wiser than the Great Khan Ögotäi has given them credit for being. If a man is not afraid of his god, then it goes without saying that he will not be afraid of his overlord.'

'Unless that overlord is more terrible than any god created by a priest to scare his worshippers into good behaviour,' said Mar'ya Morevna cynically.

Amragan *tarkhan* looked at her for several seconds, his face bland and blank, until finally Tsar Ivan said, 'Yes?' in a tone that demanded some sort of reply.

'You wife, Lord of Khorlov,' said the Türk, 'is like a Tatar woman.' Then he grinned and held up one open hand as though to turn aside the offence he saw flare up on Ivan's face. 'That was not an insult, as she well knows.' It was true: Mar'ya Morevna wore an expression more of amusement than anger, half-hidden by the pretence of rubbing an itchiness at the end of her nose. 'She speaks without deferring to the men's side.' Amragan shrugged. 'Sometimes that is a good thing. At other times, not. You know your lady best.'

The amusement on Mar'ya Morevna's face curdled like vinegar in new milk, and it suddenly became Ivan's turn to hide his face behind a thoughtful gesture. He had been prepared to hate this envoy and until he found out more about him, there was still little to like about the man; but there was a quickness about his wits that was strangely appealing, as he slid deftly between political observation and delicate social insult. If Amragan *tarkhan* had been a jester, Ivan would have rewarded him well. As it was, being the representative of both the Ilkhan of the Golden Horde and of the Great Khan of all Khans, with two hundred horsemen encamped beyond the kremlin gates, he was a man to watch.

And listen to: especially that.

'How can you speak with the voice of the Khan Ögotäi,' he asked curiously, 'when he has been dead these two years past?' His tone was so much that of simple interest that the *tarkhan* answered without any of those hard stares that suspected some hidden insult.

'No new Khakhan has yet been chosen by the *kuriltai*,' he replied. 'His *suldë*, what you would call his spirit-strength, remains with us until that time. It goes before us in the *tuk* standard of nine tails, and it gives us power. It will be so until the new Khan takes his place in Karakorum.'

'And for the present, each Ilkhan rules as he sees fit?' said Mar'ya Morevna. It was more of a speculation voiced aloud than a question, unless Amragan chose to treat it as such. The envoy said nothing, and his hard face remained devoid of expression as Mar'ya Morevna went on. 'So I wonder if the Ilkhan Batu is endeavouring to consolidate his position in Russia while there is no superior authority to order otherwise.' Still none of the Tatars gave anything away, even when she said flatly, 'After all, he was at pains not to go to Karakorum for the *kuriltai*. Gout, wasn't it?'

'Mar'yushka!' Ivan was shocked; if this was diplomacy, it was a rougher brand than he had been expecting. The silence deepened, and Tsar Ivan wondered if he was the only person present grateful for a sword still scabbarded at his hip.

Then Amragan *tarkhan* threw back his head and laughed, a great bark of mirth that shattered the stillness as suddenly and loudly as a hammer might smash a pottery jar. The shamans – and not just the shamans – were astonished. But what had broken at the same time was that slowly increasing tension, a feeling in the air like a bowstring being steadily drawn back until it had to be released or break the bow. Either way would have been damaging, but this easing of the pressure brought harm to nobody – except for the Rus, who were having difficulty accepting the fact that a Tatar could laugh at anything but destruction.

'Gout perhaps,' said Amragan once he had regained sufficient grip on himself to speak clearly. 'But also the knowledge that where he was, as the only Lord of Sarai in the sea of grass you call the Kipchak Steppe, was a better place than being one among many in a dead Khakhan's court. So now you know that which is a secret to most others. Is this not trust, by the authority I am given?'

Ivan glanced quickly at the other three faces, and saw only surprise. It was trust indeed, but to a Tatar envoy with such authority, the betrayal of secrets could quickly be concealed by fire and the edge of the sword.

'When the *Sain* Khan Batu advised me that Khorlov was different to other cities of the Rus,' said the Türk, 'I thought he meant only by your use of *kara-sechun*, the Black Wisdom, and so I brought all of these,' he jerked a thumb at the shamans, 'to protect me. But also it is because you speak plainly, and do not conceal your meanings behind a fog of fair words like the Chin of Kithai.'

'We can do that when we must, Amragan *tarkhan*,' said Ivan. 'But then, having seen the fate of other cities, what good would fair words have done?'

The Türk grinned, not pleasantly. 'None at all. Nor would speaking plain have helped had you said what she did. From the lord of a city that would have been an insult, and I would have burned this place around your ears, and had I been Ilchidai *noyan*, I would have burned it long ago in any case, since you did not bow to me as you came in.'

Mar'ya Morevna's mouth compressed as though she had just drunk vinegar, and Ivan could hear a faint, high whistling in his ears as though his blood was moving too fast through his veins. To have come so close to destruction was an ugly shock, especially since it was because they had both been fooled into thinking that this Türk could be reasoned with as though he was a Rus, all because he reacted well – or at least not badly – to some jokes. Only Strel'tsin and Volk Volkovich controlled their features, and that only through long practice in concealing either what they thought or what they really were.

'Now know this,' said Amragan *tarkhan*, abruptly all business. 'The Ilkhan Batu has determined to experiment with a new way of ruling the Rus. Direct government by *daru-gashi*, the military governor with a garrison at his disposal, is wasteful of men, of time and of revenue.'

'How revenue?' It was Strel'tsin who asked that, as of course it would have been.

'The *daru-gashi* must organise the taking of a census, so that the proper proportion of taxes may be levied. Your superstitious common people believe that the taking of a census has to do with listing their souls for the Evil One, and murder our census-takers.' Amragan *tarkhan* made a gesture of despair at such foolishness. 'This even though we made certain to leave those who till the soil alone, so that they could grow their crops for us as well. When order is restored, there is often a considerable delay before taxes and grain may again be collected from that district.' Ivan winced, not wanting to know what blood and slaughter lay behind those simple words. 'So,' the *tarkhan* continued, 'it has been decided in the wisdom of the Khan, that rulers of domains as yet undisturbed may remain there. Rulers who fled before us and who have now returned may be restored to their former positions.'

'Such as the Great Prince of Kiev?'

The Türk looked at Mar'ya Morevna and smiled slightly. 'Which one? Yuriy Vladimirovich, who was ruler before the Horde came to Russia? Or Danyil Yaroslavich? Him I saw myself at the Golden Court in Sarai, putting his case before the Ilkhan Batu.'

'What case is this?' asked Ivan cautiously. Amragan *tarkhan* seemed happy enough to talk now, but having witnessed the Türk's mercurial swings of mood, the young Tsar had become much more leery of asking questions that might seem indelicate.

'This Danyil claims that the resistance made by his brother Rostislav against us was not by his command, that he would have submitted and opened the gates, and that therefore he is entitled to rule Kiev again.'

Ivan whistled softly between his teeth. 'The brother Rostislav he mentions as his entitlement to succession usurped the throne from Great Prince Yuriy in May of the very year the city fell to the Khan's army.'

Amragan *tarkhan* was not impressed. 'Then let this Yuriy come to Sarai and contest the claim,' he said simply. 'The Ilkhan Batu will hear all sides of any argument, so long as peace is observed.'

'Peace? In Russia?' Ivan laughed hollowly, aware that he might be treading on thin ice once again; but he also knew the minuscule likelihood of any quarrel between princely claimants resolving itself without fighting of one degree or another.

'Peace,' repeated Amragan. 'The Ilkhan Batu will not countenance private war in his Khanate. He follows the wise precept of the Great Ancestor Chinghis-Khan, who said: "In war be tigers, in peace, doves." And you Princes will learn that, soon or late.'

Clearing his throat, Ivan stared at the armoured Türk and tried to judge the man's temper at the moment. It seemed reasonable enough right now, so he cleared his throat again and said,

'Amragan *tarkhan*, before I took the crown I was a prince and a tsarevich; now my right and proper title is *Tsar*.'

'No. Your title is still Prince.' The *tarkhan* cast a thoughtful eye at the fur hat which did duty for Ivan's crown. 'Call yourself a Great Prince, if you wish it – but not Tsar. So speaks the Ilkhan Batu.'

'Why?' The question was as blunt as Amragan *tarkhan*'s denial had been, and the two men studied one another as though engaged in swordplay, each searching for some sort of opening. Ivan was well aware that the Tatar envoy had a far superior force at his disposal; but at the same time, he had to know why the title he bore, the title borne by his father and his father's father back through generations, was suddenly and arbitrarily set aside like this.

The Türk sighed, evidently impatient with the stubbornness of this Rus for whom the simple word of the Khan was never enough. Ivan guessed that the man's easiest solution was to have him rolled in a carpet and smothered, or stamped to death by his guards to avoid the spilling of royal blood, as so many other lords and rulers had been executed; but there was the matter of that granting of hospitality, the gift of bread and salt at the city gate. Amragan *tarkhan* had probably been insulted, defied, bowed to, even pleaded with, but it was almost certain that he had never before been treated to the simple courtesy of welcome due to a stranger after a long journey.

'Understand and remember, so you do not ask such foolish questions when you too come to the Golden Court at Sarai,' the envoy said briskly. 'All other Rus lords are content to style themselves as *knyaz*', which is to say "prince". You of Khorlov have long styled yourselves *tsar*, and that is "Caesar". Emperor. "Khan" is also emperor, and the Great Khan is Emperor above all others. He, not you. From this day forward, call yourself a prince like all the others, and be content.'

'And why should we come to Sarai? In your own words, "rulers of domains yet undisturbed may remain there". '

'Yes.' Amragan *tarkhan* tipped back his head in a haughty manner and studied Mar'ya Morevna down the bridge of his long falcon's-beak nose. 'Yes indeed. Very like a woman of the Tatars. Even to the refusal to listen properly so as to make better space for her observations.' Though she sizzled at that, Mar'ya Morevna kept quiet – which to Ivan's mind, having seen his wife in this sort of mood before, was some sort of minor miracle and a considerable achievement on the Türk's part. 'Those rulers may remain in their domains, lady, once the Ilkhan Batu has granted his approval for them to do so. But in token that they rule by his consent, they must leave the tokens of their right to rule in his keeping, at the Golden Court of the Golden Horde in Sarai.'

Mar'ya Morevna made a small sound at that, a gasp three-quarters stifled so that it might as easily have been a sneeze. Ivan knew well enough that it was nothing of the sort, but not knowing what had provoked the gasp, didn't react. 'Tokens?' she said after a moment, carefully disinterested. 'What sort of tokens would these be?'

'Crowns, sceptres – the regalia that you of the Rus need to identify the lord of a domain.'

Tsar Ivan glowered, thinking he knew now what was troubling his wife. The Tatars were rendering those they left to rule no more than puppets; literally so, since the right to govern resided more in crown and sceptre than in the man or woman who wore and wielded them. The bearer changed from generation to generation, either peacefully or through the many acts of violence that might befall a princely monarch, but the royal jewels that passed from hand to hand and head to head remained the same. For almost a hundred years after the founding of the realm – by an adventurer of the North people more successful than his fellows – the crown of Khorlov had been nothing more than his grim, functional helmet, worn complete with its iron nosepiece. After that it had accumulated gold, jewels and all the other elaborate ornaments that made a crown more than just another hat; but even now, under all its decoration, Khorlov's Great Crown was helmet-shaped in token of the Tsar's power to rule and to protect what was ruled. Without it – Ivan thought of puppets again – he was no more than a scarecrow of sticks and rags, propped up on the throne to keep the place from someone better.

Rubbing her hands together as though they were sticky, Mar'ya Morevna looked again at Amragan *tarkhan*. 'And how many, let's say crowns, yes, how many crowns have been gathered in Sarai so far?'

The Türk thought for a moment, his lips moving as he went

through the unfamiliar names of Rus Princely states in his head. 'Twelve,' he said finally. 'The crown of Khorlov will be thirteen.'

When Mar'ya Morevna went white and carefully signed herself with the life-giving cross, Ivan knew that something more than just the loss of Khorlov's crown was badly wrong. Evidently this had something to do with the Tatars and their collection of crowns in Sarai, but though he racked his brains to think of whys and wherefores, he could dredge up nothing that might fit the facts. Amragan *tarkhan* was saying more, this time about Ivan's own reputation and about Koshchey the Undying, but the Tsar – let the Tatars call him what they pleased, he was and would remain Tsar of Khorlov even if nowhere else than inside his own head – paid the envoy no further heed.

'Your pardon, *tarkhan*,' Ivan came out of his seat at once, moving hurriedly to help his wife to her feet, 'but my lady is unwell.' Or pretending so to get us out of here, at any rate. 'There will be a banquet in your honour later today. We can talk about public matters of less importance then.'

The Türkic *tarkhan* did not get up; instead he waved an indolent hand as though *he* owned the Great Hall and the kremlin around it, and was granting Ivan permission to leave. A small snarl pulled at the corners of Ivan's mouth, though that might have been mistaken for effort when supporting Mar'ya Morevna's weight. Handing her over to Volk Volkovich, who had kept remarkably quiet during the entire conversation, Ivan nodded to one of Guard-Captain Akimov's lieutenants near the doorway of the hall.

'My guards will see you and your companions safely to the gates of the city,' he said, and whether the envoy liked it or not, his tone was that of regal dismissal. 'Armour,' he added, 'is not usually worn at my table.' Amragan *tarkhan* was silent for a few seconds while he puzzled through the levels of what had just been said; then his laughter followed Ivan all the way out of the hall.

As soon as they were in the courtyard beyond the Hall of Audience and out of sight and sound of its menacing occupant, Ivan grabbed Mar'ya by the arms and shook her with that desperate violence which is a true betrayer of fear. 'Hell and damnation, Mar'yushka! What's the matter with you?'

131

She stared back at him with huge-pupilled blue eyes that had terror barely concealed in their depths, but her voice was, as always, back under complete control. 'Hell and damnation,' she echoed. 'That has just become a very real possiblity.'

'Would someone mind explaining to me what I'm so obviously missing?' demanded Dmitriy Vasil'yevich Strel'tsin pettishly. 'After what that accursed Türk was saying, I think that – ' As a large brown hand came down heavily on his shoulder, Strel'tsin abruptly shut up.

'I think, First Minister,' said the Grey Wolf in a voice that was much less human than Volk Volkovich usually sounded, 'it would be a kindness if you found something to drink. And four cups.'

Strel'tsin gave the big man an odd look, for along with lying, alcohol was a human failing in which Volk Volkovich did not indulge. This time, however, there was a troubled look about his tanned, ruthless face that suggested he was more than willing to break his own rule. It was a look that said the Grey Wolf knew only too well what was troubling Mar'ya Morevna. 'Yes,' the First Minister said, sounding more vague than he felt, 'yes, at once. Four cups . . .'

There was a wooden bench on the sunny side of the courtyard, a pretty thing fretted with silhouettes of birds and beasts from old tales, and while Strel'tsin was off about his mission of mercy – which in Tsar Ivan's Khorlov was not likely to take him very long – Ivan and the Grey Wolf helped Mar'ya Morevna to a seat there. She was trembling, a fine muscle tremor as though she had been doing hard physical work rather than the sort of racking shudder Ivan had expected. It was only after she had been sitting down for a few minutes, with Ivan on the bench beside her and Volk Volkovich squatting nearby on his haunches, that he realised the tremor came less from the terror in her eyes than from the frantically suppressed desire to grab Amragan *tarkhan* and his shaman companions, and beat some sort of sense into them one at a time and all together.

Dmitriy Vasil'yevich returned bare minutes later, a rather chipped stoneware flagon in one hand and four turned-wood drinking bowls in the other. '*Okhotnichnya*,' he said by way of explanation. 'From one of the guards.' The old councillor smiled one of his rare, withered, but strangely sweet smiles. Dmitriy

Vasil'yevich had outlived both his wives and all seven of his children, and smiling was not something that came easily to his lips any more. 'He was on duty and wasn't supposed to have it, and I agreed not to see it. Provided he let me take it with me.'

The herb and honey vodka wasn't chilled, as it should have been, and it wasn't even a particularly good blend; but the alcohol slammed into their throats with all the heat that any of them could have desired. Except possibly Volk Volkovich, who coughed rackingly after the first swallow and wiped those wolf's eyes of his, whose dull yellow glow had been dimmed somewhat by a sudden overflow of tears. 'I don't know what you see in this snake venom,' he said wheezily. But he held out his empty bowl for a refill nevertheless.

Ivan saw the first hint of a smile at his antics flicker across Mar'ya Morevna's face, and felt as warmly disposed to the Grey Wolf as he had been for a long time. She took a deep breath and glanced from side to side as that small sound drew all eyes to her.

'The crowns,' she said. 'The Crown regalia. *You* know, don't you?' Volk Volkovich nodded, but Ivan and Strel'tsin waited silently for further elaboration.

Mar'ya Morevna stared at the vodka in the wooden bowl, and swirled it slowly as if the patterns were telling her something. And perhaps they were. 'It isn't just the taking of your crown,' she said to Ivan, 'although God knows that's bad enough. But if they gather all the crowns and sceptres of the wide white world together in one place, all that potential force contained in gold and jewels and centuries of belief, then something has to give way. We've been between the worlds and beyond the world and into the Summer Country, Vanya; but we've always done so carefully, closing the doors we open. What might – could – *will* happen in Sarai, is that all that accumulated weight of power is going to tear through into . . . somewhere else, and there'll be nothing left to plug the hole it makes.'

The vodka seemed to have lost its strength to burn his throat the way it had done before, but Ivan gulped it down anyway. 'And then what?'

'I don't know. Nobody can know, not until it happens. Maybe our world will drain away into that somewhere else. Or it might flow from there to here. Or there might be something out there that will be attracted to here like a moth to a flame.'

'Like a shark to bloody water,' said the Grey Wolf sombrely. He was no more specific than that, and didn't need to be.

'Those imbecile shamans are behind this,' Mar'ya Morevna snapped. 'They planted the idea in the Khan's head. I'm sure of it.' She swore for several seconds with hair-curling ferocity, then rinsed her mouth out with vodka as though that might do some good. 'And no,' she said to Ivan before he could ask the obvious question, 'that didn't make me feel any better. Not at all. *D'yavol!* It's been said before, it'll be said again: they're playing with forces they don't understand. All they can see is a reservoir of power that they've taken out of the hands of a conquered but still-dangerous people, not what will happen when the reservoir finally overflows its banks!'

'What can be done?' Dmitriy Vasil'yevich Strel'tsin, Court Sorcerer amongst all his other posts, looked from face to face with the uneasy awareness that he should have been able to suggest instead of just ask. But like the shamans, he was so far removed from Mar'ya Morevna's proficiency at the Art Magic that he was of no more use than . . .

Than Tsar Ivan Aleksandrovich himself.

It was a situation not too far removed from his long-ago decision to submit to the Tatars if such a submission was necessary. Both were much harder to explain or understand than the *bogatyr'* philosophy of finding an adversary that could be cut with a sword, then cutting until you were either defeated or victorious. From Koshchey *Bessmyrtnyy* to Baba Yaga to the Tatars, Ivan reflected grimly, he seemed to have a talent for attracting the sort of enemy unaffected by even the finest edge.

'All this takes away any choice we might have had.'

'About what?'

'Going to Sarai at the Khan's "invitation", or staying here.'

Mar'ya Morevna squeezed her husband's hand gently. 'There was never any choice about that any way, Vanyushka,' she said. 'You heard Amragan *tarkhan* as clearly as I – no matter what he says about deliberately mishearing. If you want to remain Tsar, or Prince – '

'Tsar!'

' – Then you do it with the Khan's authority, or not at all.'

'Um. And how likely is it that the Türk and his escort will let me leave Khorlov for Sarai without bringing the Great Crown with me?'

'Not very,' said Dmitriy Vasil'yevich. 'He looks like the sort of man who'll check the baggage train as each item is loaded.'

'So. There it is, then.' Ivan held out his drinking bowl. 'Is there any more of that foul muck left? I need another drink!'

The feast had been under preparation for most of the day when Ivan and Mar'ya Morevna finally emerged from the kremlin to examine what was being done. Both had shared steam and then a long, leisurely bath before changing their clothes for something better than mere work garb, but if anyone thought their choice of colours somewhat out of season, there was no breath of it.

Ivan's kaftan was high-collared velvet to below his knees, his breeches, wide and silken, were tucked into heeled boots of glove-soft leather; he had a high-crowned velvet hat over all, fronted with a panache of egret feathers in a brooch of pearls and silver, and there was a single pearl drop glinting at the lobe of his right ear. Mar'ya Morevna wore her kaftan to the ankles, her slippers encrusted with patterns in pearl and small cut diamonds, and her tall filigree head-dress with its pendant rows of jewels framing her face was that of a Tsar's consort rather than a ruling princess. Ivan had insisted on it, and Amragan *tarkhan* could make of that what he liked. All the embellishment was either milk-white leather or embroidery in cobweb-fine threads of solid silver bullion; all the gemstones were white diamond or translucent pearl. Everything else was black, from the figured velvet of their garments to the Sibir'yan sable that trimmed it. Though it was still high summer, they were dressed in the sombre formal garmets worn for the day of first snowfall, for the dying of the year, and if it seemed as though they had put on mourning, to Tsar Ivan's mind that was appropriate enough.

He had examined the weather – which was holding warm and sunny, with only the slightest breeze – and with that as a pretext, had issued instructions that the greater part of the banquet would not take place indoors; nor, if it came to that, within the walls of the city at all. To have Amragan *tarkhan* under his roof alone was unnerving enough; to invite the Tatar lieutenants of his guard as well, as custom dictated, was an experience the Tsar would as soon

135

avoid. The other experience, that of the banquet itself, was one he planned to enjoy to the full, and among his string of instructions had been an authorisation to Yuriy Oblomov the Chief Cook, giving him a free hand both with the kremlin pantry and the domain's exchequer. If the Tatars were intending to plunder one or the other, and probably both, Ivan meant to imitate his old reaver ancestors and get there first.

That was why a dozen huge fires of oak logs glowed and spat in the cleared space beyond Khorlov's gate, why sweating kitchen servants not just from the kremlin but from several noble households within the city were scurrying to and fro with long-handled ladles – in fact, small saucepans lashed to broomsticks – and why the slowly drifting hot air trapped against the walls seemed like a meal in itself, with nourishment in every breath.

Whole pigs, whole sheep, and a single massive ox rotated glistening on thick wooden spits above the fires, turned from a safe distance by eager hands, basted with salted fat and their own drippings by the bucketful. They were watched and sniffed and tentatively prodded now and again by the Firemasters of seven kitchens, each one with his or her own opinion of how to get the best result from a joint roasted on an open fire. The joints – Ivan could not help but smile at how they could use such an insignificant word for five thousand pounds of meat, the ox itself weighing two thousand pounds or more – had been revolving slowly for almost four hours now, and each cook was growing passionate about what should be done in the last period of cooking to bring out the finest flavour.

So far as the Tsar of Khorlov was concerned, if the aroma was an indication of how they would taste, then taking them down and letting them cool and standing out of his way was the best thing they could do.

There were fish on grills, and capons and squab on skewers, looking insignificant beside the vast bulk of beef and pork and mutton no longer quite on the hoof, but adding their own piquancy to the afternoon as they were smeared with lard or oil or butter in which onions and garlic had been crushed, then sprinkled with delicately fragrant herbs. Marjoram and rosemary, basil and thyme and dill all added their tang to their air, mingling with the

136

more pungent scents of horseradish or sour-pickled cabbage, mushrooms and cucumbers.

Ivan wandered about as the Tsar was supposed to do on such occasions – an arduous duty! – smelling and tasting and complimenting this cook or that on some new masterwork of the culinary art. Here the simple, a pot of buckwheat *kasha*, simmered in meat stock and buttered to perfection; there the elaborate, chicken *tabaka* style, boned and fried flat under a weighted lid with a fierce seasoning of garlic, walnuts and the brutally hot, brutally expensive red pepper flakes of Si-Chüan. It was food for the fingers; Ivan did not even need to draw his eating-knife and spoon from their case at his belt, but simply ripped off a piece, dunked it in *tkemali* sour plum sauce, munched it up – and then drank a lot of cold wine very fast as the red pepper set fire to his throat.

'Make sure that the envoy Amragan *tarkhan* has plenty of this,' he said to the headscarfed little woman who was tending the pans. 'It might thaw him out.'

Leaving her gaping at being addressed so casually by her Tsar, he walked on, pausing every now and then to glance with satisfaction at the festival around him. Such events had been more common in the old days. Ivan smiled bitterly; those 'old days' were no more than six years ago. Before the Tatars. His wedding; the birth of the children; his accession to the crown that he was soon to lose. Occasions when even the poorest peasant could 'eat with a long knife and a big spoon'. By his calculation there was enough food not just for the Tatar envoy and his escort and for the people from the kremlin palace, but for every man, woman and child in Khorlov. So far as drink was concerned, there was enough for twice that many. His people were Rus, after all, and drinking – especially at someone else's expense – was a joy to them. What was the adage? 'Free vinegar is sweeter than bought honey.' True enough, and never more than when the Tatars all unaware were providing both the honey and the vinegar.

The Tsar of Khorlov squared his shoulders under the ornate black kaftan, hitched his collar just a little higher behind the nape of his neck, and sauntered down to where the official reception was being prepared. It was as though the banqueting hall from Khorlov's kremlin had been brought bodily into the open air, and then its floor, walls and ceiling carefully removed so that just the furniture remained. It should, thought Ivan, appeal to the Tatars: to eat like civilised human beings for once, yet under the canopy of their god's blue sky.

'God, it is blue, isn't it?' said Mar'ya Morevna as she moved beside him and took his arm and followed his gaze upward. The words were so apt that Ivan, not for the first time in their marriage, wondered whether his wife could read if not thoughts then at least images from his mind.

'Amragan and his Blackhats should appreciate it.'

'I should hope so. We've gone to a lot of trouble on their behalf. Giving the tax collector a cup of wine, my father used to say.'

'Your father,' said Ivan, 'was a lord in his own right. He didn't pay taxes, they were paid to him.' Mar'ya Morevna punched him gently in the ribs.

'That didn't make him any less entitled to the saying, did it?'

'And if this is what he would have called a cup of wine,' said Ivan, punching back, 'then your father was wealthier than he had any right to be.'

'Are you fighting?' said a small, uncertain voice. Tsarevna Anastasya gazed solemnly at her parents, and in particular at Ivan's still-clenched fist. 'When I do that to Kolya, he doesn't like it. But I hit him much harder than that' – it sounded like a criticism of Ivan's technique – 'and then he tries to hit me back. Of course I don't let him. It would be disker–, discor–,' Natasha furrowed her brow as the words refused to jump from mind to mouth, 'discourteous-and-inappropriate behaviour. To me, anyway.'

'Strel'tsin?' said Mar'ya Morevna.

'Not a doubt of it,' said Ivan. 'He's the only man in the palace with the nerve to let a seven-year-old child run loose with words like that.' He bent down and scooped his daughter up onto his shoulder, where she first knocked his hat crooked and then carefully set it straight again. 'And no, little mouse, we weren't fighting. You and Nikolai fight. Grown-up people only argue.'

'Then was that – ?'

'Not even slightly.' Mar'ya Morevna pulled a kerchief from her sleeve and dusted at the child's boots before they could track dust all over Ivan's black velvet shoulder. 'We were just having fun.' Ivan chuckled; the low, husky sort of chuckle that Mar'ya Morevna knew only too well. She glared at her husband and he felt the tension of another potential punch gather against his ribs; then instead she patted 'Tasha on the wrist. 'But for Heaven's sake don't go telling people that you found *mam'ya* and *batyushka* having fun together!'

'Why?'

'It's . . . discourteous and inappropriate behaviour.'

'Oh.'

'You see, mouse, it's not their business to be told things like that about their Tsar.'

'Oh.'

'They'll think we can't afford a lock for the door.'

'Ivan . . .'

'Yes?'

'Shut up.'

'Should I go out of earshot and come back again?' The throaty, accented voice sounded amused, even though the only suggestion of a smile was a movement of those damned moustaches again. Amragan *tarkhan* had taken Ivan's parting words to heart. Except for the knife in his lacquered eating-case he was wearing neither armour nor weapons, even though the ten Mongols of his personal guard were wearing both, polished to mirror brightness so that whenever they moved the scales of their harness reflected the sunlight like the facets of a well-cut gemstone. Instead the Khan's envoy was wearing a simple red headband around his brows, the long braids of his hair hanging down his back, and a plain shirt of heavy linen with his usual baggy trews and soft boots. But over it all was a magnificent cross-wrapped robe of royal purple silk that shimmered whenever he made the slightest movement. It was woven with a complex pattern of curly branches and long-tailed birds, so that when the light struck just so, they shone pale violet against the purple background. The brocade of soft gold thread that edged and hemmed it was hardly worth as much as the fabric itself.

Ivan eyed it, envied it, and wondered how many lives it had cost. 'No need,' he said. 'A family matter, nothing more.'

'You do your family well, it seems,' said the Türk, indicating all the food being prepared further up the hill.

'That is for my people, not my family. But one of the Tsar's titles is "Little Father", so maybe you could call them my children after all.'

'Did we come to Khorlov on some festival holiday?'

'No. It's just . . .' Ivan couldn't really think of a good way to explain how he was making sure all his stores of the best food and drink were consumed now, by his own people for the most part, so that Amragan or those who came after him would have no chance to loot it. 'It's the day the Tatars came, and didn't burn the city.'

'Indeed.' The way the *tarkhan* spoke suggested that he was more aware of what was going on than Ivan guessed, because he looked up at the sun, just past the meridian, and smiled. 'But we are still here, and the day is not yet over.'

At least he was smiling when he said it, and more than his moustaches moved. Ivan smiled right back, and reached towards the nearest table for the jug of wine almost encased in ice, and two large cups.

Once, and not so very long ago, Ivan had been like every other Russian, whether of high birth or of low. He had drunk *kvas* and ale and vodka, and when he could get it, red wine imported at great expense from Frankish Burgundy, and white wine transported at much less expense from the Krimean coast of the Black Sea.

Then Ivan had discovered the Greeks. These were not the crafty Byzantines who had been hired to teach martial and political skills to Mar'ya Morevna. Nor were they the hairy, wild inhabitants of the equally wild Peloponnese, who were little better than animals and maybe a bit too closely related to those same animals. Certainly they wore more goatskin than ordinary folk could stomach, and as a result smelt worse than their own flocks.

Ivan's Greeks were safely pinned to the pages of a dog-eared copy of the *Il'yad* he had found in Mar'ya Morevna's library. He had been reading strategy and tactics: Tacitus, Vitruvius, Polybius, Demetrius, and just for a change from the Latin -us names, Heron and Caesar. Even though there had been brief sparks of interest, most of the reading had been as dull as listening to any elderly commander move the cutlery about the table.

But the *Il'yad* was another matter. Sarcasm and savagery, love and war. Ivan could not read the original Greek, but it had been transcribed first to equally unreadable High Church Slavonic written in the crabbed letters of the old Glagolitic script by some Orthodox monk, and then painstakingly translated into modern Russian by Mar'ya Morevna's father. Long before even the North people who were Ivan's ancestors had sailed their longships down the Volga, trading as they called it – though if the odds were right they tended to take rather than haggle – these Greeks had laid siege for ten years to King Priy'yam's kremlin at Troy. They had eaten great feasts of roasted meat, just like this one, and quaffed great quantities of wine, and Ivan, after several evenings curled up with a lamp, a bottle and the book, had determined he wanted some of that same wine.

As a result, and with some effort, he had developed a taste for the nauseating varnish that the old poet claimed was drunk by heroes. Wine mixed with resin was not something he had ever tasted before, and the first mouthful convinced him that anyone who drank it on a regular basis *had* to be a hero.

Either that, or desperate enough to drink lamp oil.

To Mar'ya Morevna's amusement, Ivan persisted. At least it didn't surprise her. She had long known her husband was a stubborn man, given to fads and fancies that he would describe at boring length until his audience either fled into the night or rose in rebellion, but she was relieved that this stubbornness didn't extend to adding sea water to his wine as well as resin. Not that Ivan hadn't tried it, though not having sea water to hand, he had dissolved salt in ordinary water instead. Once. That *once* had made him as spectacularly sick as a whole evening's indulgence in more common brews, and the sea water idea was hastily discarded. The resin, however, remained.

Mar'ya Morevna was not the only one to shake her head. The Rus were fond enough of sour, tangy things like pickled cabbage, but in equal measure, they had a notoriously sweet tooth as witness the swarms of bees kept not just for mead and *sbiten'*, mead's nonalcoholic little brother, but also to provide the vast quantities of honey that they used to sweeten their food.

And here was Ivan Aleksandrovich Khorlovskiy, Tsar by his father's abdication and by his own acceptance of it, married to the ruler of a principality, lord of wide domains, with a self-developed

taste for a wine so acid – never mind its bouquet and aftertaste of
turpentine – that all but the most depraved peasant would refuse
to have it in the house. That he admitted it was hardly surprising.
Other Tsars and Princes had admitted to other vices, more
interesting ones than this – though the most interesting of all
usually came to light only when those who had indulged in them
were safely dead – but the drinking of wine deliberately matured
in barrels made of raw pine wood was not so much interesting as
simply peculiar. It had one advantage, however: there was no
mistaking the Tsar's preferred drink, served in its own distinc-
tively shaped jug buried in a bucket of ice, and little likelihood of
anyone wanting to steal it.

The jug in his hand contained that same stuff, resinated wine
vinegar in all but name, though packing a velvet punch that no
vinegar could claim. Ivan offered one of the cups to Amragan
tarkhan, then filled the other for himself and took a long,
confidence-inspiring draught from it before pouring for the Tatar
envoy. The confidence he had meant to inspire was partly his own,
through the rapid ingestion of a favoured form of alcohol, and
partly that of the *tarkhan* so that the man wouldn't think he was
being poisoned. There had been too many people who had made
that assumption from their first sip for him to want to run any such
risk with the Khan's man. Coughs and curses were one response,
and more or less acceptable; however, torching the city was quite
another, and not.

After that, Ivan had intended to drink Amragan *tarkhan* into a
foolish stupor, to leave him sickened with his head pounding, to
prove . . .

Something that had made perfect sense earlier.

When the Türk drained his first cup and asked for more, the
game lost much of its sparkle. Amragan *tarkhan* had not only
drunk the Greek wine before, but liked it and was much taken that
Ivan shared a common interest. That was not something which the
Tsar of Khorlov viewed as complimentary, though mercifully he
was nothing like drunk enough yet to say anything of the sort.
Instead, Ivan pressed the barely reduced jug into Amragan's
hands, made some sort of excuse and stalked off to see what was
happening with regard to food.

Enough and more than enough was happening to ease the mood

of any Tsar, even one in a worse temper than he was. The various roasted beasts were being eased from their fires as he approached, to 'rest' as the cooks called it, before they were carved and served out. Ivan admired them, and let the pleasure of that simple – or not-so-simple – artistry clear various flickers of poorly targeted malice from his head. Even though they were no longer near the raked, banked beds of coals they still bubbled gravy and sizzled faintly, and their scent was that of Heaven with the angels singing. Each creature, whether sheep or pig or the titanic ox, was glazed and crackling with a baked accumulation of herb-laden oils, browned butter and its own fragrant juices, varnished onto the meat in a coruscation of tints that ran the spectrum from dainty pink to a crisp-edged, savoury deep brown. Everyone in Khorlov was there to watch them being unshipped from the great roasting-trestles, and more than a few Tatars from Amragan *tarkhan*'s guard as well. It was odd to see old enemies, or predators and victims, united in a silent, inhaling appreciation of good food.

'Smells a damn sight better than *grut*,' said Amragan *tarkhan* at Ivan's elbow, making the Tsar jump slightly. For such a tall, strong man he moved with surprising lightness on his feet, even though – Ivan went surreptitiously on tiptoe to peek inside – the jug of resinated wine was a good deal emptier than the last time he had seen it. Of course most of its contents could have been poured out on the ground, and what remained carried about like this just to impress; but the *tarkhan*'s breath and Ivan's nose said not.

'*Grut*? It even sounds appalling.'

'Marching rations,' said Amragan without much enthusiasm. 'The women separate mares' milk into curds and whey, dry the curds in the sun, then they crumble them up and pack the crumbs away – because once they're dried, they keep forever. Then if we're on a hard march and there's nothing else, nothing at all, or no time left to hunt, we mix the crumbs with water and drink it. That is *grut*.'

Ivan made a face and recovered the jug of wine, then, lacking a cup, took a generous and most un-tsarlike swig. 'Whatever reason Chinghis-Khan – '

'The Great Ancestor Temüchin.'

' – Or whatever. Why he was conquering everywhere.' He swallowed some more wine. 'It probably had more than a little to do with finding somewhere rich enough that he wouldn't need to eat *grut* any more.'

Amragan *tarkhan* stared at Ivan and raised his eyebrows at such disrespect for the first Khan of all Khans of the Mongols. His tongue passed over those thin lips as though in response to the fragrance of good roast beef, though Ivan expected it was more likely the prelude to a threat or maybe a pronouncement of punishment. What he had not anticipated was a cheerful slap on the back and another of those crashing guffaws of laughter. Ivan staggered a little and hid a crooked smile as he worked his shoulders to ease the ache; despite his steadiness of feet and speech, the wine had taken effect on Amragan *tarkhan* in no uncertain terms.

For all the looting and pillaging he had done, with the guzzling of stolen wine it had entailed, the Türk was likely far more used to the fermented mares' milk drink *kumys*. Ivan had tasted it, and though sour enough it had nothing like the potency of even the most ordinary wine. Only the wealthiest Tatars could afford to accustom their systems to stronger fare, and they habitually drank to excess – Ögotäi Khan had died of it – so that when lesser mortals had the opportunity to emulate their betters, the results were immediate and drastic. Amragan was nowhere near falling down drunk, and was unlikely to be so for a while, but it seemed that he had forgotten his dignity as an envoy.

Heads had turned at the noise, and most of the people looked on with approval and no small relief to see the Khan's ambassador so friendly with their Tsar. Others were less pleased; the men to whom an enemy was always an enemy and never someone to be reasoned with, the men whose word for friendship with the enemy was 'treason'. They glared at Ivan from the cover of all those other smiling faces, and turned away, and made their own decisions about what to do with enemy and traitor both.

Though he might have suspected something of the sort, Ivan saw none of it, for at that moment Yuriy Oblomov handed him a carving knife as big as a short sword, the largest and most impressive in the kremlin kitchens. Only when the Tsar had formally made the first cut in the meat could the revels and the proper eating begin, and with his stomach beginning to make enthusiastic and undignified noises, Ivan wasted no time in wielding the blade. As he moved aside to let the Chief Cook and his professional carvers do their work, he found himself grinning wryly at the cheer which went up from the crowd; it was an unusual sound for any Russian city with Tatars encamped outside its walls, and was made more unusual still by the shrill whoops as those same Tatars joined in the cheers.

But then, after the aroma that wafted from the roasted ox when Ivan sank his carving knife into its brisket, a stone statue would have been cheering too.

Despite the presence of Amragan *tarkhan* and his merry men – a presence increasingly merry and hard to ignore as the jugs and flagons went round – it was a good old-fashioned Russian feast. Everyone, not just the Tatars, merrily ate and drank too much. As the drink went down and the singing and dancing began, inevitably one or two fights also broke out among the peasants for this reason or for that, but they were settled amicably with fists or meat bones rather than more deadly weapons, and prompted a few amused wagers between the *boyaryy* at the kremlin tables.

Seated in the guest's place at Ivan's right, Amragan *tarkhan* leaned forward. There was a brimming wooden beaker of something or other in his hand – in fact Ivan could not remember when there had *not* been one – and the Türk was grinning. 'I begin to understand,' he said, 'more of why you laughed when I spoke of the Ilkhan Batu's intention to maintain peace in the Rus domains.'

The Tsar watched one of Khorlov's blacksmiths lift someone else above his head and fling him bodily into the piled fodder for the Tatar horses. That at least was more of a wrestling move than an attempt to do real harm. The truly pugnacious had already had their fights and were sleeping off the effects under trestle tables somewhere. 'My people are a sturdy lot, *tarkhan*,' he said. 'Enslaving them would break their spirit; turn them into nothing more than serfs, pieces of property. I would rather not live to see that happen.'

'And now I should say something ominous like, "I can arrange that," ' said Amragan *tarkhan*. 'Yes?'

'If you feel a need to state the obvious, feel free.'

'Then I shall save my breath. But the Ilkhan Batu has no need to make slaves of the Rus peasants. Their lords do that work quite

145

well enough, and Ilkhan Batu has dominion over *them*. If your sturdy people ever become true slaves, serfs as you call them, it will be because a Russian, not a Tatar, found it convenient to make them so.'

Ivan toyed uneasily with a scrap of meat on his platter and said nothing. Slavery in the sense of iron fetters had been what he meant, not the invisible bondage of labour promised by contract against a loan of grain or use of land. Such a contract might be made for anything from one year to ten, but the obligation could seldom be discharged and often the work such a peasant performed was no more than payment of interest on the original loan. Amragan *tarkhan* knew a deal too much for political small-talk with him to be comfortable for very long.

'So I will be the slave instead?' he said at last.

'As there is one Everlasting Sky,' said the Türk, gesturing sloppily upwards with his cup, 'so on the earth there should be one ruler, and that is the Khan of all Khans. The Ilkhan Batu acts for the Great Khan, whether alive or dead. You will act for the Ilkhan Batu, as I do. This is not slavery.'

'Yet he takes my crown from me, the sign of my lordship in Khorlov.'

Amragan *tarkhan* shrugged, and drank deeply. 'The lordship is what is granted you by the Ilkhan of the Golden Horde, and no man will dare to question it. As for the crown, who will know? I have not yet seen you wear the Great Crown which he demands of you, only lesser things. Wear the lesser and name them great.'

'It's not . . .' Ivan began to say, then fell silent. *Not the same, lacking in power, a pulling of my teeth? That isn't your business. Or you know it already.* 'Never mind. What must I do to gain this grant of lordship from the Khan?'

'Come with me to Sarai and pass through the fires. Bow to the East. Bow to the Ilkhan Batu and give up your crown. Pay the head tax. Then you will be lord of Khorlov by his command, and he will make war on any who would try to depose you without his leave.'

'And what about *with* his leave?' The Türk shrugged again, evidently deeming an explanation to that question superfluous. Ivan shook his head and made his mouth smile, then said, 'Now these fires . . .'

He got no further, because a shadow came between him and the westering sunlight. Aleksey Mikhailovich Romanov stood there, swaying slightly, a goblet of wine in his hand and a smile of sorts on his face. He had the look of a man who had both drunk and overheard a great deal more than was good for him.

'Equivocate, Tsar Ivan,' he said in a blurred voice. 'Make him give you concessions for the loss of your crown. Of your realm. Of whatever honour the Khorlovskiy dynasty could still claim. Don't simply do as he asks.'

'You have a place, *bogatyr*',' Ivan said softly. 'Go to it.'

'My place is here,' said Aleksey Mikhailovich. 'A *bogatyr*' should be ready to defend his lord, even when that lord is no longer worthy of it.'

'A *bogatyr*' should be ready to obey his lord's commands, and my command to you is *sit down!*'

The young man shook his head and frowned, not so much in refusal of the order but as though he had forgotten something important. He looked into the goblet as if expecting that the answer was in there with the wine, then drank deeply just in case it was.

Amragan *tarkhan* watched the performance with an expression of tolerant humour on his face, drunk enough not to take immediate offence at anything the *bogatyr*' had said so far and more amused at Ivan's embarrassed discomfiture than anything else. 'Are all your warriors such wilful children?' he asked.

'I said sit down, Aleksey Mikhailovich. Must you be made to do so, like a' – Ivan hesitated, then deliberately used the Türk's own words – 'like a wilful child?'

'Not yet. There is a thing still needing to be done.'

Ivan pushed himself back in his chair and drummed his fingers in exasperation on the table. 'By me? By you? What?'

'This!'

The remnants of the *bogatyr*'s wine hit Amragan *tarkhan* full in the face, blinding him with its stinging splash for long enough to let Aleksey Mikhailovich throw down the empty goblet and rip his sword out of its scabbard. The blade came around in a long, hard swing that might have sheared the Tatar envoy's head clean off his shoulders. It missed. Amragan *tarkhan* was still in his chair, but chair and man together were both flat on their backs where Tsar

Ivan had wrenched them in the shocked second while the sword was drawn.

But it had not completely failed to draw blood. There was a small clatter as Ivan's pearl-drop earring fell onto the table, with most of his earlobe still gripped in its steel and silver clasp. He clapped one hand to the side of his head as the ear and a long straight cut along his cheek spurted blood in the way that such wounds will, out of all proportion to their size. There was a sound inside his skull like small bells ringing, ringing . . . And then he saw the guards, both Tatar and Rus, come charging in with their weapons at the ready.

'*Nyet! Stoy! Skoroye budyet!*'

That command to stop brought his own men to a standstill with Aleksey Mikhailovich Romanov at the centre of a ring of steel but still alive, and the sheer volume of his shout made the Tatars hesitate at least until Amragan *tarkhan* regained his feet. The envoy was obviously undamaged, except for spills of wine and food over his fine garments; but he was just as obviously shocked sober and in a towering rage, his mouth contorting as it shaped the orders that would have stamped Khorlov from the face of the wide white world. Then he saw the blood running between Ivan's fingers, and his orders went unspoken. For the time being.

Mar'ya Morevna came hurrying from her place as hostess at one of the other tables, prised Ivan's reluctant hand away from his head and swore venomously at the ugly wound. He could hear his children crying somewhere in the distance beyond that clangour of bells, and a crackling sound like burning straw much closer. Ivan didn't need to see the sparks crawl down Mar'ya Morevna's arms to know that they were there, but the Tatars gasped, pointed, and drew back – which meant nothing more than that there would be fewer numbers in the queue to hack or blast or tear Aleksey *bogatyr'* into dripping shreds. Volk Volkovich the Grey Wolf was there too, and though his face was completely human, his eyes as they met Ivan's were anything but.

'Only say the word.' It was more a snarl than speech, but Ivan shook his head, heedless of the drops of blood that movement spattered over the grass like rubies sown for harvesting.

'No.' Talking hurt, since it moved the muscles in his right cheek that the sword-point had gouged. 'Not you.' He gripped Mar'ya

Morevna's wrist and felt a heat in the flesh like metal left too near the fire. 'Nor you, and,' Ivan turned to face Amragan *tarkhan*, 'most definitely not you.'

'He tried to kill me,' said the Türk. 'Because of what you did, I will forget my duty to the Ilkhan Batu, and remember only that I am *tarkhan*. If he wants my head so much, then I have the right to try for his. Like a man, not an assassin. Sword to sword.'

'I said no,' said Ivan, trying not to mumble the words. 'You are my guest. You ate my bread and salt. The treacherous son of an unwed bitch was my councillor. Any right to his head is *mine*.'

'Ivan,' said the Grey Wolf in a low voice, 'be careful of this one.'

'He's a drunken fool.'

'Fool I can't question; but I saw him draw his sword, and he was sober enough then. I think the Tatar was never in any danger. He wants *you*.'

'What?'

'He knew that you dared not let something so impersonal as the law deal with his attack on Amragan *tarkhan*, not if you hoped to avert what the Tatar might do to Khorlov. So now he has a chance to put a sword through you in "fair" combat – though I think that you too are more sober than he hoped. My good friend, your drinking habits on occasions such as this are too well known. They will be your undoing.'

'To prevent Khorlov being destroyed by the Tatars, he puts himself at risk of being killed. . . ?' The clanging ache in Ivan's head had surely driven out all sensible thought, for he felt certain that he was missing something obvious. 'Why not just sit still instead?'

'Because his father Mikhail Romanov could make himself Tsar after you were dead, and make his own pact for peace with the Khan. He has the support to do it, among the councillors and *boyaryy* who oppose your policies, your lady, your freedom with the Art Magic; you know the names well enough by now.'

'No matter what happened, Aleksey would be dead. If I didn't kill him, Amragan *tarkhan* surely would.'

'The *bogatyr*' may be a willing sacrifice for his father. Or an unwitting one. But Mikhail Romanov would be Tsar regardless.'

'And the children?' Mar'ya Morevna wadded up a soft cloth, dipped it in water mixed with tincture of poppy seeds and began to clean the ribbons of drying blood from Ivan's face, a business that needed her attention no matter what the subject of the conversation might be.

'*Gospozha Tsaritsa*,' said the Grey Wolf patiently, 'the question is unworthy of your wisdom. If the *boyar* Mikhail is content to see his own son dead, what value will he place on another man's wife and little ones?'

'Thank you,' said Mar'ya Morevna. 'I just wanted to hear someone say it aloud.'

'Lady, you may leave Mikhail Romanov to me.' Volk Volkovich grinned, and his teeth glinted. 'Unless you want him yourself?'

'Only dead.'

First Minister Strel'tsin came bustling up as quickly as his aged limbs allowed, but late for all that since his dignity in public places had not permitted him to run. 'Majesty, you are the Tsar of Khorlov,' he said at once, ignoring the look that his use of the forbidden title drew from Amragan *tarkhan*. 'And as such you may not hazard your person – '

Ivan produced a wincing smile that included both Strel'tsin and the Tatar envoy, as well as several emotional states. The pain from his ear and face was fast dying down to a dull throb, so that both talking and thinking were easier. 'I've heard that one before, Dmitriy Vasil'yevich,' he said. 'A long time ago. But as Amragan *tarkhan* will tell you as many times as need be, in the eyes of the Ilkhan Batu and the Golden Horde, I am no longer Tsar of anywhere. Just a prince. And until you take the time to rewrite the appropriate statutes, there is no law in Khorlov that forbids a prince to defend himself and his honour. In fact, if I remember rightly . . .'

'Yes, Majesty. Er, Highness. You do remember rightly. The laws of trial by combat.'

'There. So make yourself useful. Even more useful. Have someone go to my chambers in the kremlin and fetch . . .' Ivan turned slowly and stared at Aleksey Mikhailovich Romanov. 'No. Send them to the armoury. Bring me my father's sword.'

The chosen guardsman was back within a few minutes, out of breath and sweating inside his mail, but with the straight heavy *shpaga* in his hands. It was a sword of the North people, as old as the Rus themselves. Ivan took it and drew the broad blade, the weapon's heft and balance quite different to his more usual light Cossack sabre. Its massive pommel and heavy cross-guard made the hilt fit more closely to his hand, restricting any dainty finger-play, but that same restriction made the *shpaga* feel like a natural extension of his whole arm: shoulder, elbow, wrist, blade. He held it up to the light, and the edges glittered with a cobweb-fine cross-hatch of honing marks.

Aleksey Mikhailovich watched him and laughed harshly. Condemned to death by his actions unless he could buy back his life with the death of his own lord, he had given up his pretence of drunkenness and now watched preparations with a coldly rational eye. 'Will you chop me with this great sword, Majesty?' he said. Ivan stared at him but did not waste breath on a reply. 'Well, you might, you're supposed to be good with a blade. Or I might chop you. But neither way will make you right. Or any less a coward – and a traitor.'

The common people had been pushed back outside a circle whose perimeter was marked out by Rus and Tatar spears, turn and turn about. Unasked and more unwanted than he guessed, Archbishop Levon Popovich was striding to and fro within it, sprinkling holy water everywhere, accompanied by a train of priests all waving censers with such energy that the heavy smell of incense all but masked the scents of well-cooked food.

'Will you wear armour?' asked Amragan *tarkhan*. For all his efforts to be a disinterested observer, the Türk was as fascinated as anyone else right down to the lowest scullery servant crowded around the circle of spears. Ivan considered a moment.

'No,' he said at last. 'Why prolong matters? Sword and shield are good enough.' He pulled off the velvet kaftan, now sadly dark and stiff on one side of the collar, and tried the weight of one shield after another from the half-dozen or so contributed by his guards before picking a round iron-rimmed wooden one with an iron boss over its handgrip. He settled it against his forearm, looped the cross-strap around his neck, then glanced at Aleksey Mikhailovich. The soldiers surrounding the *bogatyr'* moved aside without needing to be told.

They closed behind him again as soon as he was within the combat circle, but Ivan felt sure that his adversary had no intention of trying to escape. Aleksey had stared at him in a way the Tsar remembered from other times and other places. Koshchey the Undying had that same look, hungry and hating; so had Dieter Balke, the Teutonic *Landmeister*, even though his hatred had been tempered by a brutal merriment. But the looks all had one thing in common: they wanted to kill.

Ivan Aleksandrovich of Khorlov came on guard in the proper manner for his chosen weapons, shield advanced and angled to deflect the blows rather than block them, sword poised to work around the shield rim with that vicious snapping motion as though the three-foot blade was no more than a riding whip. He did so just in time, for Aleksey wasted no time on assuming formal fighting postures. Instead he feinted a high cut and as Ivan's shield moved, hooked his own shield inside it to pull it aside, and thrust his already-bloodied sword straight through the sudden opening.

Ivan felt the wind of it go by as he jerked his head aside. The straight stab was all that saved him; a long cut would have gone through whatever space his head had left to dodge in. He hooked his own sword-hand over Aleksey's outstretched forearm and wrenched down on it, trying to pull the extended sword from the man's hand or even with luck break his arm at the elbow.

It didn't work; Aleksey Romanov's extra four inches of height prevented Ivan from gaining enough leverage either to break, pull or throw. But he was still able to keep the man from recovering his sword for another blow, and protected by that, he spun around the axis of the locked shields. For one hazardous second his unguarded back was to his enemy, but with the *bogatyr*'s arm still well caught, there was nothing that Aleksey could do, either to attack – or to defend himself as Ivan completed his turn, broke the lock on his shield and lashed backhanded with the rim.

It struck with a soggy impact that missed the spine Ivan had hoped to snap but not one of the kidneys, and Aleksey howled as he went staggering forward. The Tsar of Khorlov regained balance and came after him, sword raised to cut him across the lower back. Aleksey reeled around far enough to interpose his shield, and Ivan's sword-blade screeched as it stuttered across rivets in a shower of sparks and planed away a long curl of wood. His own shield boomed an instant later as it stopped a wild swing from the *bogatyr*'s sword, then went heavy. Ivan knew what had happened at once, and wrenched sideways with all his strength.

The shield creaked, groaned – and then its handle snapped and it went flying.

Tsar Ivan didn't care. Aleksey had sheared through the thin iron of the rim, almost clipping a handspan of meat from Ivan's bicep, but had jammed his blade immovably into the close-grained planks of which the shield was built. When it spun away, the *bogatyr*'s sword went with it. He still had his own shield, but Ivan had his father's sword. Shifting the heavy *shpaga* broadsword into both hands, clumsily because the weapon's grip wasn't really big enough, Ivan advanced on Aleksey Mikhailovich Romanov and in a score of shattering blows, reduced the other man's shield to matchwood and tatters and sent him sprawling on his back.

They stared at each other, panting, and Aleksey's look of hatred was undiminished. 'Kill me,' he managed to say between the gasps and a racking fit of coughs, 'kill me a thousand times, and still you will not be right!'

He might have been dying already, from that frightful chop across the back, but Tsar Ivan was not prepared to wait for a traitor to die in his own time. 'Maybe so,' he said wearily, putting one booted foot on Aleksey's chest and resting his sword-point beneath the man's chin, 'but you'll be no less dead.' He crossed both hands on the pommel and leaned down with all his weight.

There was a cheering, uncertain at first because of the expression on Ivan's face as he walked away from the upright sword driven through meat and bone and gristle into the earth beneath, then more full-throated with every passing second. The Tsar's honour had been vindicated and his decisions proven right by nothing less than victory in combat before the judgement of Heaven. The Tatars were still not friends and allies, but they were at least not going to destroy the city because of the actions of one stupid young warrior. There was still food uneaten and drink undrunk . . .

Mar'ya Morevna and the Grey Wolf met him at the edge of the combat circle. Volk Volkovich nodded, just once. 'There will be no dynasty of Romanov Tsars,' he said. 'At least, not this year.'

Ivan felt his mouth move in response; he felt sure that it was not a smile, and without a mirror could not be quite sure what the muscles of his face were doing yet. He had not felt frightened either before or during the fight, but now that it was over and he was still alive, he felt very slightly sick. It was not reaction to killing Aleksey Romanov, but something deeper. Mar'ya Morevna reached out and took his hand, and he was grateful for the simple contact. Then he gazed past her to where Amragan *tarkhan* was engaged in some conversation with the captain of his guard, and Ivan recognised that queasy feeling in his belly as disgust.

'We used to blame each other for surviving the invasion more or less unscathed,' he said at last, his voice miserable. 'It's gone beyond that now. They don't even have to kill us any more; we're doing it ourselves, on their behalf. I think the Golden Horde has truly won at last.'

Chapter Six

The Independent Tsardom of Khorlov;
July, AD 1243

Mar'ya Morevna was sponging at her husband's head again when Amragan *tarkhan* came over to them. She glanced at the Türk, but paid him no further heed, since the lacquer-like black crust of dried blood chose that moment to come away from Ivan's ear and he yelped like a trodden puppy.

'If you had let me take care of this mess at once, I could have saved the earlobe straight away,' she said severely. 'But no, this needs work, and all because you had to be a hero. Look at you.'

The response that it was difficult at least without a mirror was not something she would have wanted to hear. Instead Ivan gave her a wretched look and a sort of crooked smile that moved only the undamaged part of his face. 'There are some things that can't wait,' he said. 'You've ruled your own domain. You should know that.' Mar'ya Morevna grunted, but perhaps fortunately said nothing aloud on that subject.

'And you fought well,' said Amragan *tarkhan*. Just as fortunately, he had taken being ignored by Mar'ya Morevna as only to be expected from any woman, Princess or otherwise, who had a husband dripping fresh blood on her fingers and part of his ear on the table beside her. 'In my defence, no matter what your people thought of it. I shall say so when I make my report to the Ilkhan Batu.'

'Report that the Tsar of Khorlov executed a criminal.' Ivan caught the Grey Wolf's eyes and almost corrected that to 'two criminals', then thought better of it; the explanations would be tiresome and none of the Türk's affair in any case. 'That's all.'

'It is more than enough. But I remind you again, you are not Tsar – '

'Amragan *tarkhan*, at least ten days and maybe two weeks of hard riding lie between Khorlov and Sarai, even for one of the

155

Khan's *chapar* couriers with a change of horses every fifty miles and a bandoleer of bells to clear his path. For all I know I may be Tsar indeed, no matter what you might tell me – or not even Prince any more, never mind any lesser title. The Khan of the Golden Horde may have changed his mind, and you won't be aware of it. But until I stand before him, and he says otherwise, if I call myself Tsar then of your courtesy, a correction is not required each time.'

The *tarkhan* studied Ivan for several seconds, his angular face cold and considering. 'You are a strange one,' he said at last. 'You submit to the Khan without question, regardless of the wishes of your High Council – oh yes, I heard that too – to save your city; you fight and kill one of your own *bogatyr'* warriors, to save your honour before a guest and again, to save your city and its people; and then you seem willing to put your own neck under the axe by arguing about what title you should bear.'

'Personal matters and policy matters are two different things,' said Ivan. Then the significance of what Amragan *tarkhan* had just said struck through the ache and sting of Mar'ya Morevna's nursing. 'So Khorlov will come to no harm because of that young fool?' He frowned, and not this time just because of what Mar'ya Morevna was doing to his mutilated ear, but at his own choice of words. He had said 'young' automatically, even though their ages had been so close; but Aleksey Romanov's behaviour had been that of a man with a lot of growing up still to do. And now he never would. Did that mean he was growing older than his years? And did it matter any more? Ivan didn't know.

His eyes shifted past the Türk to where three of Captain Akimov's guards were busy in what remained of the dispersing circle of people. For all that the fight had taken place because of an ostensible breach of the rules of hospitality, the Cossack Guard-Captain had formed his own opinion about the real reason behind it, an opinion and a reason that had been confirmed by Ivan's not issuing any alternate orders to those that Akimov had loudly given to his men. Two of them were wrapping the *bogatyr*'s corpse in a cloak, and the third was working hard to clean any remaining stubborn smears from Ivan's broadsword. He had already used that same sword to lop Aleksey's head from his shoulders, as befitted the death of a traitor. The already half-severed neck had given him no trouble. None at all. Ivan and the wide, sharp blade had seen to that.

Amragan *tarkhan* followed his gaze, then swung back to focus briefly and pointedly on Ivan's ripped ear and the long cut across his cheek. 'No harm,' he echoed. 'You took the offence on yourself, and I, I have already forgotten it.'

Have you really? thought Ivan. He could see the same cynical disbelief flick like the beat of a bird's wing across Mar'ya Morevna's face. *I think not. Or at least, only for as long as it suits you.* He kept the thought closed away as Amragan *tarkhan* – should have done earlier, having concluded now how to play the same game as this man. Appear to take everything, every word, every gesture, at its face value while in actuality accepting none of it. Ivan was well aware that the Khan's envoy might still be able to spring some surprises on him, but there was a pride in the Türk that caused him to waste his shots on ill-advised gestures and posturing. That remark about knowing that Ivan and his High Council had not seen eye to eye over the issue of surrender and submission was just such a waste. There had been no need for anyone to know it, except that the *tarkhan* had wanted to impress; and what he had done instead was to warn Ivan, Mar'ya Morevna, Volk Volkovich and anyone else who might later be advised of it that very little could be regarded as a secret any more. Ilkhan Batu of the Golden Horde might have been better advised to employ renegade Chin of Kithai as his ambassadors; on the few occasions Ivan had met them, dealers in jade and silk and spices for the most part, their words had said little and their impassive faces still less.

'I thank you for that,' he said, and bowed courteously from his seat – so that Mar'ya Morevna smacked him irritably on the back of the head and ordered him to sit still and stop wriggling in a tone of voice he had more often heard her use on the children. They were about somewhere, though whether either of them had seen the fight and especially the end of it, he had been too busy at the time to notice.

Half his mind hoped not, that they had been taken away and fed sweets, that they had not seen their father forced to nail a man of an age to be his own twin brother to the ground in order to stifle the dissent of other men old enough to know better. The other half was less sure about the wisdom of insulating a Tsar's children, or

157

anybody's children if it came to that, from the reality of sudden, violent death that had become all too common in Russia since the Tatars came. They had seen him cut, that much he knew already, because he had heard Natasha's voice crying; Nikolai had sounded more as if he was yelling with rage. Or it might have been the other way around. It was hard to tell now, hard to remember what he had heard through the noises in his own head all that time ago . . .

'Do you want me to try to put this earlobe back where it belongs?' said Mar'ya Morevna, exasperated, 'or will I forget all about it and let you wear the earring clipped to the other side instead?'

Ivan looked down his nose at the pathetic little gobbet of flesh she was waving under it. 'If you can, then do it,' he said.

'It's going to hurt.'

That might have been a note of regret in her voice, but it sounded more like gloomy satisfaction. As Mar'ya Morevna brought the chilly, severed lobe back into contact with Ivan's sticky, overheated ear and began muttering under her breath, he hoped not. No matter how fashionable the wearing of a dramatic single earring had become among the gentlemen of Khorlov's court, he had managed to avoid having the appropriate hole bored in his person, because he had seen no reason in the infliction of unnecessary pain; on himself, anyway. Mar'ya Morevna, of course, had both ears pierced, and ornamented the scars with everything from simple pellets of polished gold – which Ivan thought looked uncomfortable – to long pendants of precious metal filigree ornamented with enough gemstones to buy a reasonably sized principality – which Ivan thought looked down-right excruciating.

'Are you trying to make me believe it's not hurting now?'

He knew it sounded stupid, but with the Türk standing by, Ivan was determined to at least try to be brave and funny. What he really wanted to do was grind his teeth and bang his fists on the table as throb became ache and ache became a jangling white-hot needle of anguish. Just when he could take no more, when he absolutely had to jump up and down and scream, the intolerable pain became a sudden spreading warmth as comfortable as a spiced cup of hot *sbiten'* honey drink on a cold winter night. Rather than yell, Ivan released a long-drawn-out sigh and sagged sideways to lean his head against Mar'ya Morevna's breast. He had to fight to hide the embarrassed grin that wanted to plaster itself all over his face, because what with that surging uncontrollable peak and then the warmth and the pleasant weariness afterwards, it felt almost as though they had just made love in public. Except that public or private, what had just happened hurt too much for him to want to make a habit of it.

He glanced surreptitiously at Amragan *tarkhan*, wondering what the Türk had seen, what he thought of it – and if he had found it funny. Ivan had no worries on that score at least; the man had taken several steps back, and he looked frightened. The expression looked strange on that harsh face, and for just an instant Ivan could not understand why. Then he realised: it was sorcery again.

The shamans who had accompanied Amragan *tarkhan* to Khorlov were physicians, besides much else. But whether they employed wizardry as a part of their medicine was another matter altogether, and even if they did, it was unlikely to be anything so direct as Mar'ya Morevna's casual, powerful use of the Art Magic. The reminder was timely, a warning of Khorlov's skill with the Art and yet not one so blatant that it might be taken the wrong way – for what was she doing except healing a hurt taken by her husband in, as he had said himself, the *tarkhan*'s own defence? Unfortunately, timely reminders about one thing can sometimes lead unintentionally to a recollection of others, and so it was with Amragan *tarkhan*.

The Khan's emissary recovered himself well, enough at least that Ivan saw no advantage in teasing the man, however gently. If sorcery, and the wariness of sorcery, was one of the reasons why Ögotäi Khakhan and his great captains had left Khorlov alone when other cities went up in flames, then he was going to be the last one to alleviate that wariness. But Amragan *tarkhan* had been given other instructions than simply 'burn' or 'do not burn'.

'The Ilkhan Batu is waiting,' he said. 'His commands are simple; it is not fitting that you should live in lands taken by conquest, claiming them for your own, and not do homage to the lord who took them. Batu *Sain* Khan requires that you be brought to Sarai for that reason.' Amragan *tarkhan* gave them both a quick, honest, open smile that sat less than well on his lean face.

'Also he desires to meet with the man who slew Baba Yaga the witch and Undying Koshchey.'

'More than once for that one,' said Mar'ya Morevna drily. 'The old bastard was well named.'

Ivan grinned, pleased enough in a wry sort of way. All of this was news to him; not that the Khan had heard of his various exploits, since they were common enough knowledge, but that a Mongol descended in direct line from Chinghis-Khan's Golden Clan, and thus one of *the* Powers in the wide white world, should make it one of the reasons why he should attend the court at Sarai. It was flattering, more or less. 'Is that all?'

'Hardly. As you know already, if it pleases him, he may grant – or restore, if you like that better – the dominion of Khorlov to that Rus lord whose wisdom is proved superior to those who call themselves his equals. You.'

'And if not, he'll give my throne, my crown and my realm to whoever *does* please him. Yes?'

'It is not my place to say.' The Türk shrugged, to show how little he was concerned in the doings of his lord and master. 'But the Khan of the Golden Horde has other, er, requirements, which knowing his wisdom should not surprise you overmuch. First, that your children come with you to Sarai – '

Ivan felt the convulsion of anger jolt like a thunderbolt through Mar'ya Morevna, so that her fingers and his clamped spasmodically together; then he felt it just as quickly subside. To fear for one's children was a natural reaction, and to restrain that reaction diplomatically was typical of a ruler trained by the wily Byzantine Greeks. Because of that training, Mar'ya Morevna had always been able to control herself better then he could, and Ivan was glad of it. He swore bitterly under his breath, furious with himself that he had failed to foresee such a stipulation as this in the Khan's commands, never dreaming until now that there might be more forms of submission than simply a lack of armed resistance.

Not that he could complain – if he were not the father of those same children – since Batu's requirement was only sensible and what Ivan would have done if the positions were reversed. A Tsar's son and heir could be a more dangerous focus of unrest and dissension than the Tsar himself, even though the lad was only seven years old. No; *especially* when the lad was only seven years old, because then there would have to be an adult to act as regent and 'advise' the child Tsar on what to do until he reached his majority.

If he ever did.

He and Mar'ya Morevna would have to do as they were told, like it or not, or there would be no point to any of the rest and Amragan *tarkhan* would flatten Khorlov after all. Even so, there was an awful temptation to push the *tarkhan*'s amiably spoken words back down his throat on the point of a sword. Suicidal, of course, and any second thoughts would come too late; too late for the Türk, but also too late for Ivan, his family, his people, for Khorlov and for everything else he was trying to protect. But there were other ways to ensure their safety, ways to get them out of Sarai far faster than even the swiftest pursuer.

There was only one problem: those ways depended rather on Amragan and his Khan not knowing about them already, and the *tarkhan* was speaking now in a tone of voice that cut through Ivan's plotting and focused all of his attention back on the Türk.

'. . . being aware of this,' Amragan said, 'the Ilkhan Batu also commands that you and your entourage ride only, ah, ordinary horses when you come with me to Sarai.'

'I . . .' Ivan bit down on anything else he might have said, and closed his eyes briefly to concentrate instead on his newly healed ear. It no longer hurt, but still felt hot and annoying, like a nettle sting. Annoying or not, stinging or not, it was a more acceptable irritant than what Amragan *tarkhan* had just said. His mood was not sweetened by the awareness that, again, he should have expected something of the sort. Black Sivka was hardly a state secret, and nor was Chyornyy. The two stallions, with their speed that paid no heed to the distances that troubled ordinary travellers across Moist-Mother-Earth, and their intelligence that was more than that of some people Ivan could name, were a source of gossip, appreciation and some considerable envy throughout the Rus lands.

To think that Batu Khan would have known nothing about them, or knowing made no provision based on that knowledge when issuing his orders to Amragan *tarkhan*, was no more than the most baseless optimism, and he had given way to indulging in it like the worst and laziest daydreamer. No ruler with any wit – and though

Ivan hated to admit it, Batu seemed both well-advised and wise in himself – would allow any subject prince to come calling on a steed which could make nonsense of the whole concept of hostages.

Knowing that added no honey to the sourness of the Khan's command. If the horses stayed behind, and there seemed no way at present to avoid it, then there was no way in which Ivan and his family could leave Sarai fast enough that the Khan's relay riders would not overhaul them within a day. Unless Mar'ya Morevna was willing to use a Gate, and, looking at her now, Ivan guessed that even asking would be a waste of breath. The Gate-spells worked in much the same way as that more natural ability of the two black horses, granting the ability to take – what did the old philosophers say? – the shortest distance between two points. Their drawback, as simple and as deadly as the risk of jumping across a chasm rather than climbing down one side and up the other, was that anyone using a Gate had to know exactly where they were going, the exact location of the Opening-Gate at the other side, and whether there was anything there. Anything, or nothing.

Like deep water, or open air over a sheer drop, or a solid wall. Any one of those things, being there already, had rights and priorities in the scheme of things, and all were fatal; some more unpleasantly so than others. To share space with height or depth was unpleasant enough, even though it was something that might come all too naturally to sailors or swimmers or climbers or the careless, but to share space with the stones and mortar of a fortress tower, however briefly, was a particularly horrid way to die. Some time after the Battle on the Ice, Ivan had heard a second-hand description of what had happened to the Teutonic Knight Dieter Balke: he had seen him go into the Gate, but mercifully had not been there to witness him come out. It was just as well. *Buried alive* could not begin to describe it.

Anyone with more than the smallest education in the Art Magic knew of the theoretical existence of such spells, but that person would also know that Gates had never been used successfully, and thus were of no practical use, and . . . and many other excuses of the same sort. Mar'ya Morevna and her father Koldun the Enchanter were the only sorcerers in all Russia to have used the Gating-spells and lived to talk about it; but not even Mar'ya Morevna used them more than she needed. Because the spells

162

were so dangerous, and so seldom used, they were also seldom spoken of. That helped to keep them a secret from inquisitive ears and eyes, and now, when those doing the prying were Tatars afraid not just of what they might find out, but of the whole subject of sorcery, maintaining that secret was easier than ever before.

Assuming, of course, that Batu Khan didn't know about *them* as well. Ivan was growing very cautious over allowing any assumptions about the Tatars to sway his plans in any way at all. Fear of sorcery was one thing, but he was beginning to suspect that the Khan of the Golden Horde was even more afraid – well, reluctant anyway – of being left in ignorance of any matter at all that might give his subject peoples an advantage. That feeling had grown so strong that it was pleasant, and almost a surprise, when Amragan *tarkhan* made no mention of the Gates.

'Are you all right again, Papa?' asked Nikolai Tsarevich.

At the sudden question right by his elbow, Ivan jumped and swore; then grinned weakly as Mar'ya Morevna glowered at him and Nikolai stored this latest phrase away for future use. Probably at the most socially inconvenient time, if previous experience was anything to go by. 'Yes, I am. But Kolya,' and Ivan's voice grew disapproving, 'honest gentlemen don't sneak around and creep up on people.'

The Prince considered this. 'Does that mean Volk Volkovich isn't an honest gentleman, then? Because Mamma says he sneaks around all the goddamn time.' The small voice was still loud enough that Ivan cringed, both at the words and at the way Amragan *tarkhan* looked ready to burst with suppressed laughter. Mar'ya Morevna was blushing bright red, and Volk Volkovich the Grey Wolf, gentleman or not, appeared to have gone politely deaf. 'Anyway,' virtuously, '*I* wasn't sneaking.'

'Oh, were you not indeed. . . ?' That the child should compound his errors by lying about them, and sound so righteous in the process, was enough to make the most patient parent angry. And right at the minute Ivan's patience was stretched thin enough to snap.

'The child is speaking the truth,' said Amragan *tarkhan*, and folded his arms as though his pronouncement put an end to the matter. Ivan turned slowly from Nikolai to look at the Türk, not at all sure that he liked a Tatar envoy interfering in family matters as

163

well as in all else. Yet the *tarkhan* had already proven himself more fair-minded than any such envoy needed to be, enough at least that he deserved a hearing.

'Explain.'

'I did not see him behind you,' said Amragan simply. 'By its very nature, such movement is slow, and not even the best hunter can sneak quickly. I would have seen your son. But I did not. I turned my head and the next minute, he was by your side. So.'

Ivan knew otherwise about how fast a really good hunter could move unheard, but he glanced at the Grey Wolf and said nothing. Regardless of Amragan *tarkhan*'s intercession on the boy's behalf, he looked forward to hearing Nikolai explain how getting close enough to make his father almost jump out of his skin didn't qualify as sneaking. Perhaps there might also be a few words about not eavesdropping on grown-up conversations, and most especially on not repeating those conversations in company. But all that could wait until later.

'All right,' said Ivan, determined to change the subject to another, any other, before his son reported more of what his oversharp ears had picked up. 'Then you weren't. But where have you been all this time?' He looked about him, but saw no sign of his daughter. 'You and 'Tasha both. Well?'

'Hiding.'

'I didn't see you.' Then Ivan shook his head and held up his hand quickly to forestall what Nikolai might have said in reply to that, knowing full well that whether the boy meant it that way or not, the obvious reply would come out sounding impertinent. 'Yes, I know, that's what's supposed to happen when people hide. But where?'

'That's a secret,' said Nikolai firmly, and a little too much so for his father's taste. It didn't matter in the slightest that sharp back-talk from child to parent was something of a Khorlovskiy family tradition. Ivan had given his son one oblique warning by uttering the last potentially cheeky comment himself, and so disarming it, but if Kolya was too busy with other smart remarks to notice, then on his own head – or more accurately backside – be it.

Then Mar'ya Morevna reached out and took Ivan by the upper arm, in a movement which looked to the casual eye no more than a light caress; but her hand briefly clamped onto his bicep with all the strength of a grip trained by wielding sword and mace and that heaviest of all weapons, the baton of command. Ivan looked at her and raised his eyebrows. 'Later, Vanya,' she said, and that was a command as well. 'Not in front of the visitors.'

Ivan could see a strange look on her face; it was an expression he had seen before, and not so very long before. This morning, in fact, on the city walls, when they were waiting for the Tatars to arrive outside the gates, and Volk Volkovich had been wearing it as well. They had both intended to tell him something, except that Amragan *tarkhan* and his men had interrupted them before anything could be said. What the envoy had commanded afterwards about loss of crown and title had apparently driven the small domestic problem from Mar'ya Morevna's head. Until now – and as Ivan got to his feet and began to make his excuses to the *tarkhan*, he felt very sure, as he had not done before, that this 'problem' was neither domestic nor small.

'Enjoy the rest of the banquet,' he said. 'With one thing and another, I find my appetite less than it was. And there are matters needing my attention, not so much as a tsar than as a father.' Ivan inclined his head slightly. It was not really a bow, nor even a salutation between equals, but the nod of one independent ruler to the servant of another. A highly placed servant, of course, and worthy of respect, but a servant nonetheless. He was slightly amused, and just as slightly irritated, to see Amragan *tarkhan* return the same courteous gesture. For probably just the same reason . . .

'Now, Kolya, tell your father what you just told me,' said Mar'ya Morevna, turning her reluctant son around by the shoulders and giving him a push in the small of the back. Ivan watched this small performance, and listened with as much interest as the day's recent events permitted as Nikolai Tsarevich produced some muttered explanation about hiding out of sight where nobody could see, whenever he wanted to. Though the child's words had a tendency to ramble off the subject before a nudge from his mother dragged them back on again, there was enough about them to make Ivan feel more than a little bewildered by the time Nikolai was done.

'You hide *behind* things?' he asked, sorting furiously for sense

165

while trying not to look as confused as he felt. 'Like you did today, I suppose, out in the open meadow without a weed tall enough for a mouse to hide behind. Kolyushka, don't play games. Your father isn't in the mood for them. Where do you hide?'

'My secret place. Behind . . .' Nikolai hesitated and waved his hand at the world in general, trying not to repeat himself but plainly lacking the vocabulary to say what he meant. 'Behind *things*. You know.'

'No, I don't. Tell me.'

'Ivan, you're not being very helpful,' said Mar'ya Morevna. 'The boy is doing his best.'

'That best isn't very good. Remind me to have a word with Strel'tsin and the other tutors. If my son and heir can't express himself properly – '

'Nor could you, in this case at least. And I'm not so sure I can myself.'

Ivan's eyebrows went up. *Magic?* He mouthed the word silently, and Mar'ya Morevna nodded. 'All right, Nikolai, don't bother trying to tell me what you've been doing. Show me. Hide in this secret place of yours for, oh, a count of five. Starting now.'

Kolya brightened up at once. 'Yes, *batyushka*,' he said, grinning. 'Watch this.'

There was nothing to watch, because there was a sound like a small hand-clap and all of a sudden Prince Nikolai Ivanovich wasn't there any more. Ivan jerked out of his chair so hard that it fell over with a resounding bang, and the only other sound was that of Mar'ya Morevna counting, ' . . . Three. Four. Five . . .' And Nikolai was back, standing not quite in the same place but with exactly the same grin, and otherwise looking as though he had never been away.

'Gnah?' said Tsar Ivan usefully, and sat down hard on a chair that, like his son, wasn't where it should have been. Once Kolya and Mar'ya Morevna had disentangled him and soothed his ruffled pride – which if they but knew it, was the least of Ivan's concerns – Ivan looked at the seven-year-old boy with the same apprehension he normally reserved for such books as *Enciervanul Doamnisoar*, 'On the Summoning of Demons'. It was hardly the proper way for a father to regard his son, but just for that few seconds before he pulled himself together, Ivan found it entirely correct.

166

'As far as I can understand it, Vanya,' said Mar'ya Morevna, 'we have two children who don't need spells to use the Gates.'

'How?' Ivan said, then made a quick 'shush' gesture with his hand. 'Wait for that a moment. Nikolai, go find 'Tasha; bring her back here. And,' he said quickly, 'do it the ordinary way.' That hastily inserted condition made Kolya look as droopy as a water spaniel kept from jumping in the river, but he nodded obediently at last and trailed out of the room. When the door had closed behind him, Ivan turned back to Mar'ya Morevna with a grin very like that of his son. 'Now again, how?'

'I don't know the *how* of it, not exactly,' said Mar'ya Morevna, 'and I'd rather not guess just now. Nikolai wasn't very clear on that point – '

'I noticed.'

' – But it seems to have come as naturally as walking and talking to both of them. And the *why* is rather more obvious. I told you a long time ago that I thought the twins were conceived in the Summer Country.'

'That night in Vasilisa Kurbit'yevna's hunting lodge. I remember.' His grin widened briefly. 'What with worrying about Firebirds, and falling in with Teutonic Knights, and falling out with Tsar Vyslav Andronovich, that was the only night for nearly two weeks when we did anything more than fall into bed like corpses into a grave.'

'It made my calculations easier, at least,' said Mar'ya Morevna, and favoured Ivan with a thoughtful look. 'And because both of us have had to work hard to gain ability in the Art.'

'One of us a good deal harder than the other. Certainly not as easily as . . . as walking and talking.' He shook his head in disbelief. 'They learnt to do that quicker than I expected, too.'

'I should have realised. Put the two facts together sooner than I did.'

'And what good would it have done, except maybe give us this present surprise two years ago? Don't worry about it. Unless,' Ivan leaned forward, frowning slightly, 'unless they might come to some harm from all of this. Passing through the Gates is dangerous.'

'How would we stop them? Make them promise? And how would we make sure the promise was being kept? I'm not casting

167

doubts on their honesty, Vanya, but they're only seven years old, and you know well enough by now what they're like.'

'The attention span of a gnat.' Ivan chuckled. 'Just like me at that age, if you believe my dear sisters.'

'It's good to know that children take after their parents,' said Mar'ya Morevna, which told Ivan something about what she had been like as a little girl. 'Yes. They'd be oh so careful for about a week, then one of them would forget, and then since the promise was broken by accident, they wouldn't need to keep it any more.'

'And it would be a secret, just like before. What made you guess?'

'On the battlements this morning. When Natasha threw that punch and missed. She doesn't usually miss, but this time Nikolai saw it coming and – well, moved out of the way.'

'I said he would be good with a sword, didn't I? Was I wrong?'

'Not really. He will be, if he doesn't grow up thinking that gives him an unfair advantage. But you saw what your eyes expected to see, which was a nimble sidestep. Volk Volkovich and I saw something we *didn't* expect to see. There was no stepping involved. There's a difference.'

'Quite so . . .' Ivan looked up out of his own thoughts and found Mar'ya Morevna staring at him. 'Yes?'

'Why don't you go ahead and say it out loud?'

'Say what?'

' "It's a pity they weren't older, but we can't involve mere children." Or something like that.'

'Older. . . ?' He stared at her without comprehension for a second, then realised what she meant. 'No. Oh, no, no, never. I wasn't thinking that at all.' Ivan hesitated, pondering about the rightness of what Mar'ya Morevna was so plainly not suggesting. 'Not until now, anyway.'

'Then what were you . . . ?'

'That the children could escape from Sarai even if we couldn't. Am I so bad a father, or so ruthless a tsar, that you thought otherwise?' Mar'ya looked a little ashamed of herself.

'Not as ruthless as I am. I thought of it first.'

'It? Is your "it" the same as mine?' Even though he already knew that answer, Ivan pursued it with all the ruthless persistence he had earlier denied. Then he relented. 'And would it put them at any more risk to steal back the Great Crown – or something that looked like it – than for us to leave it with the Khan?'

'Ivan, no! They're only children!'

'They're your children, and mine. That's enough to put them in danger whether they come with us or stay here. And if what you said is even half-right, about all the crowns of Russia brought together in one place, then they might not live to become older children if we don't do something. Anything.'

'To even think like that, you've become ruthless indeed.'

'You're wary of the Gates. I'm downright scared of them. But the children . . . You heard Kolya. It's no more than a secret place to hide in. He's less afraid than I was when I found my secret hiding place all those years ago. One of the old storage cellars behind the kitchens, that was. Its lock was broken and – well, never mind.' Ivan gave Mar'ya Morevna a sidelong glance that was half amused and half abashed. 'Wherever he's going, it obviously doesn't have damned big spiders already living in it.'

'Were they really damned big ones?' asked Anastasya Tsarevna from the doorway, which had opened silently while he was speaking. 'With horrible damned big long legs?'

Ivan groaned softly. Now that it had been drawn to his attention in a way that not even a busy and recently conquered Tsar could overlook, he was noticing more and more that his son and daughter had no need of sorcery to appear silently in places where they could overhear things they weren't supposed to. 'Natash'yushka, little mouse, you shouldn't talk like that. It's not ladylike.'

'But Mamma – ' came the inevitable reply.

'Mamma is grown up,' said Mar'ya Morevna severely. 'And grown-ups can do things that children aren't allowed to. Nikolai Ivanovich, you be quiet! Never mind what else! Just remember that children can do things that grown-ups aren't allowed to any more. When did you last see me dropping a snowball on someone coming through the kremlin gate?'

'But I got smacked!' protested Nikolai as plaintively as though the injury was still fresh.

'Afterwards. I couldn't have done it at all. Fair exchange, you see.'

'Um.' There was muttering between the twins, who despite

their often violent differences usually managed to present authority with a united front. The outcome was as grudgingly conceded as effort from a camel. 'All right,' said Natasha at last. 'I suppose it is.'

'That's very generous of you. Now come here and sit down. Your father and I have something we want to talk about.'

'Oh, that,' said Nikolai, scornful that a prince of mature years should be thought ignorant of such vital matters. 'We already know where children come from.'

'Ah . . . no,' said Ivan, after a pause to gather wits scattered for what felt like the hundredth time today. Though the accuracy of Kolya's information would have to be checked at some later date, somehow he didn't feel quite up to it right now. And from the look of her, neither did his wife. 'Not quite. We were more inclined towards, er, finding out where children *go* . . .'

'The Summer Country,' said Mar'ya Morevna once the twins had gone. They had wandered out not quite hand in hand, which suggested that as soon as they were out of earshot there was going to be a flurry of accusations over who had blabbed their secret. 'No doubt about it.'

'That's where they go to play, and hide,' said Ivan. 'But as for the rest – are you absolutely sure what they're doing?'

'Didn't you understand? For all she doesn't know half the terms of reference, 'Tasha was quite intelligible.'

'I understood enough to start to worry. Explain the rest, and make me stop.'

Mar'ya Morevna smiled indulgently and patted Ivan's hand in a way that he was starting to find annoying, not because it was an over-repeated mannerism, but because it was so usually prompted by some ignorance on his part. Usually an ignorance of the Art Magic. If even his own children knew more than he did, he had better get back into the library and start to study again, in his copious spare time of course. The awareness that if Batu Khan appointed a Tatar *daru-gashi* governor and a swarm of *baskak* tax-squeezers he would have more spare time than he knew what to do with, didn't help.

'All right,' she said. 'Will I make it insultingly simple?' Ivan gave a wry smile and nodded permission, glad she had asked –

since it was already fairly certain that she would do so anyway. 'The children can move between the wide white world and the Summer Country the way we move between rooms in this kremlin. When they come back from – '

' – The corridor outside the door?'

'Do you need an explanation at all?'

'Yes.'

'Then be quiet. But yes. The corridor makes better sense. If the Summer Country is the corridor, and our world is the kremlin, then they don't have to come back to the same place – the same room – as they left. So long as they know a room – another part of the world – is there, they can go to it. No spells, no circles, no Gates.'

'You sound jealous.'

'Of my own children?' Mar'ya Morevna shook her head; then grinned quickly and shrugged. 'Well, I suppose a little. What they can do without effort or any risk of harm, I could never match if I studied the Gating-spells from now till the day I died. Which might not be too far off, if I was as careless with the Gates as they can be. So yes. Envious, and just a bit sad. If a man invented a machine to let him fly, he would still envy the birds who can do it all by themselves.'

'I don't want to fly,' said Ivan. 'What I want is to keep my people safe. And if doing that means keeping my crown, and taking back all the other crowns the Tatars stole, and saving the wide white world from falling through whatever pit you say is being opened up beneath it, then that's what I'll do. And the children can help me do it. All they have to do is see wherever all the crowns are kept and – '

'Ivan?'

'What?'

'Have you been drinking?'

'No. Why?'

'Because if you had, and not giving any of it to me . . .' Mar'ya Morevna aimed an affectionate cuff at his head that would have raised all the stars of a summer sky if it had landed. 'You are the crookedest, most devious and nasty-minded – '

' – Man you married.' Ivan finished for her, smirking now, in a wicked and far better humour than he had been for hours. He put

171

both arms around her waist and his mouth close enough to one ear that he needed only to whisper. 'But don't stop. I love compliments.'

'Never mind the compliments. We are going to get ready for our journey to Sarai and the court of the Golden Horde.'

'And if we should first happen to visit the armoury . . .' Mar'ya Morevna shivered in his arms, and Ivan felt sure it was from more than just his breath tickling her ear.

' – Or the Treasury . . .' she murmured.

' –Then we had best make sure that Nikita Pavlovich the goldsmith is with us. Just in case the Great Crown – '

' – Or a helmet – '

'– Needs to be repaired.'

'Or gilded, trimmed with fur and studded with fine gems . . .'

The Khanate of the Golden Horde; August, AD 1243

Ivan stood up in his stirrups and shaded his eyes against the glare of the sun. All that he could see was a vague, shadowy blot against the steppes, black against the brown and green of vegetation. Nothing else. He dropped back into his saddle and looked quizzically at Volk Volkovich.

'Chernigov,' said the Grey Wolf. That was all. Ivan flinched and stared again at the distant blot, then turned to Mar'ya Morevna.

'The children will stay in the wagon,' he said. 'And with the curtains drawn, if we get any closer to . . . To that.' There were the beginnings of complaints from Nikolai and Anastasya, but those fell silent when he jerked his horse around and glared at them.

Both children knew that they could take an excessive number of liberties with their father and survive every one, but there came a point after which it was as well to sit still and be quiet. The expression on Ivan's face told them that such a point had just been reached. Watching a sword fight – or an execution, if it came to that – could be justified as a part of the education of any tsar's children, if only to teach them that life was not to be taken without good reason, since it could not be returned. Looking at other gruesome scenes such as that which he suspected was waiting closer to Chernigov was simply unpleasant, and thus unnecessary. If anyone, child, councillor or ally, needed to see rotting corpses before they understood what a war could do to the fragile creatures that they were and ruled, then it was already too late to make an impression. Even so, there was always the possibility that time was not wasted nor senses blasted quite in vain. But not those of children. Never the children . . .

It was small wonder that they were restless, because the journey to Sarai had been uneventful so far. Boringly uneventful, and for almost three weeks on end. While Ivan was the first to admit that boredom was preferable to any amount of near-fatal excitement, there could always be too much of any good thing.

'You're going to look?' asked Mar'ya Morevna. Ivan nodded. 'What good will that do?'

'Satisfy my curiosity. And those two' – he indicated Count Danyil Fedorovich and the *bogatyr*' Konstantin Il'yevich – 'can come with me. For Konstantin at least, it should prove to him how right I was not to oppose the Tatars, and how right *he* was to support me. As for Danyil Fedorovich . . . Well, he might just have his mind changed.'

Mar'ya Morevna looked at the councillor dubiously. 'So far as he and his kind are concerned, I wonder sometimes if they have a mind to change. But yes. It might work. And if it works, it might shut up the opposition back in Khorlov.'

'The method you used on Aleksey Romanov is still the most effective,' said the Grey Wolf. He wasn't smiling when he said it. 'They will try to stab you in the back on every chance they get. Every chance you give them, by being just and fair and forgiving. If one of your own Council will not agree with your decision, then get rid of him. One way or another.'

'We had this debate before,' said Ivan. 'How many times will we have it again?'

'As many times as need be,' said Volk Volkovich. 'I have decided – for whatever reason I may have had at the time, I forget which – to help you, guard you, and defend you. And your family as well. That defence does not always mean a sword and shield, Ivan Aleksandrovich, nor teeth in the night. It also means, or so your own father said, being ready and willing to say the things a

173

listener does not like to hear and by his,' he bowed slightly to Mar'ya Morevna, 'or her, rank, expect to hear. So I alone am left to say them. And I do.'

'Constantly.'

'Thank you.' The Grey Wolf smiled, a quick gleam of that excessively white, excessively ragged and sharp array of teeth. 'At least the effort is not going unnoticed.'

'Volk Volkovich, you're funny!' said Anastasya Ivanovna, leaning out of the wagon and as usual listening with more attention to things that weren't her business than anything that was. 'Have you ever thought of being a court jester?'

'No, my lady.' Again that elegant bow from the saddle, and the smile that this time had gone long-suffering, a wolf to the cub who was chewing on his tail for the hundredth time. 'My jokes have too much bite in them.'

'Very droll.' Mar'ya Morevna stared at Volk Volkovich as he straightened up, and her frost-pale eyebrows drew together in a frown. For all his declarations of defending Ivan and his family, for all that she trusted him more now than she had ever done before, she had still grown up with too many tales where a meeting between wolves and children had only one ending.

The Tatar escort eyed Ivan's party strangely as they rode out across the steppe towards the ruined city. Ivan glanced at them and even though he was too far away for details, the thoughts crossing those weathered, slit-eyed faces were easily read. *What is he doing? Why is he doing it? Doesn't the idiot Rus know that there's no profit left in a place after we finish with it*? How many of the fur-hatted horsemen had been here the first time, Ivan didn't want to know. He growled something inarticulate deep in his chest, a sound that drew a look of surprise from the Grey Wolf, and laid his whip across his horse's flanks to make the stupid thing move faster than a trot.

Sivka would not have tolerated such treatment, but then Sivka would not have needed it. This bay gelding, however, was a dumb animal in every sense of the word and needed all the riding aids ever invented by the agile mind of man to make it do other than eat grass and look handsome. Ivan wondered whether spurs might not work better than the more usual *nagayka* whip, but suspected that the dogmeat-with-hoofs under his saddle had too much mule in its ancestry even for that. It would look impressive stalking into Sarai, but that was all he could say in its favour.

And it had a rotten line in conversation, too.

Volk Volkovich drew level with him after a few minutes, when the bay slackened its gait and Ivan had grown tired of trying to encourage it to greater effort. The Grey Wolf had no such trouble. He had long since reached some sort of unspoken rapport with the rangy grey mare that was his usual mount while in man's shape. Ivan had never asked, but he suspected the arrangement ran along the lines of 'do your best or be eaten'.

'Why in such a hurry, friend Ivan?' he said, reining the grey back to match Ivan's pace. 'And why so concerned with what the children will see? Chernigov fell four years ago, and the wolves – ' He fell silent and had the decency to look ashamed of himself.

It was indeed a decency, a politeness, and nothing more than that, since shame about the completely natural doings of his real self – and his relatives – was not something that the Grey Wolf ever felt. Ivan wondered how many hours Volk Volkovich had spent in front of a mirror to perfect the expression. He was glad that Mar'ya Morevna was still far enough away not to see it or hear the words which had caused it.

'I'm in no hurry to look at Tatar leftovers,' he said. 'But any excuse to move faster than that damned amble is good enough for me.'

'It's the way the Tatars march. And it's taken them all the way from the high steppes to the gates of Vienna.'

'I know that. I don't have to like it. And anyway, old friend,' Ivan slapped his horse's neck and raised a little puff of the red dust of the steppes, 'I'm just a little spoiled by Sivka. If it wasn't for Amragan *tarkhan*, we could have been in Sarai and away again by now.'

'It's the "away again" that was concerning him,' said Mar'ya Morevna, coming up to them in a cloud of russet dust. She brushed in a half-hearted way at the sleeve of her riding-coat, knowing that it was a gesture matched only by mopping up an incoming tide with a sponge. 'If he hadn't known about the horses – ' Then she shrugged. 'Ah well. The price of fame.'

Ivan opened his mouth to speak, but what came out instead was an oath as his bay horse shied at something in the long, dry grass.

He stared downward, then began to concentrate on calming the horse rather more gently than the others might have expected. His voice, when he spoke at last, had become hushed as it might have done in Khorlov's cathedral, and he was still staring at the ground as he made the sign of the life-giving cross over his heart. 'Some prices,' he said, 'are higher.'

The skulls were everywhere.

It was not as though Ivan was taken by surprise; he had heard reports of Tatar sieges and their aftermath from Volk Volkovich and others, and knew what to expect. Except that reports and forewarned expectations did not do justice to the reality, and the reality here was a field full of skulls stretching from where he sat towards the blasted patch of land that had been Chernigov, for as far as he could see. There were so many of them that they looked at first glance like a harvest of turnips, and that rustic image was preferable to the alternative. His eyes and mind, which had in their time encompassed many more gruesome sights, could not immediately accept that these, so many of these, had once been living heads attached to living bodies.

'No ribs or arms or legs,' said Mar'ya Morevna, crossing herself in turn. 'Someone has been making themselves a little victory monument. Her voice was as quiet as Ivan's had become, but it had retreated into the coolness he had heard before. Not quite unconcern, not quite lacking grief for the dead, but certainly not the same level of awe-struck shock. Mar'ya Morevna had looked upon such scenes before, and had caused some of them herself – Ivan could still remember three thousand dead Tatars strewn from one horizon to the other. But that had been a battle.

These skulls had been pulled free of some of the ghastly pyramids of severed heads by which Tatar commanders indicated their displeasure at a too-stubborn defence, a too-reluctant surrender – or whatever else had moved them to irritation on that particular day. As Ivan rode slowly closer to the blasted brown patch of ground that had once been a city of forty thousand souls, he discovered that even four years of being washed by the rain and bleached by the sun, of being picked at by birds and gnawed by – he glanced at Volk Volkovich – other creatures, had not been time enough to completely flatten out this monument to savagery.

It had been too big.

Cawing wildly, crows erupted from the pile of skulls that even after so long still rose as high as Ivan's saddle. He reined in with a soft oath and blessed himself again with a hand that shook, though whether with anguish or anger, he didn't know. The poor, scattered bones through which he had been riding were long since clean and smooth, scoured to the colour of ivory. These were not.

Heaped and tumbled together as though still trying to protect each other from the weather and the scavengers, the remaining skulls were a hideous reminder of the mortality of man. Patches of hair and shreds of dried and blackened flesh disfigured them, and untouched by sun or rain or beak or fang they had become instead a banquet for the smallest vermin of the steppe. The hot, still air was heavy with the buzz of carrion flies, and a stench had soaked into the ground so that it seemed the place would never be truly free of it again. At least it was old, faded like the skulls themselves. Ivan had smelt the sickly-sweet gagging reek of fresh putrescence three times before, three times too many. This was more tolerable. Almost.

He jabbed his heels into the bay gelding's flanks, but had to put his whip to it again before the shuddering beast would move. That reaction at least he understood. He would have preferred to turn back himself, but there were two reasons why he did not, and they were riding up behind him now. Ivan heard the stifled cries of horror and disgust from his two councillors as they came close enough to see the more repulsive details of the skull mound, and he suspected that they too would have chosen not to go any further. Only the presence of their Tsar in front, and Mar'ya Morevna and Volk Volkovich behind, kept them in their place.

He tugged a rein, dug in a knee, and walked his horse slowly all the way around the mound, not looking at the thousands of eye-sockets that seemed to stare at him, but at the four eyes that were so reluctant to meet his own. The young *bogatyr'* Konstantin was signing himself with the cross over and over again and muttering some litany of prayer under his breath, but his companion was not giving way to any such display.

Count Danyil Fedorovich had flouted Ivan's authority on the day of his father's abdication, and had been slapped down for his trouble. The *boyar* had never forgotten it, and had made it his business to oppose Tsar Ivan thereafter for no reason other than the attainment of some obscure satisfaction. His had sometimes been the sole voice of dissent in matters where Khorlov's Council was otherwise unanimous, but his reasoned arguments in those matters – as well as his position and the support it commanded – had meant that there was no way in which he could be accused of simple obstruction. As a token of displeasure, Ivan had removed him from his place as a member of the *druzina*, the Tsar's personal retinue, but it had not deterred Danyil Fedorovich.

Even when Ivan had made the momentous and scandalous announcement of unconditional surrender to the Tatars that had almost provoked swordplay in the Council Chamber, Fedorovich had objected so smoothly that there had been nothing the Tsar could do about it. By that time, of course, unanimity less one had become so much an expected part of any agreement that the *boyar*'s words had not swayed the ultimate decision; but it had not made the man any less aggravating, and there were times when the Grey Wolf's advice regarding badly behaved councillors seemed as practical as any. The only problem was that if Tsar Ivan killed off every councillor who disagreed, he would soon have no Council left, and the standard response of '*Kill them all, then, and have some peace for once*' had seemed less coarsely funny since the Tatars came. Killing them all had happened far too many times already. He had only to look around him to see that.

'Do you still think Khorlov should have fought?' asked Ivan.

Fedorovich blinked like a man awakened from an ugly dream and looked his Tsar in the face for the first time. That look was not hatred, such as Ivan had been expecting. Instead it was contempt. 'This is an uncouth way of driving home a point,' the *boyar* said. 'I had expected better of your father's son.'

'My father's son,' said Ivan wearily, knowing that once again he was not going to get a direct answer to his question, 'has spent six years and more in trying genteel methods, and none of them have worked. Well, Danyil Fedorovich? Have they? Explanation, logic, even appeals to what in another man would be common sense. At least now you've gone so far as to admit there *is* a point I'm trying to drive home. That's an improvement of sorts.'

The nobleman uttered a disdainful grunt, but it sounded less sincere than other such grunts that Ivan had heard down the years. Certainly it was nothing like as heartfelt as the noise of Konstantin

Il'yevich leaning from his saddle to be sick. Doing the *bogatyr'* the consideration of turning away until he had recovered his composure, Ivan wished that he too could give way to the churning in his guts. Or the stinging in his eyes. But while Count Danyil's cold gaze was on him, he had to maintain that dispassionate façade, and be a tsar.

Mar'ya Morevna stopped her own horse beside his, and the look on her face was plain. She was ready to support any decision he might make, whether it was to go on or return, and ram any clever observations or objections from the count back past his so-white teeth with the butt of her riding whip. Not that it would do any good; but Ivan felt certain it would make her feel much better.

'We go on,' he said. 'I've come this far, and seen this much. I might as well see the rest. And you' – he did not trouble to more than glance at Count Danyil Fedorovich – 'will come too.' There was no answer from the *boyar*, and Ivan had expected none, but the presence of Volk Volkovich between him and retreat was assurance and reply enough.

The city, or what had been the city, was both less ghastly and more distressing than the scattered pyramid of skulls. Ivan had been in Chernigov only three times in his life, and two of those had been since becoming Tsar in 1236. The place had struck him with its similarity to Khorlov; not just in the usual way that one walled city with a kremlin resembles any other, but in many small ways that made it comfortingly familiar. All that meant now was to make it easier to visualise the same destruction visited upon Khorlov, and only that familiar layout of walls and streets and buildings made it possible to know where the parts of the city had ever been.

Because they were gone.

Nothing remained except that flattened expanse of ground where the city had once stood. Ivan had expected ruined houses, burned-out wooden shells with the grass of the steppes a second invader now that the Tatars had left, and the full weight of what it meant for a place to be so destroyed that its site was ripe to be ploughed and planted had never really struck home. Not until now. There was not even grass; the soil was so choked with ash and charred, blackened shreds of timber that no plant could survive in it.

One image kept creeping back into his head, a childhood memory, and not one to be proud of. Ivan, ten years old, had found a nest of red ants busily doing whatever it is ants do, and had squatted down to watch them. He learned within minutes that one of the things these particular ants did was to bite, and bite hard.

After the usual interval of squealing and running to his mother to have it all made better, Prince Ivan had come back. He had brought a flask of lamp oil and a taper, both stolen from the kremlin kitchens, and had slowly and carefully burned the ant nest, pouring the oil in ever-decreasing concentric circles to better enjoy how the little creatures ran frantically about, and thrashed, and crisped, and died. Then he had ground even the site of the nest out of existence with the heels of his boots, and had later been smacked for scraping the gold work from the leather. But the smacking had been worth it, because that burnt, smashed patch of ground remained until the next winter as a reminder of his mighty power to deal destruction on those who had offended him.

Was that what had happened here? A demonstration of power and nothing more? This was how the Khan of the Golden Horde saw Russia and all the rest of the world that his horsemen could wrest from its rightful owners. Mere nests of insects to crush beneath his feet. And if they should dare to cry out and fight back against that destruction . . .

Tsar Ivan Aleksandrovich of Khorlov sat in the midst of desolation on his stupid, stubborn horse, and wept silently for the stupid, stubborn people of Chernigov.

He rode back towards the column of Tatars, staring at them, breathing shallowly, trying to control the black rage that was not just righteous wrath, but a desire to do unto others such as he had never felt before in all his not-quite-thirty years of life. Up until now he had been fair-minded, more so indeed than most of his contemporaries, reluctant to do anything so irreversible as the taking of life for fear that he would later be proven wrong. That was then, half an hour and an eternity ago.

If every man, woman and child of every tribe that made up the Great Khan's empire had just one throat, and he a razor, he would not have hesitated for the taking of a single breath. And never mind the specious arguments about how could he hold the women

180

and children to blame? because Tatar women had given birth to the men who had done this, and Tatar children would grow up to become, or to give birth to, yet another generation of them. Otherwise what he wanted to do would bring him a moment's satisfaction before Amragan *tarkhan*'s men cut him to pieces and then turned back to do to Khorlov what they had done here. If he was going to kill Tatars, he would have to kill them all. Nothing could remain. No survivors, no retribution, nothing. Just bones, and ash, and dust on the wind.

No-one dared speak to Ivan as he rode slowly past them; not his wife, not his friend and most certainly not his councillors. They had all seen his face, but neither Danyil Fedorovich nor Konstantin *bogatyr*' saw other than the dry-eyed, expressionless mask of a man stoically trying to hide tears or nausea for the sake of his dignity. Mar'ya Morevna and the Grey Wolf knew more than that. What was hidden by those dispassionate features was something made all the worse by being held on so tight a leash.

Mar'ya Morevna was the first to shake free of whatever spell this grim place had laid on them all. She overhauled Ivan – not a difficult task, since his horse was moving no faster than a walk – and rode beside him in silence for a few seconds before he even noticed she was there. 'Vanya,' she said, 'whatever you're thinking, forget about it.'

'I was trying not to think about anything for a while.'

'Only trying. And not doing it very well. Vanyushka, I won't give you a lecture. Now isn't the time. But I will give you two pieces of advice. One is something my father said: revenge is like wine – it keeps well, and tastes better for it. The other is my own philosophy about Amragan *tarkhan* and all others like him: any man who completely trusts an enemy's surrender has put a knife at his own throat.'

'If you run with the wolves, howl,' said Volk Volkovich, who had come up almost silently on Ivan's other side. 'But if you run with the dogs, just wag your tail.'

Ivan looked from one to the other and slowly, like a fire whose draught has been cut off, the heat faded from his eyes and the stiffness from his features until at last he gave them something that the charitable might have called a smile. 'So many proverbs,' he said. 'All right. You say wait. I'll wait.' Then, mocking gently,

'But to make it all convincing, you'll have to wag your tails as well . . .'

Chapter Seven

The Khanate of the Golden Horde;
August, AD 1243

Ivan Aleksandrovich was weary. He was weary of the featureless vastness of the steppes, so flat and unchanging that the presence of a scrubby tree was an event. Weary of sleeping in a *yurt* that smelt strongly of whatever creature's fur had been hammered together to make the felt which covered it, more strongly still of the ten Tatars who had slept in it on their journey up to Khorlov, and positively reeked of the camel which carried it during the day. Weary of being pleasant and courteous to Amragan *tarkhan*, watching his smile and listening attentively to what he had to say, when what he really wanted to do was shear off smile and head together.

And most of all, he was weary of *grut*.

There had been enough and more than enough of what the children called proper food when they left Khorlov; Mar'ya Morevna and High Streward Strel'tsin had seen to that. They had meat from every bird and beast in the storage cellars under the kremlin kitchens: barrelled hams of pork and mutton, beef trimmed lean and packed in preservative spices, joints of roasted geese packed in jars under a sealing layer of their own fat. There was dried meat, salted meat and smoked meat; there were bales of crimson-black sausages as long as a man's arm, hard enough to be used as cudgels and spiced like the hearths of hell. There were cheeses in small tubs, cheeses in cloths, and cheeses in thick coats of beeswax. There was wine, and ale, and *kvas*, and various flavoured vodkas in small stoneware bottles. It was enough food and drink to last Ivan and his people all the way to Sarai, and part of the way back.

Or it would have been, if someone – neither Ivan nor Mar'ya Morevna then or later admitted responsibility, though both of them blamed the other for playing trustworthy subservience a

183

little too far – had not invited Amragan *tarkhan* and his officers and shamans to as formal a dinner as could be contrived in tents of beaten hair. Ivan had seen how vassals ate, and how peasants ate, and how even less human creatures ate; but though he had dined with Tatars before, he had never seen how they ate when someone else was providing the food and they were not – as they had been at the banquet outside the walls of Khorlov – on their best behaviour.

They had watched in appalled fascination tinged with disbelief as Amragan *tarkhan* and nine other Tatars of more-or-less average size ate their way through a feast that in Khorlov's banqueting hall would have more than satisfied three times their number of Rus noblemen and warriors.

'Storing up for hard times,' Mar'ya Morevna had said behind her hand. The joke would have been funnier if there had been any indication that it might be the truth, but though broad and stocky enough, none of the Tatar captains had any spare flesh worthy of comment, and the shamans were positively gaunt. Where all the food and drink was going was a mystery, but go it did. The quartermaster had come to them the following morning with the hardly surprising news that instead of ample food for forty days of wandering in the wilderness that the Tatars had made of southern Russia, they now had barely enough to last for twenty-five.

That was when the Rus contingent added *grut* to their diet. As the days went by, they ate more and more of it; not because they were growing accustomed to the taste, but because there was less and less of anything else. But there always, unfortunately, seemed to be plenty of *grut*, and plenty of water to mix it into that particularly nasty granular sharp-cheese soup or porridge which was the accepted method of consumption. The 'unfortunate' part of it was Ivan's own opinion, and it had grown from an awareness that while there was enough of the wretched dried curds, none of the Tatars felt inclined to go hunting for fresh meat – and they weren't about to let any of their Rus 'guests' go galloping over the horizon with a bow and arrows either.

It gave the lie to what Amragan *tarkhan* had said about *grut* being only a ration of last resort; but then he was a Barlas clan Türk, and every other man in the Tatar column was from one or other Uighur or Mongol tribe. Perhaps a fondness for the flavour went with high cheekbones, slanted, Oriental eyes, and an excessive respect for the memory of that old butcher Chinghis-Khan, but except for Amragan they all seemed actually to enjoy the sour crumbly soup rather than eat it only from sheer necessity. The Türk, on the other hand, wasted a lot of his breath in reminiscence about *yogurt*, which to hear him talk bore as much relationship to *grut* as a strip of drief beef to a gravy-dripping roast served up with all the trimmings.

Ivan reserved judgment on that. As a Russian, he liked sour cream; but he ate it as a relish, not as the main dish. One food made from maltreated milk was probably much like another, and *grut* washed down with mares'-milk *kumys* went a long way to explain why the Tatars were the way they were. Sour on sour made sour, so far as he could see.

The Tatars laughed among themselves, presumably cracking jokes like any other group of soldiers whose duty has turned out a good deal easier than it might have done; but there was always a harshness to the laughter. He was honest enough with himself to accept that without a knowledge of what they were saying, his own mind was lending its own shades of meaning. But no amount of error could erase the fact that these men, or others like them, had turned the city of Chernigov into an infertile waste of bare, sour soil – and there was that 'sour' again! – and piled up the severed heads of its people as children might heap the stones of eaten plums in autumn. From what he had heard, and now seen with his own horrified eyes, the Tatars could take any land of milk and honey and transform it to a desert of ash and *grut*, so that their Khan could state without any fear of contradiction that there was peace in his domain.

The dead are very peaceful.

Ivan was dozing on the elaborate Persian couch that did duty for a bed in his appointed *yurtu* tent when he heard the travel-camp start to wake around him. The sun was barely above the horizon, and there was just enough light to see the faintly glowing verticals of where the tent's door-curtain didn't quite align with the doorway. Certainly it was too early even to think of getting up, and anyway Oleg Pavlovich, his Groom of the Bedchamber and head of the servants he had brought from Khorlov, had yet to arrive with hot water for washing and shaving. Just because a group of civilised persons was obliged to travel with barbarians was no reason to live like them. Ivan rolled onto his back – quietly, so as not to disturb Mar'ya Morevna who was fast asleep and snuggled tight against his ribs – then crossed his arms behind his head and resumed thinking the same sort of unpleasant thoughts about Amragan *tarkhan* as had occupied his idle waking moments for all the days since he had seen the ruins of Chernigov.

Mar'ya Morevna called it unhealthy; Volk Volkovich called it a waste of time; but Ivan called it just an indulgence. There was little likelihood he would ever have the Türk at sword's point without having to worry about the consequences of killing him; but not even Batu Khan of the Golden Horde could police a man's thoughts.

Sometimes it was a slim, curved Cossack sabre like the one he wore each day; sometimes a heavy broadsword like the one with which he had fought Aleksey Romanov. Sometimes it wasn't a sword but a dagger, like the one with which he had ripped up Dieter Balke before shoving the Teutonic Knight into the maw of an unformed Gate; at other times it was a slender iron mace with a flanged steel striking-head the size of an apple, that could burst the man's skull open like a raw egg. And sometimes, just sometimes, it was one of the spells from the less savoury side of the Art Magic, the spells that could shred meat from bone with a word and a gesture, that could boil the blood in living veins, that could . . .

Then he realised that the undertone of distant shouting was in fact not just the ordinary camp-waking noise that he had grown all too familiar with over the past few weeks. Ivan had often wondered what a Tatar would sound like when in terror for his life, when emitting the sounds he had so often caused in others.

Now he heard it. And Ivan realised in that instant that it was a sound he would have preferred to hear somewhere else, in a place far away from his wife and his children. He rolled sideways off the couch and grabbed for his clothes with one hand. The other hand had already closed around the belt-wrapped scabbard of his sword.

Mar'ya Morevna had been asleep and snoring in a tiny, charming way when he began to move; but at the first sharp, muted clatter of sheathed steel she was wide awake and sitting up, with the dagger that he knew only was somewhere under the tumbled pillows drawn and glinting in her hand.

'What is it?'

Ivan stamped his foot to get one hastily tucked-in boot in place around his ankle bones. 'Damned if I know,' he said, then belted his sword in place over his shirt and breeches without bothering about an outer tunic. Not the most enlightening of observations, it at least had the virtues of accuracy and brevity. 'But I intend to find out.'

'Wait for me – ' shouted his wife, but anything else she might have said was lost in the noise as Ivan plunged out of the *yurt* and into the middle of more chaos than two hundred Tatars and forty Rus should have been capable of causing. The first man he asked for an explanation was a waste of time, a Mongol archer whose eyes were as wide and staring as his facial structure permitted. The man didn't speak Russian and wasn't listening to Farsee. He flung off Ivan's restraining arm and ran off in a way that the young Tsar would have thought was someone taking cover, had the archer not been a soldier of the Golden Horde and thus an accredited part of the Scourge of God. Everyone knew *they* didn't run away, except in some elaborate tactical withdrawal to entice the enemy onward, except that Ivan could have sworn with a clear conscience on a stack of Bibles that this particular Scourge of God was looking for somewhere to hide. The way the man dived under a wagon did nothing to correct such a wrong assumption, though even now, Ivan had seen no reason for all the confusion.

Certainly whatever was going on was a matter for men and nothing else, because he could hear no sounds of disturbance from the animal pen on the far side of the *bok* camp. The morning was beautifully clear, with only a few fine skeins of cloud high up in the sky, so that the newly risen sun was throwing hard-edged black shadows across the ground from tents and running men alike.

Then Ivan squinted frowning at the sunrise and turned quickly to look at the *yurt* from which he had just emerged. Lying in bed, he had seen that same sunlight burning beyond the heavy curtain-flap that covered the doorway – he had been awake enough not to have dreamed it – and yet it could not have happened. In common with all the Tatar tents of the *bok*, it had been set up so that the door-opening faced towards the auspicious south rather than impudently towards the sunrise; moreover both the doorway and the whole southern side of the tent were in the shadow of the *yurt* beyond, and from the length of that shadow would be so for another half-hour or more. So where had the glare of not-sunlight come from. . . ?

Then Ivan laughed out loud, remembering another time and another place in another world than this one, and ran to a clearing beyond the cluster of tents where there was enough space for him to see more of the sky.

'Firebird,' he said quietly, not summoning but inviting as he stared up into the vast blue vault of the new day. Small wonder, on a morning like this, that the Tatars claimed it as their god. 'If you seek me, here I am.'

Nothing moved, nothing responded, and he began to wonder if all of this was nothing more than his own imagination coloured by wishful thinking. 'A Firebird?' said Mar'ya Morevna, who had just caught up with him with the children in hot pursuit, and overheard what he had said. She shook her head regretfully. 'Hardly. They don't cross into the wide white world unless someone calls them, and then they come to where they're called. A pity . . .'

'A pity about what?' Volk Volkovich the Grey Wolf arrived on soft feet, moving almost as quietly in human form as in his natural shape. From the look of him it was fairly certain that he had not been sleeping this past night; there was a relaxed, lazily well-fed air that Ivan had come to recognise and not ask about.

'Firebirds,' said Mar'ya Morevna shortly, still never at her best with Uncle Wolf around, and especially in the early morning before breakfast when he had so obviously eaten already.

'Then you saw it too? Good.'

That put an effective end to any further speculation as to who had or had not been imagining things, though not to the children's joy. 'He's here! He's here!' Ivan heard 'Tasha squealing delightedly; she was jumping up and down and clapping her hands, giving absolutely no impression of being frightened or worried, or anything but being completely thrilled at the prospect of seeing a Firebird. Kolya was waving both his hands at the sky, alternating between cheering like a small but very piercing adult, and whistling between his teeth like the merest peasant at a horse race.

Ivan watched them bounce around for a few seconds, and found himself frowning at such a display of pleasure. No more than a month ago, he would have put such excitement down to nothing more than the uproar in the camp, augmented by the chance of seeing a *zhar'yanoi* fire-creatre which both Nikolai and Anastasya had heard their parents talk about. Now he wasn't so sure. It was not *a* Firebird that they were hoping to see, but very specifically *the* Firebird, because all this looked far more like the reaction to an unexpected visit by a friend. Given the way they had been casually popping in and out of the Summer Country where the Firebirds lived, that didn't surprise him as much as it should have done. It worried him, though; one more worry among the many that a father doesn't usually have where his children are concerned, to keep company with the many that he does.

'Calm down, both of you,' he said. 'If there was a Firebird here at all, it's gone now. So behave.'

'He wouldn't have gone away without saying good morning to us,' said Anastasya firmly. Ivan blinked and Mar'ya Morevna stared, both of them suspecting that their daughter's use of 'us' was entirely accurate and specific. The twins, it seemed, were on good terms with a creature more potentially explosive than the largest fire-bombs of the Tatar siege artillery, and again, though shocked by the potential risks, Ivan was strangely unsurprised. Even without the sorcerous location and circumstance attending their conception, any friendly relationship between these children and other creatures capable of extreme violence was singularly appropriate.

'Did you call it here?' said Mar'ya Morevna, managing to combine suspicion and resignation in the same short sentence. Nikolai and Anastasya shook their heads. 'No,' they chorused.

'But we could,' Kolya added hopefully. 'Do you want – '

'No!'

'No need.'

Ivan twisted around to stare at the Grey Wolf, because there had been an edge to his voice that had turned his words into more than just an announcement. He turned fast enough that he caught sight of one of the tall man's ears twitching, listening to a sound that no-one else could hear; human shape or not, it seemed there were some aspects of the wolf-shape that remained besides his eerie eyes. Those eyes were gazing thoughtfully at the empty sky, not as though he could see something that others could not, but in the anticipatory way of someone who knows where to look before anything is there to see at all.

Then Ivan heard it too. At first the noise was like a cloth bedsheet being torn in half, if one could imagine a bedsheet that big. Then the noise slurred, and slowed, and deepened, until it was no longer just the biggest bedsheet in the world, but the very canopy of the sky that was being ripped asunder right down the middle.

Why wasn't there a noise the first time? Ivan's brain was screaming at him through that impossibly huge sound. *Why didn't you hear something?* The answer was fairly simple, in fact brutally obvious if he thought about it at all: the Firebird didn't want anyone to hear it that first time. They had seen it, though. And now Ivan saw it too.

The last time he had seen a Firebird fly free in the sky had been almost eight years ago. He and Mar'ya Morevna and the Grey Wolf had stood on a hillside somewhere in the Summer Country and watched one of the creatures flit across the peach and indigo heavens above a magnificent sunset. It was a memory that Ivan kept safe and cherished in his mind, taking it out every now and again to admire and polish as though it was a fine enamel painting. And yet, then and there it had seemed – well, natural, because that Firebird belonged in the Summer Country.

Just as this one did *not* belong here.

It appeared in the part of the sky where Volk Volkovich had been staring, high up and far away, riding the noise of its passage across the blue as foam rides the crest of a wave, the air tearing apart around it and slamming together in a long, thunderous roar all along its wake. That wake remained engraved on not only the ears but the eyes of everyone beneath it, because the Firebird's passage left a long bright track across the sky like the mark made by a nail scratched across a piece of dull grey lead. At first sight the Firebird was not a bird at all, but just an unendurably brilliant speck of fire gilding the loose weave of the lofty clouds as it descended through them. Then huge wings unfurled from the centre of that incandescent speck, curbing its descent from an uncontrolled plummet out of the heavens to an even more ominous falcon's stoop, and the sound became a high, shrill whistling of wind through white-hot feathers.

There were double shadows everywhere, those cast by the sun and those cast by the Firebird; but at least the common shadows remained in one place. The others stretched out across the steppe as their source moved across the sky, overlapping and parting like the shadows cast by children making finger-play by lamplight. After only a few seconds they became impossible to watch, because their movement provoked a near-drunken unsteadiness in those who stared too long, as if the earth itself was moving and not just the shadows.

It seemed to Ivan that things had gone strangely slow, because he had enough time to register the expressions and reactions of everyone nearby: from Mar'ya Morevna's astonished oath to the children yelling with delight and the Grey Wolf's silent satisfaction; from the near-panic of the ordinary Tatars – and some of the more susceptible Rus as well – to Amragan *tarkhan*'s glare laden with the shocked fury that he dared not vent. Trying to prevent matters from getting any worse, Ivan managed to keep his own face schooled to careful neutrality; but inwardly he was exultant. If the Khan's envoy needed an occasional reminder that in this instance at least, he was not dealing with the usual sort of Russian prince, then such a reminder as this would do him no end of good.

The Firebird dropped vertically through the last thousand feet of its descent, braked almost to a standstill with three huge, heat-scented strokes of wings feathered with tongues of fire, then landed softly right in front of –

– Nikolai and Anastasya.

'Hail, my friends!' it said, giving them the flare of wings and crest and tail that Ivan knew of old was its version of a salute. 'Greetings and well met. Be welcomed back into the Summer Country, you and all your' – the beaked head went on one side and then the other as its hard raptor's eyes took in the scene – 'guests.'

That it had chosen to greet only his children in the hissing metallic voice that Ivan remembered only too well came as no great shock. But the way it had greeted them, and the place in which it evidently thought they were, was more unsettling.

'Hail, *gospodin* Firebird!' he said, drawing an immediate sharp-pointed predator's stare. It was a relief to see recognition

191

cool the hot, gold-rimmed black jewels that did duty for the Firebird's eyes. This might not have been the same Firebird he had encountered before – one flame-hot falcon with an eight-foot wingspan looked very much like another – but all the *zhar'yanoi* were inveterate gossips, and if he didn't know it, it at least and fortunately had heard of him.

'Ivan Aleksandrovich. Then the Tsar of Khorlov's duties must have grown lighter at last,' said the Firebird, rather sarcastically. 'My companions in adventure' – it indicated the two children with a jerk of its head while Ivan and Mar'ya Morevna wondered just exactly how the twins had gained *that* particular title – 'say constantly that you are too busy to return to the Summer Country and exchange a pleasantry or two with the friends of your youth.'

'*Gospodin* Firebird, the passage of eight years does not make then my youth and now my dotage.' The Firebird looked at him and though it didn't actually possess any, Ivan had the distinct feeling that it had sceptically raised its eyebrows. 'And despite your welcome, this is *not* the Summer Country.' The Firebird gave him a long stare, glanced about, stared again and then produced a series of blinks that suggested it was completely nonplussed.

'But – ' it started to say, then clattered its beak and fell silent. A Firebird struck speechless by surprise was not something Ivan had ever encountered in his last dealings with the creatures, and it was a sight worth seeing since usually they had views about everything under the arch of Heaven, and no reluctance about voicing them.

'Not the Summer Country,' Mar'ya Morevna repeated. 'This is – was – lately the southern part of the principality of Pereyaslavl' and is now a province of the Khanate of the Golden Horde.' She managed by great effort to keep her voice neutral, though another twitch of its head and a snap of that hooked pickaxe beak suggested that the Firebird had heard what lay behind her toneless words and didn't like it. 'But it is not the Summer Country, and never was.'

'I was not summoned.' It was not a question, just a flat statement of fact, and one which saved the twins from a possibly unpleasant interview later. 'I was in the Summer Country,' it said, the iron voice scraping harsh with anger, 'and then . . . And then I was not!'

The Firebird spread its wings in a sudden passion, lashing them through the air in trails of sparks while it gouged its talons into the dry grass of the steppe. Small fires sprang up at once, then choked in curls of blue smoke as they died out for lack of the fuel that their own brief fury had consumed.

Ivan sympathised with the Firebird, an empathy he would never have dreamed possible until now. It knew no enemy to strike at for this insulting behaviour, and while he knew his enemy, striking was out of the question. Either way, the frustration was the same. 'Apologies for inconvenience,' he said weakly. 'You'll go home now, of course?'

He didn't know whether he wanted it to do so or not, because from the appalled expressions on various Tatar faces, its presence might prove a useful club to beat concessions from the Khan. But it was also a liability, an opinionated one at that, and obvious besides. Natasha was tugging at his shirt with the probable intention of making him ask it to stay, but Mar'ya Morevna's face suggested an urgent need for a few minutes alone to discuss the whys and hows of its being here in the first place, and preferably after it had gone back to where it came from.

'Is this, ah, change of scenery a trouble to you, *gospodin?*' said Volk Volkovich. He sounded more painfully polite than ever, and only those who knew the Grey Wolf well could hear the soft rumbling growl down in his chest that coloured the words, warning the irritable Firebird that any trouble it felt had better not be visited on his companions.

'No trouble, wolf,' said the Firebird, staring at Volk Volkovich speculatively for such a long time that Ivan felt an overpowering desire to back away and leave them room to sort out their differences. Fortunately none of the Tatars, not even Amragan *tarkhan*, thought that 'wolf' was anything more than a mild insult aimed at the magnificent cloak Ivan's sinister henchman was wearing. 'No trouble at all.' It scratched its beak briskly with one sickle claw, so that a shower of sparks went skipping across the already-charred grass as though someone was sharpening a sword on a grindstone. It sounded like that too; in fact it sounded, with a high, steely singing, as though the sword was entirely too sharp already.

Then the Firebird flapped its wings once in a flurry of heat and sprang into the air. It hung there like a kestrel for a few seconds, hanging on the rising thermals of its own creation; then went spiralling upward in the same way as a dry leaf might escape from an autumn bonfire. As it rose, it flared impossibly bright until it was casting heat and light like the very sun itself, and once again two shadows instead of one went stretching out from everything on the ground. Abruptly the yellow glare surrounding it went blue-white, the colour of a lightning flash, and all the other colours of the world were bleached to black and white.

Then light and heat and Firebird disappeared together.

Squinting and dazzled like everyone else, Ivan wondered if they shared his thought; that though the world's colouring had returned, its tints and shades were somehow plain and common, grown more drab with the Firebird gone. Though with their – entirely natural – tendency to hot temper, they *were* somewhat unsettling to have around.

'Name of Tängri, man!' rasped Amragan *tarkhan*, sounding most satisfactorily appalled. 'What under the Blue Sky was that?'

Ivan turned and looked him up and down, a slow, insolent stare that had the Türk not been so shocked, he would have found insulting. 'You know so much about me and my doings, Amragan,' he said. 'That was just an old friend of the family. Surely you recognise a Firebird when you see one?'

'I . . .' Amragan *tarkhan* fell silent. Faced with the revelation that even Ivan's children were acquainted with demons from the sky, and the uncomfortable choice of admitting he had never seen a Firebird before or compounding the error by making easily disproved claims, he had evidently decided to say nothing.

Mar'ya Morevna had other interests, though from the sound of it, not very important ones. 'How far from here to Sarai and the Khan's court?' she asked, her voice only mildly curious. That lack of any excitement suggested the encounter with the Firebird was an everyday occurrence. It might never have taken place, for all it mattered to her. Ivan smiled inwardly. Such a display of unconcern might not, and probably would not fool Amragan *tarkhan* – but he would wonder how much of it was real and how much was pretence, and that would help keep him off balance until the time came to make his report to Batu Khan. It was fortunate that with the exception of the children and the various lesser dignitaries, all of whom could be excused for one reason or another, Ivan's people had remained calm and untroubled. It made the present display of nonchalance that much more convincing.

The Türk stared at Mar'ya Morevna for a few seconds and Ivan could actually watch the man pull his confused mind back into some sort of order. Amragan covered well, but Ivan had the advantage of having seen variations on this same reaction a dozen times. The eyes shifting rapidly about as though checking that the rest of the world had returned to a semblance of normality; the dry tongue licking dry lips on a sweat-damp face; the hands clenched into fists to conceal their shaking. Ivan's hidden smile grew broader. The envoy could not claim that he had been threatened, far from it; but his own imagination was doing far better work to encourage future respectful behaviour than any number of Rus soldiers armed with swords.

'We are – ' The *tarkhan* stopped and coughed savagely to clear an unmistakable squeak from his voice, and when he tried again, it sounded much more businesslike. 'We are only three days' march from the Golden Court. Maybe less,' he looked from side to side, glaring at his own Tatars in the way he no longer dared to glare at Ivan and the others, 'if this camp is struck within the next hour! Get to it! We're wasting time!'

He strode off, bellowing.

Ivan watched him go, then looked sidelong at Mar'ya Morevna. 'How far to Sarai, eh? You don't ask idle questions, even of Tatars – so what was that all about?'

'Use your brains, my dear.' Mar'ya Morevna gave her husband a sour little smile, but no hints. 'You don't usually ask idle questions either. At least you ask less of them than most people.'

'I don't think I've been insulted,' said Ivan to the world in general, 'and I'll go on thinking that.' He lowered his voice. 'It's about the crowns, isn't it?'

Mar'ya Morevna nodded. 'The Firebird thought it was still in the Summer Country,' she said. 'It felt nothing during the transition – and when it left us, you saw how that transition usually looks and sounds and feels.'

'Not quite,' said Volk Volkovich. 'That Firebird wasn't in the best of tempers – although in my opinion they seldom are. But what you were seeing was the equivalent of a door being slammed.'

195

'When I want your opinion I'll ask for – '

' – But then you'd never get it, would you? *Gospozha tsaritsa*, this matter has gone beyond your – I beg pardon – ' and the Grey Wolf gave her a bow worthy of a courtier, '*our* petty differences. But lady, though you know things that I do not, so I know things that you do not – and if you constantly refuse to listen, how will you ever learn what those things might be, never mind if they might be useful?'

Ivan heard the way Mar'ya Morevna drew in her breath at that, and laid one restraining arm on her shoulder. That might not have had any effect – as well he knew – except that Nikolai and Anastasya simultaneously tugged at the skirts of her long riding coat. They said nothing, knowing well enough not to abuse the privileged position of being present during an adult argument, but Mar'ya Morevna looked down at their anxious faces and swallowed whatever she had been about to say. Then stared accusingly at Volk Volkovich. 'Are you trying to steal my children from me?' she said, her voice flat and cold. 'Because I think you're succeeding.'

The Grey Wolf stared at her with glowing yellow-green eyes that never blinked. 'I am trying,' he said, 'to prevent Death stealing them from you,' and with huge dignity turned his back. He did not stalk away, as might have been expected; but his silent presence was more of an accusation than any dramatic exit might have been.

Face expressionless, Ivan looked at his wife, then pointedly walked around until he was face to face with Volk Volkovich. They stared at one another for several seconds of silence before Ivan inclined his head a few barely perceptible degrees. 'Later,' he said. That was all. He hoped it was enough.

When he turned back to Mar'ya Morevna, he knew it was impossible to be angry with her. She had told him enough of why she felt the way she did about the Grey Wolf for Ivan to understand all the parts she hadn't dared to explain; but he had hoped she might be able to control such feelings for the sake of that political abstraction 'the greater good'. Not today, it seemed.

Perhaps Volk Volkovich would understand that. Perhaps he already did understand, and all he wanted was the simple apology that cost nothing but a little buckling in that terrible rigidity of her pride. And he might receive it. But not today, it seemed.

Ivan let the matter drop. It was not something that could be easily dealt with here, in the open, in front of the children and in front of the Grey Wolf and in front of as many of Amragan *tarkhan*'s Tatars who had ears sharp enough to hear what was being said. He hoped Volk Volkovich would understand that, as well.

At least – and there was a gloomy humour about it – Ivan's brain had been shaken out of its indolence in a way not even the appearance of the Firebird had been able to do. He knew exactly why Mar'ya Morevna wanted to know how close they were to Sarai, and exactly why the Firebird's unexpected arrival – unexpected even by itself – concerned her so. Things were already beginning to slip to and fro between the boundaries that kept each world separate from the next. The doors leading into the corridor were no longer locked, and some of them were hanging ajar. A Firebird was impressive enough, but it was nothing by comparison with some of the, the *things* that dwelt in the cold dark.

Things that might find the bright warmth of the wide white world as appealing as a candle to a moth. Most moths burned up in a candle flame; but a big enough moth could put the candle out. Ivan shivered, and all the eminently sensible things he was going to say fell out of his mind. 'Back to the tent,' he said finally. 'There are things I want before it's packed away.'

That was sensible enough for now.

The rest of the journey to Sarai took less time than Ivan feared; but it still took more time than he might have hoped. There was a taut, unpleasant atmosphere about the caravan that had not been there before. Some of it came from the incident with the Firebird; some of it from the sharp exchange between Mar'ya Morevna and the Grey Wolf; and some of it, quite simply, from the all too human curiosity of the many, Rus and Tatar both, who were watching to see if a juicy scandal was in the offing.

Was there more than just honest duty between the Tsar's handsome henchman and the Tsar's beautiful wife? Was there more than that between the Tsar's handsome henchman and the handsome young Tsar himself? Was it true that the Tsar's twin children were as close to the henchman as to their own father, and if so did that simply mean they were as close to their own father as to the Tsar? The possibilities and permutations were endless and delicious.

Ivan officially heard none of it, and neither did Mar'ya Morevna. If Volk Volkovich heard any, as seemed likely with his sharp ears, he did not pass the information on – and for that much at least, Ivan was grateful. What he was not told, he was not obliged to know. But there was a list of names taking shape at the back of his mind, a list cross-referenced with other such lists that went back almost eight years, a list that one day quite soon he might have the pleasure of signing and sealing and handing over to Khorlov's under-worked executioner. And if any of what he had – not – heard was reported back to him by either of the children, he would not even wait that long.

And in the meanwhile, he tried to find out why it was that the Firebird should have appeared where it did, when it did. The why of the matter he knew already, but for a long time the rest was more puzzling.

Mar'ya Morevna was of little help. There had been more words between them, as they lay in bed together on the night of the – was it a quarrel, really, when it had not been between the two of them? There had been other fallings-out in the course of their marriage, sharply worded differences of opinion about one thing or another. But both of them had long been content that those had been nothing more than bickering. It was only human nature that even when two people were very much in love, if they were both well-educated in the same subjects then sometimes there was a reluctance to allow one to score what the other felt was an undeserved point. It was an almost childish silliness, the sort of thing that within an hour might be laughed or grimaced at. And if this business had blown up out of all proportion into a really serious quarrel, what was only one of those in eight years? Unusual? Remarkable? Hardly; Ivan knew the real answer.

It was one too many.

The words they had exchanged had been pointless for the most part, spoken in such low tones for the sake of privacy that they had been robbed of whatever impact they might have carried as they went wandering around and around the subject at hand without ever piercing to its centre, to where it would have done some good.

'Apologise,' he said at last. Not to whom, not for what. Just, 'Apologise.'

That was when she had looked at him with eyes that were as cold and hurting as daggers of blue crystal; cold, and guilty, and ashamed. And unbendingly proud. 'No. I can't apologise.'

'Why? *Why?*'

'Because . . .' Again the cold daggers, pride and shame together, aimed not at him but through him, at someone beyond him; and he knew who that someone might be. 'Because I can't find the words. Because I don't know how.'

Ivan took those daggers full in the face without a word, understanding while not understanding, and not daring to say so because that was the last thing in all the world that she would want to hear right now. Instead he had taken his wife's hand in his, and held it. He had held it all that night, while they lay on their backs in the silence of two people with nothing left to say, staring at the low, dark, musty ceiling of the felt tent as they tried to sleep. And all that night, fingers entwined, their hands had remained together; wrist to wrist, elbow to elbow, shoulder to shoulder.

It was as though a bared sword lay between them down the centre of the bed.

Sarai, capital of the Khanate of the Golden Horde; September, AD 1243

There was an escarpment where the dreary flatness of the steppe became the valley of the River Volga, just as wide, just as flat, simply marsh-wet instead of dust-dry. Ivan reined his horse to a standstill on the crest of that low eminence and looked down towards Sarai and the Court of the Splendid Khan. He did it not so much because he wanted to, as because he thought he must. There was a feeling of portent and significance about this moment, though whether it would turn out good or bad rested, as so often, in the hands of a man Ivan had never met, but who controlled his destiny as surely as though he pulled the strings of a puppet.

The city had not been built so much as it had grown – like a poisonous fungus, Ivan thought – on the old Bulgar lands near the mouth of the Volga, eighty miles upstream from where the river poured into the waters of the Caspian Sea. Once it had been no more than just another *bok*, a vast trading camp whose walls of mud and straw enclosed hundreds upon hundreds of hunched felt tents, whose magnificence rested solely on the plunder strewn haphazardly here and there as magpies might strew shiny gewgaws.

That had changed. Ilkhan Batu of the Golden Horde was not known as *Sain* Khan for nothing. His splendour in dress, his fondness for jewels and adornments, his extravagant generosity when giving feasts for his commanders and lieutenants, all that had gained him the title 'Splendid'; but it was what he had done to Sarai that confirmed it.

Amragan *tarkhan* had told Ivan all of that, in the friendly and slightly relieved fashion of a man glad to be home after a task which had turned out more difficult than at first suspected. Ivan had smiled and nodded thanks for the information, as he had nodded and smiled almost all the way from Khorlov, with just enough vinegar spiking the honey to make the Türkic envoy appreciate what a quiet, well-behaved hostage he was all the rest of the time. Hostage, not guest. He made sure that he remembered the difference even as he took pains not to show it. If any man had the wealth of empires at his disposal, he thought as Amragan rode away, and the slaves taken from those empires to do his bidding, and enough constructive stirring of his imagination to want to live in something other than a felt *yurt* then that man could make a city like Sarai.

It was not a compliment.

Sarai was still a trading camp, just as it had been in the days of the Volga Bulgars a hundred years and more ago. It was still an infestation of tents encircled by a wall, and even at this distance Ivan could smell it. The city stank as badly as every other Tatar camp he had ever encountered; but now, after four years of occupation by Batu *Sain* Khan, four years of backbreaking work by only God knew how many slaves, it was more than a mere *bok* on the steppes.

The wall was no longer bound together by pounding straw into mud before allowing it to dry in the sun. Instead it was constructed of worked stone, an elaborate ring of fortifications, battlements, ramparts and ditches surrounding buildings of half-a-dozen styles from half a dozen conquered countries. Ivan had seen none of those styles in their proper place, but he had read Dmitriy Vasil'yevich Strel'tsin's chronicles and studied their tiny, beautiful illustrations. Even from where he sat he could recognise curved, peaked, red-painted roofs from Kaï-t'ing and T'ung-hüan and the other fallen cities of what had been Sung China. Here was elaborate latticework in carved brick and inlaid patterns of blue and turquoise tiles from Bokhara and Samarkand in Khwarizmid Persia. There were low, blocky, ponderous houses, each one its own fortress, like the caravanserais of Kashgar and Khokand in the Syr Daria at the Roof of the World.

Ivan knew them all, the strange names from the strange places; places as far away as last night's dream, places that once he had wanted to visit, places with names like strange jewels, capable of creating their own bright images from mere black letters and coloured inks on a sheet of parchment. Names to conjure with, and make a far more wholesome magic than the jarring syllables of true sorcery. Images like the fortress of the Bala Hissar and the great port at Basra; the weavers of Isfahan and Tashkent, the swordsmiths of Nishapur and Khandahar; the mountains of the Hindu Kush; the crags of Koord-Kabul; the ship-lined curve of the Golden Horn beyond Byzantium; and the gleaming spires of the Hagia Sofia.

Ivan drew in a deep breath, and sighed, frowning as the heavy stench of Sarai filled his nostrils. Long ago, before the realities of being a tsar's son had begun to weigh upon him, he had wanted to be a *bogatyr'*. Not one of the wretched self-seeking political creatures who now made up the greater part of his *druzina* retinue, but a true hero-knight, a wanderer, a journeyer to the far places of the world.

And now they were here.

But not really here, because the city had been built by men whose minds and bodies had been stolen from where they belonged, so that the buildings they made were no more than a cheat and a deception, like false, cheap jewellery of paste and coloured glass. Tsar Ivan Aleksandrovich of Khorlov had not been stolen like the slaves and artisans. There were no ropes binding him, no chain shackling him like a leashed dog to Amragan *tarkhan*'s saddle. He had come and would enter as he had been invited, freely and of his own will.

Ivan smiled, a smile that was no more than a skinning back of lips from far too many teeth that Volk Volkovich would have been proud of. Once invited within those walls, so the old legends said, he would be like one of the *oupirchiy*, those who once were dead and now were risen again – and that at least was true enough, thanks to Koshchey the Deathless. He would be free to come and go as pleased him; to do what pleased him; to visit whatever mischief as seemed right and proper on the people there . . .

He smiled again and leaned forward in his high-peaked saddle, gazing down on Sarai through eyes slitted by more than the glare of the sun as its light pierced like a sword blade through the western clouds, and entertained the thoughts of a Tatar *voevoda* who would see not a city but a nest of ants. As he stroked the lashes of his riding whip slowly through his fingers, he dreamed a secret, ugly dream from long ago, of his boot-heel coming down, and down, and down again until that nest and all the ants within it had been stamped from the face of the wide white world. Sarai, and Khanbalik, and even Karakorum on the high steppes of Central Asia; all of them, and all their people, no more than a bloody smear on the crushed wet earth.

Ivan played with that for a few moments; then his mouth twisted in distaste as he felt a shudder run through him. He knew that he could do all those things in a red rage; but coldly, methodically, in the Tatar fashion . . . ?

No.

Keeping the screams out of his dreams afterwards was a trick he had not yet learned, and he had no desire to learn it. A good conqueror did not make a good tsar, and he had no desire to be remembered as Ivan the Terrible. Someone else in later years could have that title, and be welcome to it. The word *grozniy* had many layers of meaning in Russian – menacing, threatening, awe-inspiring – but none of them were kindly meant. Only someone ruled by the useless, short-lived passions of an adolescent, like Aleksandr *bol'shoy*, Aleksandr the Great who had been Ivan's hero until he learned the truth behind the glittering legend, could truly do what needed to be done and still have any hope of sleeping at night. Because he did not truly understand or care about what he was doing; because everyone but his own people were just nests of ants. . .

And did crushing one nest bring another back to life?

No.

So why bother? Surely it was better to hold back and watch that nest go about its business because you, and you alone, knew you could have flattened it, and held back because you were so much better, stronger and wiser than the ants who called themselves the rulers of that nest.

Except that killing was easier, destruction was simpler, and it made your power more easily understood to more people than any amount of grand, merciful gestures that they would only see as weakness anyway. Ivan grinned down at Sarai, a horrible, humourless grin like any one of the thousands of skulls piled up outside Chernigov, and wondered who would understand what in a thousand years. And who would really care? He shrugged, and dismissed the matter from his mind.

Broken clouds like great grey sailing ships were sliding heavily across the sky. Ivan, who had never seen a ship, watched them with gloomy indifference. They had been threatening rain all day, and already a thin drizzle was sweeping over the city, hanging from the lowering heavens like a skein of fine grey silk. He had watched such intermittent showers march across the steppes, barely enough for now to lay the dust, but that would change. *Rasputitsa*, the time of bad roads, was on the way. The autumn rains were already overdue, and that usually meant they would be excessive when they arrived at last. And right now there was a certain fitness to the concepts of Tängri the Blue Sky hiding his face and weeping heavy tears on Sarai.

'A pity that's no more than drizzle,' said Mar'ya Morevna behind him. Ivan hid a start of surprise as best he could, so lost in his own thoughts that he had not heard her approach, and twisted around in his saddle to look back at her.

'You want to get wet?'

'Never mind the wet. I wouldn't object to a good thunderstorm.'

'Bored with the rain already? God, what are you going to be like when it's been falling non-stop for a week?'

'Vanya, I . . .'

'What?' Ivan saw her shoulders slump in a sort of reverse shrug, and bit his own lip as he realised why. His immediate, unthinking sharpness had been part of an unfortunate family characteristic he shared with his sisters. In the right mood, any of the Khorlovskiy could cuddle a domestic disagreement like children with a favourite toy, and now that they were in sight of Sarai, and all the fears he had hidden so well were beginning to surface, Ivan was in that mood right now. The true annoyance came from knowing it, knowing how to prevent it, and still displaying that instinctive talent for saying the wrong thing in the wrong tone at just the right time to be most hurtful.

That Mar'ya Morevna knew all about that trait, and had been trying in that magnanimous and forgiving way of hers to patch up the squabble, only served to make him feel worse, more irritable, and more inclined to continue it until matters could be solved on his terms instead of hers. Small wonder that all of Tsar Aleksandr's children were known for their peaceful family lives, free of the petty frictions that plagued ordinary folk. It was because they avoided cause for discord as a reformed drunkard tried to avoid the bottle. Enough quarrels of the intensity they could maintain for days at a time, and there might well be murder done. Ivan muttered an imprecation at himself under his breath.

Like Mar'ya Morevna about the Grey Wolf, simply saying *I apologise* was a more difficult task than he could face right now. They knew each other that well at least. The apologies would be made, sooner or later, and they might have more value later than not. Hastily saying nothing but the words – just making the proper noises at what seemed the proper time – counted for nothing unless they were meant sincerely, and that sincerity was not for public display. Later, perhaps. Somewhere behind closed doors. He could think of nothing worse than baring his soul in plain sight and hearing of the entire caravan; because it suddenly seemed that he and his wife were the focus of attention for every idler and for a good number of those who should have had better things to do. Ivan had never been one for wearing his heart on his sleeve, but Mar'ya Morevna was the only woman he had ever met in all his life who could tear that heart right out of his chest and leave him unharmed.

'Start again, Mar'yushka,' he managed at last. 'And try to forget' – *and forgive* – 'everything I said.'

Mar'ya Morevna gazed levelly at him with those blue-grey eyes, and Ivan felt as he had often done before, that she was looking right inside his head and reading the unspoken thoughts from the very surface of his brain. If that was so, then surely she had also seen what it was he would have said had they been alone in some private place where a tsar could become just another man. And perhaps it was true after all, because the cool sadness in her eyes thawed like ice in sunshine, and even though she made no mention of it, Ivan knew his hard words had indeed been forgiven.

'I was wishing for thunder,' she said as though merely continuing an interrupted conversation. 'Since we're going to be rained on, we might as well have some drama to go with it.'

'Indeed?' Ivan looked at the heavy sky, then back at Mar'ya Morevna, and raised his eyebrows slightly. The onlookers, sensing that the moment for drama had passed, lost interest in what was evidently going to be a mundane discussion of the weather. 'There's more to it than that, isn't there?'

'Tängri's displeasure.'

'Now you really are getting devious.' Ivan found that he was guarding his speech with great care just at the minute, and rightly so. He was getting into another of those situations where he would too easily end up being forced to admit ignorance of something Mar'ya Morevna had tried to teach him six months or a year ago, and he was still smarting enough from one demonstration of his stupidity to want to add another to it. 'Displeasure about us? What are we to a Tatar god, or him to the Rus?'

'A token of warning, maybe. According to what few sources I've been able to mine' – of course Ivan immediately wanted to know which and where and when, but had the sense to keep his mouth shut until she was done – 'thunder is the only thing the Chingisid line are afraid of. Chinghis-Khan Temüchin was supposed to have some especial reverence for the Blue-Sky god. Any sign of irritation from Up There was taken personally – and Ilkhan Batu is the old butcher's grandson.'

'I see,' said Ivan, and did, for once. 'If we rode into Sarai to the accompaniment of a good roll on Tängri's drums, and some juicy rumour was planted to get to Batu's ears, then it might give us some extra weight during whatever bargaining needs to be done later.'

'Alternately it might just get us all killed out of hand,' said Mar'ya Morevna drily, though from the sour smile that accompanied her words, it didn't look as if the threat concerned her much.

Even though the rain had died away, and with it any chance of hearing what Ivan had called the Sky god's drums, there were drums enough to keep their ears occupied for the next while. The Tatar band had been busy this past few minutes, unwrapping their instruments from the oiled silk that protected them from inclement weather. Now there were shrill squeaking noises as reeds were checked for damp, and sullen rumblings as the heads of the great *naccara* kettledrums were re-tensioned.

Then, instructed in an eerie silence by nothing more than movements of Amragan *tarkhan*'s yak-tail standard, the column closed up from its somewhat straggling line of march into a tight military formation. Only then did the Türk give a signal for it to advance beyond the crest of the escarpment and into plain view of Sarai. And the silence came to an end.

The band played, as it had done during the approach to Khorlov: a squeal of *shawms*, a thunder of drums, a brazen blare of trumpets. But this time, there was a reply.

After a long silence when the first flare of music from the marching column had died away and only the distant twinkling spear-points of the sentries moved along the ramparts of Sarai, there came an answer from the mighty horns and drums of the Court of the Golden Horde. That sound, scream and thunder blended together in one single awesome blast of noise, was both terrible and splendid. It rolled across the flood plain of the river Volga, was caught and channelled by the valley carved through centuries from the face of Moist-Mother-Earth, and its full strength smote like a tidal wave against those who dared approach the city of the Splendid Khan. It was a sound of welcome in the ears of the Tatars who had gone forth and returned, but an ominous warning of power beyond human comprehension to those who came to bow and ask for favours.

Only those who were too young to understand the layers of

meaning behind it could truly enjoy that huge magnificence, and there were only two such in the entire caravan. Nikolai and Anastasya Khorlovskiy had been allowed out of their wagon and onto horseback for the entry into Sarai, and now they bounced in the saddles of their small ponies, clapping their hands in wonder at the sights and sounds laid out before them.

Ivan and Mar'ya Morevna looked at one another across the heads of their children, and though no words were spoken, their still-unresolved quarrel was not merely forgiven, but laid aside once and for all. It was as if the awesome sound of the Khan's music had reminded them of how insignificant their own disagreement was in the face of such an adversary. Continuing with it would have served no purpose – if like any quarrel it had ever served a purpose now, before, or afterwards – and the subject of that quarrel had not ridden with them this two days past.

Amragan *tarkhan* had passed no remark about Volk Volkovich's absence. The Türk had made little enough comment about his presence that it was likely all Russians looked the same to him and that one more or less was not worthy of his attention. At least, he had said nothing about the *man*. However, Amragan and several of his Farsee-speaking lieutenants had been cursing the presence of a 'damned big wolf' this two days past. One of the column's outriders had vanished, or rather, he had failed to appear the morning after his night on duty. For some hours there had been little concern; even a Tatar pony could miss its footing at night, and on a couple of past occasions the night picket had come trailing in near noon, bruised and muddy, leading a limping horse. But not this time.

There had been a search, and someone had stumbled across marks in an area of soft earth that had been more than just circumstantial evidence. Both sets of tracks indicated plainly that they had been made by creatures running at full speed, and the unshod hoofs of the outrider's horse were distinctive enough. But beside them were the paw marks of a wolf. That was all: there was no sign of a scuffle, no blood, no discarded clothing and not even a drag-trace to indicate that the missing remains of man or horse had been taken away. Just the double line of tracks – that ended with shocking abruptness two full strides short of the end of that betraying bare ground, almost as if some hand had reached down out of the sky to snatch up wolf and horse together – if any hand would dare to snatch up the wolf that could leave such tracks as these.

Its pad-prints could barely be spanned by a full-grown man's fingers spread as wide as they would go, something demonstrated several times by several different people, each of them more nervous than the last. That was indeed a 'damned big wolf', impossibly big, because those tracks meant it stood maybe four feet high at the shoulder. It was a good guess. Both Ivan and Mar'ya Morevna knew exactly how good; but Ivan at least took a malicious pleasure in speculating just how much bigger than the biggest guess this wolf might really be. And thus – with a little reminder of the Firebird that was hardly needed – how unlikely it was that the maker of those tracks had been 'just' a wolf.

He wrapped up his conclusions in enough hunter's jargon that they sounded entirely convincing, so much so that every Tatar in the column, and most of the Russians as well, had been in a state of apprehension bordering on terror for the past two days. Only Ivan, his wife and his children were unconcerned; and all of them knew better than to say a word about it.

The missing Tatar outrider, or what was left of him, was probably in the Summer Country by now, and so was Volk Volkovich the Grey Wolf. And now, in the same way as he had achieved previously on more than one occasion, he had clothing and a mount that would not mark him out as Russian. What Volk Volkovich was planning to do, he had not confided to anyone else. But Ivan was sure that it would prove . . . interesting.

He bowed low in his saddle, and with a courtly gesture to Mar'ya Morevna, invited her to ride beside him down to Sarai and into the Court of the Golden Horde.

Chapter Eight

Sarai, capital of the Khanate of the Golden Horde;
September, AD 1243

Ivan Aleksandrovich, whether Tsar or Great Prince or whatever
his title might finally be by the sufferance of the Ilkhan of the
Golden Horde, did not flatter himself that the drums and trumpets
of Sarai were sounding because of his approach. He did at least
think – for the space of almost twenty minutes – that it was to greet
Amragan *tarkhan* on his return back home at the end of what had
obviously been a most successful mission. In that he was mistaken.
The same great blast of sound welled up from within the city walls
some several minutes after Amragan's column had reached the
floor of the river valley, and though Ivan did not slacken the
dignified pace of his horse, he rose in his stirrups and peered about
him to see what had provoked this new salutation.

Thanks to the recent shower of rain, there was no scarf of russet
dust hanging above them to reduce visibility in the various
directions it was driven by the wind. Instead the air was clear and
clean, newly washed and sparkling in the sunlight that was still
trying to break through even though night was drawing closer.
That sunlight struck sparks from the armour and weapons of
another group of riders who were pouring down into the Volga
flood plain at a good hand-gallop. They were almost a mile away,
certainly too far for him to make out any details, but they were
Tatars. The horns of Sarai sounding welcome had told him that
much already.

'Their commander isn't half as orderly as our Amragan,' said
Mar'ya Morevna, watching the distant horsemen break out across
the plain whatever way they chose. 'I wonder how long they were
waiting.'

'Waiting for us?'

'Certainly. I don't believe in so much coincidence that they
should so fortuitously put in an appearance just when we do.'

209

'Just for the sake of showing off,' said Ivan, putting his finger with remarkable exactness on the flamboyant way the other Tatars were behaving. Riding at such a speed, they had closed the distance that separated bright metallic specks from easily distinguished mounted men in a matter of half a minute or so. And those men weren't mounted at all, as often as not. He could see several of them hang down from their saddles on one side or the other – usually the right side, that being nearest to Amragan *tarkhan*'s staid, slow-moving, disciplined formation – to take half-a-dozen huge, bounding strides alongside their racing ponies before swinging astride again. All of it was done without slackening their headlong pace, or from the unbroken sound of the high, barbaric yelling, even pausing for breath.

'Nothing but noisiness and flash,' he said dismissively, without thinking, and so unconsciously sounded just like Guard-Captain Akimov, who as a Kuban-Zaporozhiyy Cossack could have shown these Tatars what real flamboyant horsemanship was all about. He heard Mar'ya Morevna snort a small, inadequately stifled explosion of laughter and glanced curiously at her; but it was the children who made him think back to that casually voiced opinion, and so brought home what he had done. Neither of the twins saw any reason to moderate their mirth just because the person speaking in silly voices was their father the Tsar. Indeed, that very fact probably encouraged them to the sort of eye-rolling, thigh-slapping extravagance which has no real place in a child's laughter except to stretch the moment of amusement as far as it can go.

'All right, you two. Enough. Behave.' The voice this time was not a comic imitation, but their father's own, and its tone was one which indicated there would be no repetition of the order. There was no more uproar after that, and Ivan ignored the occasional outbreak of muffled giggling when either Nikolai or Anastasya caught the other's eye, and had to resort to knuckles stuffed in mouths if they were to observe the letter of the law just laid down with every suggestion of severity.

Mar'ya Morevna eyed him dubiously, and even more so when his response was a grin, but Ivan paid no heed. That laugh of hers had been like a loaf of bread to a starving man; it had been real laughter for the first time in far too long, and not the false, brittle sound that he had never been able to hear as anything other than a mask in the shape of a smile. He supposed that his displays of 'humour' had looked and sounded much the same to her. They had both been, and still were, as nervous as kittens in a kennel full of hounds at the prospect of what would happen when he finally met Batu *Sain* Khan, and learned his ultimate fate. The possibilities were all too various, and few of them pleasant.

Whatever title he might bear at last, Ivan the erstwhile Tsar of Khorlov might remain the ruler of his own domain – but with one or all of his family held back as hostage in Sarai against his good behaviour and that of his subjects. Or he might not be allowed to return home at all, and he and his wife and children would remain indefinitely as 'guests' of the Khan while some figurehead was appointed to act in his name. Worst of all, the Ilkhan Batu might simply set up a *daru-gashi* governor to administer the wringing of taxes from his newest fiscal district, and dispose of the Tsar and all related to him as nothing more than an outdated anachronism.

All those numerous prospects had been lurking at the back of Ivan's mind as if they were the shadow of a kestrel and he was a fieldmouse in an open meadow. Small wonder his temper had been none of the best and his tongue had developed an indiscriminate razor edge. It would be ridiculous to assume that the same fears had not been haunting Mar'yushka's thoughts and darkening her moods; but he was honest enough with himself to accept that nineteen times out of twenty, he had been to blame for any harsh words and useless sharpness. To hear a genuine laugh, no matter how brief, and know that Mar'ya Morevna could still produce such a sound and mean it, took a great weight off his shoulders. Perhaps it was only optimism as foolish and groundless as his previous gloom had been, but Ivan found himself daring to hope that everything would be all right.

For all Amragan *tarkhan*'s care to draw up his troops in parade order before they entered the city, there were no crowds lining the streets as they rode into Sarai. Perhaps it wasn't the Tatar custom; but more probably, and no matter how significant the Tsar of Khorlov and his companions might have thought it, the Türk's mission simply hadn't been important enough to justify any public celebration. The few women and children who ran alongside the silent files of horsemen were so obviously wives and children of the

Tatar warriors they shouted for that their reception didn't count as more than the most private sort of welcome.

Ivan caught Mar'ya Morevna's eye and jerked his head towards Nikolai Tsarevich. Their son was staring from side to side, just like his sister – but instead of Anastasya's expression of delight at seeing so many strange new things, Kolya was glowering and his mouth was fixed in a pout of annoyance. Ivan smiled wryly to himself, knowing at once what was wrong. It looked as though simply being ignored even by the enemy was not something that Nikolai enjoyed, even though the possible alternatives had been explained to both the children. Being cheered would have been pleasant, even at second-hand as part of Amragan *tarkhan*'s triumphal procession. Being derided as prisoners in that same procession would have been less agreeable, though it was something that had to be expected. But to be glanced at and then dismissed as being of no importance was not to Kolya's taste.

For his part, Ivan was content enough. It gave him a chance to stare around like a yokel, rather than have to play the part either of an important guest or of a haughty captive. It also meant that nobody was paying enough attention to notice that this yokel and his wife both had an eye more to the possible ways out of Sarai than any grandeur it might have possessed. There might be no point to knowing the escape routes, as Mar'ya Morevna had said earlier, but that was no reason not to make a note of where they were.

When the squad of guards assigned as escort turned to one side and off the muddy thoroughfare that did duty for Sarai's main street, Ivan discovered – along with an inclination to pout like his son and for just the same reason – that another of his notions had been grounded only in his own self-esteem. He had been assuming that after so long a journey, he and the rest of the Khorlovtsy would be taken straight to Batu Khan. Not so. He was informed – by one Ilchidai *noyan*, nobleman of the Golden Court – that he was no more than the ex-lord of a domain which had submitted to Tatar rule, and as such could wait his turn like all the others.

Others? That was when Ivan had started to look around him with more interest than mere curiosity. There was nothing to see that he had not seen already; but in the days between now and being taken before the Khan, that would change. The blaring horns of Sarai would warn him when to look for new faces among those he knew already, and that warning would give him and the rest of his party the opportunity to recognise – or hide their recognition of – any other Russians who might appear in Sarai.

They were taken to a group of houses that had been set aside for their lodgings while they were in attendance at the Khan's Court; well-appointed places that Ivan could see were comfortable enough – with the riches at the Khan's disposal, even the kennels for his dogs were most likely examples of luxury for lesser monarchs to aspire to for their own palaces – but which were not in the least defensible.

He had hoped that they might have been installed in one or other of the massive Kashgari dwellings that were nothing less than self-contained citadels, for no other reason than that years of apprehension had bred a fondness in every Rus for thick walls when there were Tatars in the vicinity. The possibility of needing a last-ditch refuge against some attack or other had flashed through his mind when he saw those thick-walled houses, but it had been a foolish concept that had skittered around inside his skull like a drop of water on a hotplate, and to as much purpose.

Defence against what? The Tatars, at the very heart of their Khan's own realm? If Batu Khan concluded that he had no further use for the Tsar of Khorlov, then walls however thick would only delay the inevitable. Thus it was best that the inevitable be avoided whenever possible.

Ivan had found that avoidance halfway down a bottle of very fine *pshenichnaya-yezhevekaya*, whole blackberries macerated in triple-distilled wheat vodka. It was not the alcohol which calmed him, though an outsider might have thought so from the way he drank it *zalpom*, each small frost-coated silver cupful put down in a single shot to the back of the throat, and the back of the brain as well. Anyone not knowing a Rus – nobleman or commoner, it didn't matter – might have suspected the young Tsar was trying to drink himself into a stupor, and would have been much surprised that his eyes remained bright, his speech did not slur, and his mind stayed as sharp as a razor. But the squat stoneware bottle and its partners were quite small, despite being bulked out by a crust half an inch thick of clear ice from some pit dug deep in the earth and filled in wintertime with stamped-down snow. The Ilkhan's own private glacier, thought Ivan, drowning a chuckle with another swallow of the excellent spirit.

The vodka was so heavy with the flavour and scent and sugar of the fruit, and so thick with cold, that it flowed from the bottle like syrup. It smelt of the warm autumns of years ago, when there had been no Tatar invaders and no need to reach accommodations with men bearing the power of life and death over everything a man held dear. It tasted of fresh fruit at the end of a long day, and the slow burn of a low sun in an azure sky, a burn that flowed like a sweet hot acid down inside to light some fires and quench others that were less healthy. And it looked . . .

Ivan stared down into the cup of solid silver that he had brought from Khorlov, because in all their lootings the Golden Horde could never have found a thing so fine, and swirled the three fingers' depth of icy liquid from side to side.

It looked like blood.

'Four days, Vanyushka,' said Mar'ya Morevna angrily. 'Four days they've kept us cooped up here, and never a word from the Khan or even from Amragan *tarkhan*.' She slapped the table so that the vodka bottles jumped and rattled together, spraying ice splinters from the wide, deep tray intended to contain their dripping.

'Not quite cooped up.' Ivan looked up from the vodka-cup as his mind refocused rapidly. His left hand, the one without the vodka-cup in it, flicked out with startling speed and control to catch the outermost of the three bottles just as it pulled free of the bed of crushed ice that formed the floor of the tray and began to topple down towards the floor. He twisted it back into the socket made by its own meltwater with a small crunching sound, and saluted his wife with the still-brimming and quite unspilt cup.

Mar'ya Morevna's eyes flicked from it to Ivan's face to the tray and its three bottles, then narrowed as they went back to his face again. 'If you have another cup,' she said, sitting down, 'I'll have some of that.'

There was indeed another cup, small and dainty and no bigger than a lady's thumb, blue and white Khitan ceramic ware so fine that when the deep red drink went into it, the colours changed to purple and pink. Ivan poured vodka from a bottle held more than a foot above the fragile vessel's rim, all without spilling a garnet

214

drop, then twisted the bottle sideways to catch any drips as flamboyantly as any table-servant and returned it to the ice. 'Can't waste this on Tatars,' he said, saluting her again before snapping his wrist to send the cup's contents down to keep the others company. 'They wouldn't appreciate it. There isn't a one among the few who were brave enough to come with me that I would share it with, not even Konstantin Il'yevich; and the *mal'chiki* are still far too young.'

Frost-pale eyebrows lifted almost audibly. 'Oh indeed? I sometimes wonder about that.'

'So long as they look seven, they're too young for this stuff.' His grin was brief, and despite his words it was not the loose, sloppy grin of a drunk – though it would have taken one who knew him well to know the difference. Mar'ya Morevna knew, and betrayed none of it by word or deed or even the merest flicker of a facial muscle. 'Their hard luck. That leaves just you and I.'

Mar'ya Morevna sipped her *yezhevekaya*, made a wordless sound of approval, and flicked the rest of the cupful past her teeth and down to where no Tatar could get at it before holding out the Chinese thimble for a refill. 'As you say. Their hard luck.' Her voice dropped to a murmur no louder than the tiny tinkling sound as more vodka trickled into a cup as thin as a premature eggshell. 'Playing some game?'

Ivan nodded as he repeated the twist and flick of the bottle to catch the last drops on its lip, making the movement of his head a part of what any spy with one eye to a peephole would now think was part of the Rus ritual of getting drunk together.

'Um. I see.' Mar'ya Morevna dipped the top joint of her left little finger into the cup, then licked thoughtfully at the crimson drop of vodka beading it. 'Drunken despair? Or dignified resignation?'

'I'll tell you the name when I know the game.' Ivan leaned closer, the conspiratorial huddle of a man in his cups. ' 'S'all right,' he said, as loud as anyone confiding secrets might have done when they were too far gone to care, 'they don't mind. Old Khakhan Ögotäi liked a drink as well. Died of it. But that din't – didn't – matter. Ilchidai *noyan* the Jeläyr chieftain said so. 'S' on – it's on – record.' The latest cup of vodka went the way of all the others.

215

'The Great Khan was a drinker of wine and *kumys*,' said Mar'ya Morevna. 'He died an old man, after many years of active life. Too much of this' – she lifted one of the vodka bottles and shook it disapprovingly – 'and old age will be the least of your worries.' Her face froze momentarily as Ivan's chair abruptly scraped backwards, but then his hand made a little gesture that she knew well enough from innumerable weary sessions with Khorlov's High Council.

After their initial scandal at having a woman foisted on them, the councillors had bored her along with everyone else, and she and Ivan had developed a series of hand-signals when one or the other left a meeting for five minutes' relief: in the nearest privy, or with the handiest drink of tea or wine or even water, or for just a breath of air that was not already laden with seventy-year-old opinions. So that the old men would always have to treat them as equals when one or the other took a break for cover, the little hand-signals meant things like 'accept with reservations and enumerate them', 'deny absolutely', 'be slowly swayed by reason, your choice of speed and form of reasoning'. Things like that, which could be disguised as something so simple as a rub at the nose or a quick scratch.

This one, an open hand laid over the closed fist that Ivan used to push himself back from the table, said 'Cover for me', as clearly as words. As he stood up, Mar'ya Morevna immediately began an elaboration on her lecture about the dangers of drinking, drawing on examples real and legendary, approved and disapproved, and didn't lower the stridence of her voice until Ivan was back in his seat.

He looked pallid and slightly sweaty; but that was only to be expected from someone who had slipped quietly into the curtained privy-alcove and forced two fingers past his own tonsils until all the drink he had so ostentatiously swallowed had gone into the bucket underneath the nicely carved seat. Especially since he had managed the whole unpleasant operation in virtual silence.

Mar'ya Morevna took his damp, clammy hands between her warm, dry ones and stared into eyes that she plainly found all too coldly clear. 'Why all of this, Vanyushka?' she said softly. 'Why?'

'Wait a while.' Those cold eyes of his stayed with hers for another few seconds, then shifted their focus momentarily to

216

glance at the riot of moulded flowers and leaves decorating the panels which covered one wall of the room. Though it would have meant nothing to eyes a degree or so to either side, from where she sat it was a gesture as plain as a pointing finger. Mar'ya Morevna lowered her head in a movement far too slow to be a nod of understanding, and waited while he took another drink, sipping slowly at the fruity liquor to clear the foul taste of regurgitation from his mouth.

After a few minutes he relaxed, and this time it wasn't the feigned slouch of impending inebriated sleep. Mar'ya Morevna was glad to see it, and said so.

Ivan nodded shakily. 'They're gone now,' he said, and leaned across the table to lift another bottle and watch her lips compress in the beginning of a protest. But instead of pouring out still more vodka, he rapped the bottle sharply against the tray to loosen some of the ice that crusted it, then picked up a double handful of the splinters and scrubbed his face with them. He gave a gasp at the sudden shock, and a protracted shudder as rivulets of chilly water ran down inside his loose collar and over his chest. Then he grinned at Mar'ya Morevna again, the grin this time a little strained, but still not that of a drunkard. '*Slava Bogu!* but I needed that!'

'I should think you did. A peephole?'

'Yes, blast their eyes to blindness. Over here.' He stood up again and walked over to the panelled wall, then passed his hand quickly over a cluster of ornamental embossings made of gilded plaster and glue in the shape of a spray of chrysanthemums. 'See it?'

'No.'

'Neither did I at first. Watch again.' This time his hand moved slowly, and further away from the wall, so that its shadow rather than the hand itself was what crossed the surface. Mar'ya Morevna's eyes widened, then went narrow as she said several things learned in the course of her leadership of armies that young Nikolai Tsarevich would have loved to memorise. The shadow, cast by the light coming in at the open window and thus a steady source of illumination, had been constant as it passed over the domed shapes of the plaster flowers; always a series of convex curves – except for one place where it had gone briefly flat over a pattern not moulded but merely painted to match the rest. So briefly that she almost missed it.

'I should have inspected that wall myself,' she said venomously. 'Not even the Chin use that much complicated design unless they're concealing something in the middle of it. And anyway, now that I look at it,' she stalked over to give the wall and the panelling a closer inspection, 'this wall's half as thick again as the others.'

'It *is* the outside wall of the house,' Ivan pointed out.

'And I've been running spies of my own for longer than we've been married. So I should have noticed.' Mar'ya Morevna peered at the whorls of gilding and grunted softly. 'Or maybe not. This is all very clever. Not one large hole, but a lot of tiny ones. There'll be a section behind this with all the appropriate plugs, something you'd pull out then swing to one side.' She shook her head in reluctant admiration. 'But even when the damned thing was open, if you didn't know what you were looking at, you'd only think there were worms in the panelling.'

'Instead of just a single big one.'

'Very droll.' Mar'ya Morevna went back to the table and picked up her vodka, obviously torn between drinking it and throwing it. Ivan could see her running through a mental catalogue of her activities in this room during the past four days, recalling all the things she would prefer not to have done in front of an audience. He knew, because his thoughts had travelled down exactly the same path, and thanks to that – and to the way her face suddenly went deep scarlet – he was able to step forward and snatch the half-full cup out of her hand just before she flung it at the wall.

'What's past is past,' Ivan said, and if he sounded calm it was only because he had rehearsed this same speech half-a-dozen times before he had cause to use it. 'At least they don't know we've spotted them, so let's not advertise the fact with red stains on an unblemished white and gilt wall.'

Breathing hard through her nose, Mar'ya Morevna glared at him, at the wall, and at the world in general, but was practical enough to admit the sense of that. 'All right. All right.' She took another few deep breaths until the angry flush began to fade from her cheeks, but her eyes stayed hot and bright. 'Agreed. No stains. No needles pushed through the holes the first time I see one of them open. Now. How did you spot this? And when?'

'The when is easy. This morning – '

'God *damn* them. . . !'

' – When someone opened it to take a peek at me. They couldn't have realised I had the lamp over there,' Ivan pointed at one of the room's two oil-lamps, set on a low clothes chest by the wall, 'and that its light was reflected on the gilding when it moved. Otherwise I still wouldn't know.'

'So why the play-acting?'

'To give them something to report. Something derogatory, to make them maybe just a little careless. They think we're dangerous, Mar'yushka, and that scares me. The Grey Wolf overheard it on the march, and he told us both, but' – Ivan gave his wife a severe look – 'you weren't listening to much from that source. What with the Art Magic and our past reputation, Amragan *tarkhan* was expecting trouble at Khorlov. He didn't get it, and was grateful for that much. But some of his men have been wondering what we're plotting, when it's going to happen, why we did nothing before we got to Sarai and what we're going to do now we're here.'

'And the Firebird didn't help.'

Ivan laughed. 'Like using oil to put a fire out. So what I was doing was just this: giving them a demonstration of a failing they might be able to use against all of us. If they think I'm like all the Rus – or the old Khakhan – and drink too much, then they'll be off guard when they find out otherwise. It's like the children. Or like the Grey Wolf. Anything they don't know; anything they think they know and don't. It's all useful, all a dagger in our boot.' Ivan ran the tip of one finger along Mar'ya Morevna's jawline from ear to mouth, and tapped lightly against her lips. 'Remember those words, loved. Because they're all yours.'

'Indeed.' The edge in her voice was sharp enough that Ivan hastily moved his finger back, because Mar'ya Morevna looked as if she might bite it. 'So are these. Remember them as well. From tonight, before we go to bed, the lamps go *out* . . .'

The summons came two days later, and instead of the supercilious old man Ilchidai *noyan*, it was brought by none other than

Amragan *tarkhan* himself. The envoy's appearance had changed somewhat from that of the man who had kept them company on the three-week trek from Khorlov. He was more richly dressed than he had been even at the banquet outside the city, but more than that, he had shaved his head in the old Türki style. His three long braids and the fuzz of black bristles between them were gone, and only a single long scalp-lock remained so that he looked strangely like the three-century-old portraits of Great Prince Svyatoslav of Kiev.

Another bloody-handed reaver, thought Ivan. *But a Rus for all that*. The Türk might have been paying his well-behaved hostages a compliment of sorts, but Ivan was less certain about the scroll of authority the *tarkhan* carried. It looked ominously like a warrant he had seen drawn up by First Minister Strel'tsin while his father was still Tsar in Khorlov, a vaguely dangerous document until certain specifics were added at the Tsar's pleasure. Then it became lethal.

This scroll had that same look, a sleepy menace like a coiled snake, its serpentine image only increased by the writhing letters of the three languages in which it was written: Arabic, Uighur and Kithan. Amragan *tarkhan* did not trouble himself with reading all of it aloud, but the opening words alone would have sounded foolishly grandiose to anyone unfamiliar with the Tatars. Such a person, if there were any still alive in the wide white world, would see only slit-eyed nomads wrapped in furs and stolen finery, with bowed legs from a lifetime in the saddle. They would not see what such consummate horsemen had achieved; what they thought of themselves as a result; and so the salutation of the Khan's letter would have been no more than the posturing of noisy children. They would have carried such an impression into the grave – within no more than a minute.

Tängri in Heaven, the Sky above the Earth, it read, *On Earth Ögotäi, Khan by the Power of Tängri, Khan of all Khans of the Mongols, Ruler of Men. By this Batu, Ilkhan of the Golden Horde, commands* . . . And then it too got down to those specifics that could put a cutting edge on a sheet of parchment. Testing their sharpness was a suicidal waste of time, and in any case, after six days of kicking their heels in enforced idleness, Ivan and the rest of his party were more than willing to be taken before the Khan.

He suspected, and Mar'ya Morevna agreed, that a strategy of generating willingness through nervous boredom was as much a reason for the delay as any 'waiting for the others', even though the 'others' were in Sarai by now. The blare of welcoming trumpets had sounded enough times that the entire High Council of Khorlov might have been somewhere in the city – and neither Ivan, nor Mar'ya Morevna, nor anyone else, would have known it.

Keeping an eye open for strange or familiar faces had been at first an interesting challenge, and latterly a waste of time. The Tatars assigned to guard and escort them from place to place had done their work so well that the occupants of one house often did not even see the people in the houses to either side of them from one day to the next, never mind setting eyes on other parties held in different quarters of the city.

Ivan had not set eyes on the Grey Wolf, either. There were times when he wondered just how seriously Volk Volkovich had taken offence, and whether he would ever return at all. Then there were the other occasions when good sense prevailed and he realised how little good the shape-shifter would be to anyone, caught with the rest of them inside the walls of Sarai like a . . .

Like a wolf in a trap.

'You may bow to the Ilkhan Batu in the manner of the Rus if it pleases you,' Amragan *tarkhan* cautioned all the Russians when they had assembled in the courtyard of Ivan's house. 'But you will also do him honour in the proper fashion, and failure to do this will not be excused.'

'*Droog* Amragan, are the proper words not "Bow down before the Khan, or be destroyed,"?' Nikolai Ivanovich piped up. There was a ripple of nervous laughter from servants and councillors, but not from Ivan, not from Mar'ya Morevna and most definitely not from Amragan *tarkhan*. The Türk stroked his drooping moustaches as he stared down at the small boy – who stared back, Ivan was pleased to see, with all the bravado of a child who didn't know any better. That might have been something to do with the way he was manfully ignoring how his sister was poking him in the ribs for butting into a grown-up conversation. 'Your son,' said Amragan thoughtfully after a few moments' consideration, 'has been listening to wise advice.'

That might have been another veiled threat aimed at everyone present, but here in the very tiger's den, Ivan was growing tired of anything hidden behind oblique observation. When one had already knelt before the block, comments about how one's head might be at risk were already superfluous. He gave the *tarkhan* a thin, resigned smile that disarmed the warning. 'Both my children listen to everything, whether I want them to hear or not. Wait until you hear them swear.'

There was more uneasy laughter from the Russians, though this time it was because some of them were not entirely sure whether their Tsar was making a joke or being deadly serious. Ivan glanced back at them and raised one hand for silence. 'Let all of us listen to wise advice, Amragan *tarkhan*. We are required to do honour in the proper fashion. So then. What fashion is it?'

The Türk gazed at Ivan for a few seconds in silence, then slowly clapped his hands together in applause that was not quite as ironic as it might have seemed. 'I see,' he said, 'where your son has learned his wisdom. Ivan Aleksandrovich, of the many lords and would-be lords of the Rus that I have seen enter the Court of the Golden Horde, few of them unbend their pride enough to ask what might be required of them.'

'Does it make any difference in the long run?'

'That, *gospodin*, is entirely up to you. It depends on whether you listen, or merely hear.'

'As I say. What must we do?'

Amragan studied the dozen or so faces like a tutor ensuring that his class was more or less awake. He seemed to be noting those who would pay attention and those who would not, but Ivan had no need to look at them to be able to tell where any trouble lay. Count Danyil Fedorovich was much in his mind, the only man among all of them who could do something wrong from deliberate malice rather than simple blind stupidity. Even Khan Batu might be prevailed upon to excuse the one, but the other, never.

'There will be two fires burning beyond the threshold of the *Sira-Ger*, the Golden Pavilion of the Ilkhan Batu. You will pass between these fires to be purified, to render void any harmful magics you might wish against the Khan, and to drive away the chill of the world outside before you enter the hospitable warmth inside. Refusal to do this is forbidden, and will not be excused.'

Instead of the protest against intended wizardcraft that he might have been expected to utter, Ivan nodded sagely. He had been talking to Mar'ya Morevna about other matters than spies, and was expecting something of the sort. 'I know,' he said. 'The fire-spirits will do all this. We of the Tsar's line of Khorlov,' and the smile that curved his lips was nasty, 'are familiar with creatures of fire. As you saw.'

The Türk cleared his throat with sudden vigour, obviously not wanting to be reminded of the Firebird more than was necessary. 'Yes.' He coughed again, and Anastasya Ivanovna made a little noise of sympathy for the poor man's sore throat that came from a source that was – probably – too young to be sarcastic. 'You will not,' Amragan continued, 'step on the threshold between the cold outside and the warm inside. This is forbidden, and will not be excused.'

Ivan released a gusty sigh that might have been impatience. 'Amragan *tarkhan*, I know that much already. It's an insult to tread on the threshold of any *yurtu*, and make a bridge for the cold outside to intrude on the warm inside. It's an insult to whistle inside like the cold wind outside. It's an insult to bring a whip for beasts into the dwelling-place of men, and so suggest the men inside are no better than the beasts outside. So much and so many and so on and so forth.' Then he grinned quickly to take the sting out of his words. 'The Tatar rider who gave over his own *yurtu* for myself and Mar'ya Morevna told us all those things, and more. When he wasn't grousing about having to eat *grut* again for dinner.'

'He did not tell me this,' said Amragan in a tone of voice that suggested the Tatar soldier would have some explaining to do about such an embarrassing oversight.

'He was probably busy, and forgot,' Ivan suggested generously.

'Certainly you were. Now: what else is forbidden, or compulsory, and will not be excused?'

'You should guard your tongue more closely, Rus. It's sharp enough to cut your throat one of these days.'

'Truth cuts both ways, Amragan *tarkhan*. The Khan might appreciate honesty more than flattery once in a while.'

'I will let the *Sain* Khan judge that for himself,' said the Türk, and the menace in his voice was tinged just a little with admiration.

223

'Just remember this if you wish to live long enough for him to hear your honest flattery: bow to the East in honour of the Khakhan yet unchosen, who is above the Ilkhan Batu as he is above mere vassals; and before you speak at all, bow to Batu Khan, the lord and master of these lands and all who dwell within their borders.'

'Thank you, Amragan *tarkhan*,' said Mar'ya Morevna, her voice silky. 'Especially for troubling to explain the reasons behind so many rituals foreign to us. I will not even wonder why you failed most signally to tell us the manner of bow which Batu Khan will be expecting, but will presume no more than forgetfulness through being busy, just like your soldier.' The Türk coloured slightly. 'That bow should be in the Tatar manner, yes? Hat on the ground, belt laid about the shoulders, and an inclination of the head . . . three times for an Ilkhan, I should think. Six for the Khan of all Khans, and nine for Tängri of the Everlasting Blue Sky. Yes?'

'Yes.' He snapped the word.

'And how low should one bow?'

Amragan *tarkhan* glowered at her, as close to real rage as Ivan had seen since Aleksey had tried to kill him. '*Gospozha* Mar'ya Morevna,' he said through clenched teeth, 'if your bow is not low enough, the Khan's guards will instruct you with their spears. Be assured that I will make certain of it . . .'

At first sight, Batu Khan's Golden Pavilion was just a bigger version of a Tatar *yurtu* tent, hunched and low and dome-shaped, its door facing south, and everywhere wrapped criss-cross with cords to keep the sheets of felt that were its walls and roof tight against the latticed wooden frame beneath. The felt, necessary for warmth no matter how rich the occupant might be, was usually black or white, but in this instance the fabric, slightly shiny from the pounding that had matted it together, was a distinctive yellow. The colour and the dull sheen were both good enough reasons for the title 'Golden'. It was only as they walked closer, and then closer still, that Ivan and the others became aware that its yellow tint did not come from any dyed felt, but from great hangings of cloth-of-gold draped over the entire tent and held in place by broad, braided straps woven of solid gold thread. Even the wooden poles supporting the awning in front of the doorway were covered with gold leaf, laid on so thickly that they were not so much gilded as plated with the metal.

That was awesome enough, but sitting as it was in a cleared space at the very centre of Sarai, there was nothing close by the *Sira-Ger* to give an indication of its true scale. Six ordinary tents could have been raised under the Golden Pavilion's roof, with room to spare for the occupants of those six tents to walk freely to and fro.

A group of men in the clothing of Rus noblemen were standing on the far side of the huge tent, apparently warming themselves at the two great iron braziers that flanked the doorway. For the first time since he had heard them spoken of by Ilchidai *noyan*, Ivan saw the Others he had mentioned – and with a little thrill of shock, recognised at least one face.

Prince Aleksandr Yaroslavich Nevskiy had changed very little in the years since the Battle on the Ice; his golden beard had tarnished down to silver to either side of his thin, mobile mouth, and the lines in his face had engraved themselves a little deeper. But otherwise he was still the same arrogant bastard that Ivan remembered all too well. When his idly roving gaze fell on Ivan and Mar'ya Morevna, his eyes widened and his brows shot up; but just for a moment, and then he was back in full control of himself again. The bow he gave them both was deep, leisurely, elegant, and a masterpiece of understated insult, and when he straightened up again he was smiling in a way that even before he spoke had set Ivan's teeth on edge.

'Tsar Ivan Aleksandrovich!' he exclaimed loudly, so that other heads turned, then just as loudly corrected himself. 'Of course if you're here, that can't be right any more, can it?'

'I understand that's for the Khan to decide, Nevskiy. Not you.' Ivan laid two fingers on the pommel of his *shashka* sabre to make certain it was settled firmly in its sheath. For all his annoyance at finding this worthy in Sarai instead of the half-score or so of others who would have been far preferable, he returned the bow; then, gaining a certain small gratification that they had not done so without his bidding, signalled that his councillors and attendants should do the same.

'I would have thought,' said Aleksandr Nevskiy after a moment of consideration, 'that a great hero such as yourself would have given the Golden Horde your defiance. Obviously not.'

' "Your face is dirty, as the pot said to the kettle," ' snapped Mar'ya Morevna, deliberately pushing in front of Ivan as he began to advance on Nevskiy. This time his fingers were on the grip and not the pommel of the sabre, and a handspan of its blade was already gleaming in the dull daylight. '*Radi Boga!* You two should have been brought up in the same kremlin, and then maybe you'd have knocked this nonsense out of each other. For two grown men, you act in a way that would shame these children!'

'Children fight, *gospozha*,' said Nevskiy, his own long, straight broadsword poised halfway drawn. 'Why should we not?'

Mar'ya Morevna shot him a contemptuous glance. 'If you still need to do so after you've both spoken with the Khan, Aleksandr Yaroslavich, then I'll stand aside. But right now I would have thought there were more important matters to concern the last surviving lords of the Rus people. Like maybe keeping those people alive?'

Ivan stared at Aleksandr Nevskiy for what felt like an age; then nodded in response to the sort of sense only a mother could speak. The sound of two blades slamming back into their scabbards were like two sticks broken across a bent knee, the sounds so close together that one seemed a continuation of the other. 'Later,' he said. 'If we have to.'

'Later,' said Nevskiy. 'And I'll be glad to.'

'Children indeed.' Mar'ya Morevna glanced at them both, but mostly at her husband. 'You at least,' she said quietly, 'should know better than to act like this: to charge like a bull at the first red flag waved at you.'

'*Batyushka*, don't! Papa, wait! Let me fight him!' 'No! Let me!' The small voices came from about waist level, each as shrill and angry as the other, and Ivan looked down and then at Mar'ya Morevna.

'Children indeed,' he echoed harshly. Natasha and Kolya were both grabbing alternately at his and their mother's coat-tails, jumping up and down, and generally behaving in Ivan's opinion like a pair of street guttersnipes. It mattered not at all that they were defending their father; it was the manner of that defence that made him angry. The reason was obvious. Aleksandr Nevskiy's smile just at that minute would have persuaded a sanctified Roman Pope to set fire to all the world and leave God Himself to

226

sift through the ashes, and Ivan was no saint, never mind a Pope. Right now he was not even a tsar but just a man with a sword on his hip, facing another similarly armed who had given him offence.

'Defended by a wolf the last time we met,' said Nevskiy. 'Defended by a woman now, and supported by children. But not a warrior or a *druzina* or an army in sight. Why not just hang up your sword, Ivan of Khorlov? For all the good it does you, it might as well not be here at all.'

Ivan swore venomously and laid hand to his sword again, then remembered a custom of Captain Akimov's Cossack people. He drew the razor edge no more than half an inch and deliberately let it nick his finger, so that the quick stab of pain gave his overheated brain something to concentrate on besides the words of his opponent. The swelling red glare faded from his eyes almost as if it was leaking away through the tiny cut, so that he was able coolly, calmly, to lift the sabre, still hooked to his belt, and shake it so that the sharp, tightly scabbarded steel rattled loudly against lacquered, silver-mounted wood.

'So what if I do put my sword aside, Aleksandr Yaroslavich?' he said. 'Unwed and childless, lord through your father's brother but not your father. If we were alone, or I less courteous of the ears of the woman and children you make mock of, I could tell you what weapon *you* should put away from lack of use . . .'

At that, blood might have been shed or lives spilled out to soak into the ground, had Amragan *tarkhan* not laughed aloud. The sound of his laughter was like a bucket of cold water flung on two aggressive drunks; if the shock did not completely cool their ardour, at least it gave them something else to think about for long enough to let it cool of its own accord.

'Enough,' said Ivan, glowering at the Türk with all the heat of redirected hatred. 'I won't fight a fellow Russian.' He folded his arms across his chest so tightly that the tips of his fingers went pale as the blood was crushed out of them, and stared at Aleksandr Nevskiy to see what he would do.

The Prince eyed him thoughtfully; then he too glanced at Amragan *tarkhan* and did something very strange. He unhooked the straps that secured his sword to his waist-belt, wrapped them around the scabbarded weapon, and handed straps and sword together not to Mar'ya Morevna but to Anastasya Ivanova, staring at Ivan all the while. 'The child may be your daughter, Ivan Aleksandrovich,' he said, 'but I trust she is too young for treachery.' Then Aleksandr Nevskiy's wary expression stretched momentarily into another of his unpleasant smiles. 'Although one can never be too sure with a Khorlovskiy. If the need for one arises, I can always find another sword.'

'You can claim that one back just as soon as you think you need it,' said Ivan, ignoring the insult. He made no move to take the sabre from his own belt. 'But here and now, before the Khan, I think you're too sensible to entertain the thought that any sword might help you.' He studied Nevskiy speculatively. 'And what brings you to Sarai anyway? The last I heard, the town of Vladimir was a smoking ruin for lack of anybody to defend it, and your uncle Yuriy's own men had hacked his head off in disgust at how he ran away.'

Though his face darkened with anger at such crude phrasing of what was nothing but the truth, Aleksandr Nevskiy did not rise to the bait. Instead, and even though the sound rang false, he laughed. 'I long thought Khorlov lived in a little world of its own, and that proves it. Know this: my late uncle gave defiance to the Tatars without my late father's authority; he left the city undefended by his own decision; and what his soldiers did to him merely pre-empted the punishment he would have suffered anyway.'

'Meaning you're here to ask Khan Batu if he'll let you rebuild Vladimir and be its Prince, because everything that happened was nothing to do with you. How very . . . pragmatic of you.'

'And how very out of date you are, Ivan Aleksandrovich. By the Khan's generosity, I *am* Great Prince of Vladimir, and the city is already nine-tenths rebuilt.' Ivan caught his breath at that, and Nevskiy smirked. 'Yes. I thought that might be a pleasant surprise.' He made a little half-bow and extended one hand in the direction of the Golden Pavilion, ushering Ivan and his party towards the doorway. 'Shall we enter the Presence and see what the Khan might be persuaded to do for – '

Nevskiy broke off at the sound of raised voices from the other group of Russians nearer to the fires, looked for the cause of it, then swore under his breath. 'May he be damned for a stubborn fool,' he snarled, 'and doubly damned if he brings us down with him!'

The source and focus of the commotion was a man of about twice Ivan's age, big and broad inside his rich garments, his features set in an obstinate grimace and framed by a black beard shot through with streaks of grey. He was pointing at the two fires, and from the few words that could be distinguished through the general babble of the man's supporters, he was refusing to submit to the purification ritual. 'Who is he?' Ivan asked Aleksandr Nevskiy, 'and what's biting him so hard?'

'Don't you know? I thought you and your lady wife knew everything about everyone in the wide white world.'

'Let be, Aleksandr Yaroslavich. You've set aside your sword; set aside your sarcasm as well, and just give me an answer.'

'You make a better job of controlling your temper than I might have believed,' said Nevskiy with approval. 'All right. The noisy one with the black beard is Mikhail Vsevolodovich, and he's the sole surviving claimant to the principality of Chernigov – '

'I rode past Chernigov on the way here. There's not much for him to claim.'

'There wasn't much of Vladimir either,' snapped Nevskiy. 'But backed by the Khan's authority, Mikhail could have the city well on its way to reconstruction and prosperity within two years. Except that to get the backing of that authority, he must first accept it, and from the look of things, he's balking at that jump. Face it, Khorlovskiy, the Tatars rule us now, and the wise among us have come to terms with that. More or less. Yes?'

'I . . . Yes.'

'Then watch, and learn what happens to those who don't.'

Ivan stared at him, then at the gaggle of men who had given up on persuasion and had reverted to shouting at one another again. There had been an undertone to Aleksandr Nevskiy's words that raised the hair on his nape; not anticipation exactly, but a definite note of foreboding that promised little good for Mikhail the would-be Prince of Chernigov. Mar'ya Morevna had heard it too, because when Ivan turned to her, he could see apprehension bordering on fright in the darkly dilated pupils of her eyes. It was so uncommon for her to be afraid of anything that the sight of it scared him as much as anything yet to happen. 'Get the children into the Pavilion,' he said sharply. 'Do it now. And don't let them out again until we all leave together. Move!'

He did not feel more at ease until Mar'ya Morevna had shepherded Nikolai and Anastasya inside Khan Batu's great tent. They went reluctantly, sensing that something was about to happen, neither of them quite old enough – for all their born experience in the Art Magic – to know the difference between exciting and terrible. They would learn soon enough, but Ivan had no desire to hasten the process.

'I have come here at the Khan's behest,' Mikhail Vsevolodovich was saying to his followers and to the world in general, 'to bow before him as my overlord, and that I will do. But I will not bow to the East like an infidel, and I will not pass through fire as though I were a wizard!'

There was a flurry of activity as the shamans who had been feeding sweet-smelling wood onto the fires went inside the Golden Pavilion to report what they had heard to Batu Khan. After a few seconds a Tatar officer followed them. He had evidently fulfilled the same post with Mikhail as Amragan *tarkhan* had done with Ivan, because he looked more than reasonably angry.

'That one,' said Ivan quietly, 'must have told Mikhail what all these rites are about, and been ignored.'

'Maybe he did, and maybe not.' Amragan *tarkhan* sauntered past Ivan, managing to look as though he had overheard by accident rather than by deliberate eavesdropping. 'You at least took the trouble to ask. This fat fool' – he gestured at Mikhail of Chernigov's ample figure – 'may have considered that asking anything was beneath his dignity.'

Ivan might have asked something, but at that moment the cloth-of-gold door curtain billowed open and the Tatar officer stepped out of the tent. The shamans were not with him; but there were six soldiers at his back. 'Hear the words of Batu, Ilkhan of the Golden Horde,' he said, speaking in passable Russian. 'The Khan says, why do you ignore his command as though you have the right to do so? Obey, and earn your princedom; refuse and lose your life. Bow down, or be destroyed!'

'I have told you already that I will bow to the Khan,' said Mikhail Vsevolodovich, sounding less bold and more desperate, 'since he has gained his status by conquest and by the glory given him out of the Hand of God. But the rest I may not do. What shall it profit me to gain the sovereignty of all Russia, yet lose my own soul?'

'Idiot,' said Aleksandr Nevskiy. But he signed himself with the life-giving cross for all that, and Ivan followed suit.

The Tatar officer stared at Mikhail for a second or two, but whether there was pity, or contempt, or anything at all in his slitted eyes, Ivan was too far away to see. 'Mikhail Vsevolodovich of Chernigov,' he said, 'you are a dead man.' He clapped his hands and gestured the six guards forward, watching as they seized Mikhail and flung him to the ground on his back, held flat by wrists and ankles with his face looking up towards the Everlasting Blue Sky, grey now with clouds and the promise of more rain. 'But take comfort from this in your dying: the Khan of the Golden Horde compliments you thus, saying your blood is royal enough that it shall not be poured out for the black earth to drink.'

The officer made another little gesture and the two guards not holding Mikhail down began to stamp on the Russian's chest with their booted heels. The Tatar soldiers were well practised at this work, and they were finished with their victim in a matter of minutes, but it seemed to Ivan's ears that the thudding flurry of blows went on for a long time. The man who would have been Prince of Chernigov went black in the face and uttered a hideous gurgling noise, convulsing up like a gaffed salmon against the grip of the men who held him. It mattered not at all whether something burst within him or whether his heart was shocked to stillness by the stamping, but when he sagged back from that huge spasm, he was dead.

The threatened rain began to fall, drizzling from a heavy sky onto the living and the newly dead while Ivan swore a soft oath that was more like a benediction, and signed himself with the cross again; and if his hand was shaking as he did so, for once he was not ashamed of it. Aleksandr Nevskiy's hand was shaking just as hard. The Prince of Vladimir stared at his own trembling fingers, then clenched them into a fist so tight that the knucklebones showed white through the tautly drawn skin. 'In case you think it might have been,' said Nevskiy quietly, 'that was not a demonstration for anyone's benefit. Batu Khan has no need of demonstrations.'

Inside the Golden Pavilion, Mar'ya Morevna was standing as near to the doorway as a group of guards in full lamellar armour would allow. She watched in silence as Ivan and Aleksandr Nevskiy came in, having passed between the fires beyond. Those fires were hissing as rain fell on them, but even had the rain been falling and the fires been hissing earlier, neither that nor the buzz of voices within the warm, stuffy, tapestry-hung vault of the Khan's court would have been enough to drown out the sound of stamping feet. Ivan looked at his wife and saw that she knew what that rhythmic noise had meant. He only hoped the children were still ignorant of it.

A shaman took him by the arm and swung him around to face the direction in which the Great Khan's palace of Karakorum lay, countless hundreds of miles away in the blue distance of the high steppes of Central Asia. Ivan bowed; but he still had enough pride, or maybe even arrogance, that it was not the kneeling forehead-to-the-ground obeisance he had seen before. Instead he gave the proper salute of a Russian nobleman doing honour to a superior, bending forward from the waist with his right hand extended towards the ground. He stayed like that while silently counting up to three, then straightened up again, his shoulders itching the whole time in anticipation of a spear-shaft slamming into them to encourage him to bow still lower.

It didn't happen, and Ivan could only presume that the Khan, or whoever acted for him in matters of protocol, was content. When the shaman swung him in another direction, he therefore gave the same bow to the stocky, middle-aged Mongol who sat on a pile of silken cushions underneath a scarlet canopy; but this time he counted to ten.

Whilst his head was lowered, Ivan took the opportunity to glance from side to side, rather than stare about him when he was supposed to be paying full attention to the Khan. It was an enlightening ten seconds, for the Golden Pavilion was an awesome place. Not so much in terms of size, for while it was remarkably large when considered as a tent, once inside where the tapestries and hangings disguised the fact that it was a tent at all, it felt more like any room in any kremlin. There were rooms in Khorlov's kremlin palace that were four times as tall, six times as wide, ten times as long. But none of the rooms in Khorlov, or anywhere else on Moist-Mother-Earth, were so filled with drifts of bric-a-brac and trinkets.

And such trinkets! Rolls and bales of costly fabric; raw and worked gold and silver; gemstones cut and uncut; small casks overflowing with discs of precious metals stamped with the heads of foreign kings that Ivan recognised as coined money, rather than the scraps of silver-by-weight that Russians had used as currency since the days of Ryurik the Norseman and the old North people. The choicest plunder of the Western Empire had passed through Batu Khan's fingers at some time or another, before being set aside to be given out as praise-gifts when the Khan thought that such things had been earned. It was a sight to take the breath away.

Having just witnessed another way for a man to have his breath taken away, Ivan kept his thoughts to himself, and his face without expression.

It was just as well. The brief glimpse of Batu as he ducked his head had given him the impression that the Khan of the Golden Horde was nothing more than a short, fat and ridiculously overdressed man looking foolish in silks and satins rather than furs and steel and leather. He was wrong. Ilkhan Batu was of clan Borjigun, descended in right line from the Great Ancestor Chinghis-Khan Temüchin. It meant that while he was stout enough, the fleshiness of good living was overlaid on solid muscle. Instead of being rotund, his body looked almost rectangular, like a statue roughly carved from a block of timber with a hatchet. On such a body, the silks and satins looked anything but foolish.

What if he had gout brought on by the Chingisid family vice of drinking too much? His swollen feet were clad in Persian slippers of purple velvet, glittering with small jewels. When he drank now, *kumys* and wine and all the other liquid trophies of endless campaigns, he did so from cups of hammered gold, and pipes and cymbals sounded when he raised those brimming cups to his mouth. What if his hair was turning grey instead of the ruddy black that characterised his clan? He still wore it in the strange Mongol tonsure that shaved the crown of the head down to the skin, but left a lock of hair hanging down between the eyebrows and enough at the back to braid into a long, looped plait behind each ear. Gemstones and gold thread were in those plaits as well as hair, and the skullcap covering his naked crown, bald now as much as shaved, was quilted satin sewn with seed pearls. His title was well deserved, for he was a Splendid Khan indeed.

Amragan *tarkhan* was beside him, muttering and pointing, and Ivan suspected he had just reached the part of his narrative where the Firebird dropped out of a clear morning sky to exchange pleasantries. Khan Batu's pouched, slitted eyes opened as wide as they could likely go, then went narrow and speculative so that they were no more than two seams in the Mongol's weather-beaten face. Batu waved the *tarkhan* back to another cushioned seat, studied Ivan, Mar'ya Morevna, Nikolai and Anastasya once more, then crooked one finger at Aleksandr Nevskiy.

The Prince of Vladimir moved closer to the Khan, most likely to reduce the chance of his words being overheard, and went down on one knee in a way that Ivan noted. It was halfway to the subservience of the Eastern bow, and thus more likely to keep the Tatars happy, but except for an initial inclination of the head, it otherwise preserved enough straight-backed dignity to keep *boyar* and *bogatyr'* observers happy also. But if Nevskiy had hoped to preserve the secrecy of whatever reason had brought him here by whispering it to the Khan in private, he was mistaken. Batu clapped his hands and another Tatar came up from the gaggle of dignitaries to either side of the tasselled canopy, bowed, and then began to translate the Khan's words into Russian. Loudly.

Had he not just seen a man killed, and had that death not awakened frightened second and third thoughts on certain matters in his own mind, Ivan would have found the situation funny. Instead he found it merely interesting, since in Aleksandr Nevskiy's doings he could see the precursors of what he himself might be reporting to the Khan some time next year.

Prince Aleksandr Yaroslavich Nevskiy was not simply paying a courtesy call on his overlord, no matter what he had tried to make Ivan believe. He was here in order to discuss the matter of the latest tax-census, and to intercede with the Khan for his vassals in the domain of Vladimir, who had risen against the head-counters and the assessors yet again.

Again? thought Ivan. *How many times before?*

Nevskiy himself had quelled the rising, by persuasion and in places where that had failed, by force. It was an admission that shocked Ivan to the core, until he realised that it had been done to keep the local *daru-gashi* governor responsible for the Vladimir tax area from sending in a half-*tuman* of Tatar horsemen to do it themselves. Now Nevskiy had to apologise – not only for his own Russian people, but also for his having taken military action against them without first asking permission . . .

The case was heard, considered, and then to Ivan's mild frustration, set aside for a later pronouncement of verdict. He could guess the reason why. Batu Khan had seen Nevskiy before; he wanted to get on to other and more interesting guests.

'Step forward,' said the interpreter. He pointed first at Ivan, then at a word from the Khan, included Mar'ya Morevna and the children. 'Amragan *tarkhan* has informed the Ilkhan Batu of all things that have occurred since the *tarkhan* was sent from Sarai. The Ilkhan Batu will hear more of these matters when it pleases him. But first, it is his command that the Great Crown of Khorlov be placed with the other crowns and sceptres of the Rus domains who have made submission to the Golden Horde. Bring it here.'

For a few seconds the Pavilion swam in Ivan's vision, and he felt certain that he would either fall down or throw up. In the event, he did neither; breathing deeply helped, but also the resigned knowledge that it was far too late to do anything about a scheme which had seemed so very clever back in Khorlov. One of the Rus servants put a carved wooden box into his hands, swinging back the lid, and Ivan stared down at it as though he had never seen the box or its contents before. The jewelled, fur-trimmed conical shape of Khorlov's crown glittered up at him from the velvet embrace of the padded lining, and Ivan could see neither gold, nor fur, nor jewels, but just a man flung on his back and stamped to death for refusing to bow correctly.

What would the Khan do to a man who –

Seeing only hesitation where Mar'ya Morevna had already seen terrified reluctance, one of the eldest shamans who stood in the shadow of the Khan's throne walked forward and lifted the crown from its box, held it up before the Khan of the Golden Horde, and made to put it down at Batu's feet. Then the shaman snatched up the crown again and stared at it; turned it over and over in his thin, age-shrivelled hands; stroked it with his fingertips; and finally gave a thin, piercing screech of rage.

The forged Great Crown of Khorlov clanked loudly as it was flung into a heap of other golden things, then rolled down onto the floor amid a small avalanche of brooches, arm-rings and the like.

Those sliding metallic noises were lost in the shaman's shrill voice as the old wizard-priest danced with fury and delivered a stream of vituperation at Ivan's impassive face.

When they had made up the fake crown in the armoury, it had seemed like such a good idea. It would have kept the real one out of Tatar hands, kept it from adding its unstable source of power to the already dangerous accumulation of energy that was locked away somewhere in Sarai, and it would still have been convincing enough that Batu Khan would have accepted it as the proper token of submission and given Khorlov back to Ivan. Neither of them had suspected that the power in the real crown might be so intense that any lack of it could be detected simply by picking up the forgery. And now they knew, and it had all been a waste of time, and Ivan might as well have died heroically in the burning ruins of his city in the way that all the heroes of the *druzina* would have preferred. At least his reputation would have stayed intact, instead of losing it first, and everything else now.

The six guards that he remembered all too clearly were advancing on him, and for one wild moment, with his sabre on his belt, Ivan realised that he could go down fighting after all. That would leave Mar'ya Morevna and the children to fend for themselves; but maybe if he made a good enough show, the Khan might be moved to clemency, and if not, they would be in no worse case than as the wife and children of the treacherous Russian Prince who had tried to pass off a fake crown as a real one here in front of everyone. Then, before he could lay hand to hilt, Batu said something in Mongol and the six guards stopped.

Ivan felt short of breath, as though he had been running. It was too early to be certain, but he had a feeling he had just heard a stay of execution – and couldn't understand why.

Batu Khan looked at him thoughtfully, then waved back the soldiers and had them sheathe their sabres. 'That was a brave gesture, Ivan of Khorlov,' he said, and in token of great honour and respect, he spoke Farsee so that Ivan could understand without need of an interpreter. 'I love brave men. But I love wise men better. They live longer.' The Khan laughed at that, and his court joined in the joke whether they caught the humour of their lord's words or not. Ivan did not laugh; instead he just raised his eyebrows and smiled very slightly in pure relief, as though he was the one who had made a sly observation of wonderful subtlety and Batu Khan was the one overreacting to it.

Batu's laughter trailed off rather sooner than it might have done, and he eyed Ivan dubiously, wondering if this Rus might have made some impudent, dainty thrust in the manner of his people. But no; with his wife and children in the same trap as himself, he could not be so stupid as to dare any such thing. That much was clearly written on his face, and Ivan – trying not to wipe his sweating palms on his own breeches – was grateful for it. *If your tongue is sharp enough, it will cut your own throat*, Amragan *tarkhan* had said not half an hour ago. He hadn't said anything about eyebrows, or sardonic smiles, or adversaries clever enough to read your thoughts from the very posture of your body. Any one of those could be as fatal as the wrong word in the wrong place.

'You are supposed to be wise, but you have been brave instead,' said Batu. 'This,' he gestured at the crown, 'is stupid. The time for such bravery is past, and you should know it. Bow down, or be destroyed.'

To Ivan's shock he spoke this time in Russian; carefully pronounced, thickly accented, but Russian for all that. If the Khan spoke it, it was more than likely other Tatars spoke it too. Neither Ivan nor Mar'ya Morevna needed to turn around to know that numerous guilty glances were being exchanged by other people as they tried to recall impolitic statements made in a language they had been sure was safe.

'If you and all these others' – a quick, all-encompassing wave took in every Russian *boyar*, *bogatyr*' and nobleman in the hall – 'had been as brave all together and all in the one place, then maybe I might not be here saying this to you.' Batu shrugged, in that ponderous, studied and deliberate way that only heavy men with a sense of their own dignity can truly manage. 'Or you might all be dead, and I would be saying it to your successors. All that is in the past. I am here. And you are still here, for which you may thank Amragan *tarkhan* and my own curiosity. You saved the life of an able commander, and I give you your life back in exchange. But even without that,' the broad, slit-eyed, cruel face became momentarily childlike and eager, 'I could not have you killed until I heard you speak of your adventures.'

237

The Khan shuffled himself into a more comfortable position among the cushions and drank half of a cup of *kumys* while the pipes played and the cymbals clashed, then threw the empty cup to a servant who caught it with the ease of long practice. 'But for the peace of my realm and the content of its least tax-paying citizen, this matter must be settled. So tomorrow you will approach me and make whatever recompense for your stupid bravery that I may think necessary. If it does not please you, then the fault and the blame and the penalty is on your own head and not on mine.'

It was not an excuse or an apology, any more than an observation that water is wet. The Splendid Khan of the Golden Horde did not waste his breath on such inconsequential matters. Batu struck his hands together, two sharp claps like the strokes of a whip. 'Go.'

Ivan gathered up his family and retinue, and went.

Chapter Nine

Sarai, capital of the Khanate of the Golden Horde;
September, AD 1243

'Go back to Khorlov? Don't be bloody ridiculous, man! We've only just arrived!'

That was not strictly true – they had been in Sarai for five days before Batu Khan deigned to notice their existence – but Ivan knew well enough that Mar'ya Morevna had never been one to let accuracy stand in the way of a well-justified blaze of indignation. Nothing would stop her outburst. Not Amragan *tarkhan*'s presence, angry as only a man can be who has been played for a fool by those he had thought defeated, nor even his own signals to be quiet and calm down. She was far from calm right now, and with good reason.

'I referred only to you, *gospozha*,' said the Türk. 'All the others stay here. It is the Khan's command.'

'What?' Even as he protested, Ivan knew that he was wasting his breath. For all that the original suggestion had most likely come from the man in front of him, put forward as a means of revenge on those who had made him look stupid, this had to be the Khan's command in very truth. Ivan stared at Amragan *tarkhan*, and knew he was looking at someone whose delayed arrival back at the house had been caused almost entirely by his lord and master voicing opinions of stupidity, promises of punishment and orders to set the matter right. Had Amragan not already spoken his piece about how his life had been saved by the Tsar of Khorlov, who had fought a duel on his behalf, those words would never have been uttered. And that same Tsar would have suffered whatever punishment the Ilkhan of the Golden Horde decreed for forgery and a vassal's attempted deception of his overlord. 'I will go instead,' he said. 'Let Mar'yushka stay with the children.'

'No,' said the Türk. 'You will stay. Your children will stay. Your servants will stay. Your wife will not. The people of Khorlov will not rise in rebellion to support her as they might do with you, and the presence of the brats will persuade her not to try any other little tricks.'

Amragan *tarkhan* smiled, a bleak movement of his moustache rather than his lips, which stayed as thin as the stroke of a sword. 'But to be doubly certain, an escort, Beyki the chief shaman and a *käshik-minghan* of one thousand, will accompany her, to make sure that this time the crown is the one required. By post-road. First thing tomorrow morning. And that is not the Khan's command. It is mine.'

It would be.

'You to the Black Pit, Amragan *tarkhan*,' snarled Ivan, the curse soft and venomous.

This time the Türk's grin was a wide flash of white teeth, the delight of a man who has won the game at a stroke. 'And you before me to hold the door, Khorlovskiy.' He bowed mockingly in the silence he had created, and stalked from the room.

Ivan sat for a long time in that silence, trying and discarding a hundred things to say. Anger, blame, guilt and recrimination all fought for precedence, and the person deserving them changed with every passing breath. But someone had to take responsibility, and it could not be Mar'ya Morevna.

From Sarai to Khorlov and back by the Tatar post-roads would be a brutal journey at the best of times, and these were not such times. The weather had begun its change already, and the sky was seldom without its clouds, for *rasputitsa* was upon them. The rain was pounding on the roof overhead, a sound like impatient fingers drumming on a table. It would seldom cease from now on, leaving Moist-Mother-Earth sodden with red mud, untill the rain became snow as winter closed its jaws on the world, and then rain again in the spring. The Time of Bad Roads seemed sometimes to last for most of the year, and it was small surprise now that the Tatars had chosen to invade during winter, when the ground underfoot was at least frozen hard and not mud or drifting dust.

And there was something else besides.

'What,' said Ivan at last, 'will I tell Kolya and Natasha?'

Mar'ya Morevna gripped both his hands in hers, then curled herself down beside him in the wide, over-cushioned chair. 'I'll see them before I go,' she said, and affected a smile for him. He could almost see her putting it on, as bright and artificial as any cosmetic. 'They'll understand better than you think, you'll see.'

'You're angry.'

'No. Yes. But not with you. The Khan, yes. Amragan *tarkhan*, yes. And everything else, perhaps yes too. But not you. Never you.'

'Never?' He tried to tease, to do something to lighten the despair that was threatening to fall like a leaden cloak over both of them.

'Not about important things. Not even about Volk Volkovich any more.'

'Promise?'

'I promise.'

'I'll hold you to that, if he ever comes back. The children miss him.'

'Well, I don't . . .' She hesitated, shook her head, and snuggled it into the comfortable angle between his neck and shoulder, then stared at the bronze and ceramic stove in the corner of the room for so long that Ivan began to think she might have gone to sleep. But she hadn't. 'I didn't think I would ever say this. But yes, I do. I miss the sarcastic bastard, and I believe you when you say he means us no harm.'

Ivan stroked her hair lightly. 'Really?' he said, not teasing now, nor even digging for an honest answer; just wondering. 'When did you change your mind?'

'When he was gone. Not just because it left you angry, and me angry, and neither of us willing to say "I'm sorry" to the other. But because I felt . . . less safe.'

Less safe without an oboroten' *werewolf than with one*. Ivan shifted his position in an attempt to see her face, but it was still turned towards the glow of the banked stove pouring in amber stripes of hot light through the slots cut in its iron door, and the crown of Mar'ya Morevna's frost-blonde head was giving away no secrets. Yet he knew exactly what she meant. To know that at least one of the deadly shadows in the darkness was a friend, an ally who had promised to defend you and yours against all enemies and odds; that was a comfort granted to few men and women, regardless of their skill in the Art Magic or their lack of it. And he might still be out there, somewhere in the shadows,

241

watching, waiting, hopefully guarding. Ivan only wished he knew for sure.

'I wish I knew for sure,' said Mar'ya Morevna, choosing her words with an eerie prescience that made Ivan start a little. 'Whether I was right or wrong about him. Whether I offended him so much he washed his hands of us.'

'Shouldn't that be "paws"?'

'What? Oh. Yes. Very funny. It was, really. I – I just don't feel like laughing very much right now. I'm growing so afraid of the dark, Vanya. Hold me. Just hold me.'

Ivan put his arms around his wife, and held her close.

Eaten through at last, the last logs he had laid criss-cross in the stove collapsed with a crash and sent up a crackling plume of sparks. Little tongues of yellow flame licked up the chips of dried bark that had fallen into the bed of red coals underneath. Their light shone back in strands of gold from the tear tracks on Mar'ya Morevna's face until she abruptly pulled clear of Ivan's embrace, cleared her throat, sniffed vigorously and dried her eyes with a kerchief from her sleeve.

'That was supposed to make me feel better,' she said, and smiled damply. 'Who makes up such lies?'

'The sort of person who says "this won't hurt". Because it always does. Always.' He stood up, a little awkwardly from having held his cramped position for as long as she needed him not to move, and stretched to ease the kinks from aching joints before going to the table and pouring them both something to drink from the always-replenished flask. It was vodka again, *okhotnichnya* this time, flavoured with herbs and honey, and while it was good enough cold, Ivan considered moving it to the top of the stove. Hot honey and alcohol would help them sleep, and from the look on Mar'ya Morevna's face, she would need as much help as she could get. Later, perhaps. Right now there was a question needing to be answered. He gave Mar'ya Morevna her cup, sipped delicately at his own, and then said gently, 'Why the dark? You were never afraid of it before.'

'I had hoped our trick with the crown would work,' said Mar'ya Morevna obliquely, swallowing half the vodka at a gulp as if trying to get as much heat in her belly as the stove. 'I hoped it as I hoped for an easy birth of healthy children – and if a man can't imagine what that means to a woman, be grateful.'

Ivan sat down on the arm of the chair. 'They *were* healthy, their birth *was* easy – if you and the midwives weren't sparing my tender sensibilities – and the trick didn't work. But my head's still on, and Batu still doesn't have the Great Crown of Khorlov for his collection.'

'He will soon enough. I've run out of deceptions, Ivan, and he won't listen to the truth. He wouldn't believe it. Not after what we tried to do. He would think it was just one more excuse. And you heard the Türk. No more excuses.'

'Would the Khan ever have listened? I don't think so.'

'He might. That's what makes me so angry. I pictured a degenerate old tyrant, steeped in cunning. This one . . . This one seems almost civilised. At least he has a practical mind.'

'This practical, civilised Khan had Mikhail of Chernigov stamped to death for refusing to bow to him.'

Mar'ya Morevna laughed. It was a shocking sound after her tears and soft speech, brittle and cynical and all too worldly-wise. 'That was the excuse. The *reason* was that he was part of a failed rebellion, and the only one of its three leaders too proud to submit and too brave to run away. Too stupid to do either, if you want my opinion.'

'So why did he come here at all?'

'He thought that he could do some sort of merchant's deal with the Khan to keep both his honour and his lands.' Mar'ya Morevna finished her drink. 'He, an unrepentant rebel, making bargains. Stupid, as I said.'

'But he has his honour.'

'That should be a great comfort to the refugees living on the open steppe who could have started to rebuild Chernigov if there had been a lord to stand between them and the Golden Horde. A great comfort indeed. Especially with winter coming on. Yes. Winter. And the dark. You wanted to know about the dark.' She held the empty cup out abruptly. 'Give me another.'

Ivan splashed vodka into her cup, replenished his own, and returned to his perch on the chair-arm. Then he reached down and took her hand and held it. '*Lyubimyy* Mar'yushka,' he said softly, 'tell me or not. Whatever eases you.'

'You're very sweet, love.' Mar'ya Morevna laid her cheek against his hand like a cat, and sighed. 'And you really want to be told. Well. It won't ease either of us, but you're better knowing than not.' She tasted her vodka, no gulp this time, no more in fact than a moistening of her lips, and sat up straighter in the chair. 'The equinox is next week,' she said. 'Day and night will be of equal length. After that the nights grow longer as the wide white world slides down the throat of another winter.'

'Until we reach the bottom of the year and the pendulum swings again.'

'Unless something stops it.' Her voice was flat, the words unequivocal. To ears acquainted with the Art Magic as Ivan's were, deny it as he might, there was a shuddersome brutality about the statement. 'Autumn equinox, then winter solstice, and the darkness growing stronger all the way.' Mar'ya Morevna took a long drink of the honied vodka, although it was having no more effect on her than if it had been honied water. 'You know it, I know it, the shamans know it too. But though they can sense the difference between a true crown and a false one well enough, like the heat from coals in a closed jar, they can't sense that there might be anything bad or dangerous in it. A fire to warm your house – or burn it down.'

'Like a rotten egg,' said Ivan. 'You can't tell until the shell's been broken, and by then it's too late.'

'Except that if this egg breaks, the one we call our world, then the rot will come in from Outside. Oh, Vanya – ' Mar'ya Morevna stared at him with wide, haunted eyes that held a degree of fear he would have sworn she did not know, and her fingers closed on his in a grip tight enough to hurt, ' – I wish they had come for the crown in the springtime. . . !'

'I could take you out of the city without them knowing about it, Papa,' said Nikolai Ivanovich, peering over the ramparts and pointing to the distant line of shallow cliffs where the steppes tumbled downward to become the valley of the Volga. 'I could take you right out there.'

'So could I! So could I! So could I!' Anastasya shot her brother a glare for leaving her out, and gave him a push. 'We both could, and I could do it better than him. I'm sure I could. But *he* just wants to sound important.'

'No I don't! And anyway, if we both did it together, we could go even farther away from here.'

'As far as Khorlov?' Ivan spoke casually, trying hard to keep the eagerness out of his voice, but the twins had sharp ears. Natasha's face fell and her lower lip came out.

'No, Papa. Not home. It's too far. We couldn't do it ourselves, and we couldn't do it with you either.'

'I just wondered.' Ivan shrugged, making light of it as best he could. He had been spending a lot more time with his children than he could normally spare; but then, he didn't have a tsardom to take care of right now. Whenever he was able to forget the why of that, he was able to relax and enjoy his unaccustomed liberty. But when the wheres and the whys could not be ignored, he had also been doing a good deal of 'just wondering'. Especially since Mar'ya Morevna and her escort – he had forgotten just how imposing and threatening a thousand armoured horsemen could look – had ridden off to Khorlov last week. Wondering how long it would be until he saw her again, for one. At best speed in this foul weather, and it was certain that the *käshik* commander would be driving his troops at best speed all the way, she would not be back for another four weeks. With the crown.

With the oil for the fire that might burn down the house.

The twins had been complaining recently: about heat, and cold, and wet, and dry. About being itchy; about having headaches. Ivan didn't know how long it had been going on; being so damned busy with one thing and another, nobody had thought it worth-while to tell the Tsar and Tsaritsa that their children seemed to be catching something. Except that even to Ivan's inexperienced eye, neither Kolya nor 'Tasha looked in the least bit unwell. They had missed their mother loudly and inconsolably both before and after she left; but within a day they had bounced back from that with a healthy anticipation of her return. For the rest of it, they ran about almost unsupervised while within Sarai's ring of walls, playing the sort of games with the swarms of Tatar children in the city that seemed to require no skill at language but merely the ability to emit piercing shrieks.

It was only outside the gates that there were reminders of being less than guests. Ivan was allowed to ride out with only one child at a time, never both together, just as they were allowed to ride out together on their fat little ponies, but never with their father. And always, whether Ivan was with them or not, there was a ten-strong *arban* of Tatars shadowing them wherever they went, as if those small animals could suddenly develop wings and fly away before a patrol could be despatched from the city itself. The ponies couldn't, but the twins – well, that was another matter entirely.

Except that they had made it plain, with all the defiant stubbornness and crooked logic of which the seven-year-old mind was capable, that they wouldn't leave without him, even if they could. Explanations of how much easier it would be for both their parents, of how much less there would be to worry about, even how much of a score it would be over Amragan *tarkhan* – whom neither child liked – fell on deaf ears.

'Either we all go, or we all stay,' Nikolai had said at the beginning of this wet afternoon – wet? what other sort was there? – when Ivan put the suggestion to them once again. The adult phrasing and delivery in that child's treble voice had been so, so comical that Ivan had to go away for a few minutes. And if he fought to conceal tears instead of laughter, it was no-one's business but his own. All the discussion after that had been fairly light-hearted wrangling about just how far various combinations of people and things could travel by way of these natural Gates.

Less far than Ivan had hoped, was the conclusion, and certainly less far than the powerful, elaborately constructed Gating-spells that Mar'ya Morevna used so warily and rarely. Of course, one did not expect unaided human muscles to perform as well as a machine of gears and counterweights and levers, so why should the same difference not apply in sorcery? Ivan could think of several reasons why not, but none of them would stand up even to his under-educated evaluation. And besides, sorcerers from birth they may have been, but Nikolai and Anastasya were still only seven years old.

Mar'ya Morevna would have been better able to explain it in the proper long words beloved of sorcerers and scholars; but from what the children had been chattering about, he could no more expect them to perform prodigies of sorcerous travel and transport than he could reasonably expect any other adult display

246

of strength or skill from a child. But the limitations of weight and distance seemed to apply only when their Gates were being used as a short cut between one part of Russia and another. It made a sort of perfect sense, at least in that way the Art Magic had of twisting anything it touched to conform with its own convoluted rules.

Because in the last extremity all of them – or at least the children – would be able to get away completely, without any hope of return, to the Summer Country; where it was obvious Nikolai and Anastasya had friends to care for them until they grew up, even if those friends were not always of human shape. The trick, if it became necessary – and Ivan did not like to think of what sort of threat would make such a step necessary – would be in persuading them to do it.

And for the meanwhile, if none of them looked too closely, they could ignore the guards and the closed gates and pretend that they were merely visiting a friend.

At times – times when Amragan *tarkhan* and his sardonic smile were not around – that friendship was easy to believe. The attitude displayed by most of the Tatars in Sarai was a straightforward one: since Ivan was still alive, the Ilkhan Batu had forgiven him, and there was an end to the matter. If their Khan exonerated instead of executed, it was not the place of Batu's loyal *nökud* retainers to reinterpret his ruling. Thus Ivan found himself the subject of more interest and curiosity than anything else. Accustomed to and knowing how to deal with either armed rebellion or absolute subservience, the Tatars of the Golden Horde were confused, amused and often utterly bemused by a polite, courteous, diplomatic and only mildly insubordinate Russian Prince who did exactly what he was told ninety-five times out of every hundred. It put them off their stride, so much so that they took refuge in the good-humoured wariness that Ivan was coming to recognise as their most common alternative to destructive ferocity. Since he didn't know what he needed to say to make that particular coin spin to show its opposite face, one was as unsettling as the other.

It was never more so than now.

Ivan settled himself as comfortably as he could onto a pile of cushions in the *Sira-Ger*, and tried not to move. Those cushions were covered in sleek silks and satins rather than a nice fuzzy velvet, so that the least change of pressure sent them squirting out from underneath him. He glanced around and did his best not to look as though he was listening to the mutter of voices as Ilkhan Batu concluded his business of the day. Not that listening would have been of much use, since both the Khan and the court official he was dealing with were speaking Mongol; but Ivan had long since decided that an obvious show of disinterest was more polite than otherwise. Safer, too.

Thanks to some whim of the Khan's which might well have had some basis in putting either Amragan *tarkhan* or Aleksandr Nevskiy back in their place, he had been adopted as Batu's 'pet Russian'. Since Mar'ya Morevna and her escort had left for Khorlov, he had been summoned to the Golden Pavilion almost daily to sit carefully on cushions that didn't want to be sat on, and drink *kumys* he didn't feel like drinking, and talk about what seemed like every subject under the sun.

At first Ivan had thought that if this was the punishment he was suffering for insubordination, then it was far lighter than he deserved. Then he realised that it was far from light. While he was here, warm and dry, taking his ease with a drink in his hand while he listened to the rain beat against the fabric of the pavilion, his wife was somewhere out on the steppes and the rain was beating against *her*. No. Batu Khan had once again shown himself an admirable judge of character and human relationships. It was not a light punishment at all.

Ivan pushed the thought from his mind, in case it might somehow be seen on his face or heard in his voice and only serve to make matters worse. He glanced to one side, stared briefly at the Khan's gouty, slippered feet which were the objects closest to his head, then looked beyond them, grimaced and turned away. It was not the proximity of Batu's feet that was the problem. Though it might have been.

The Khan, like his subjects, observed the *yasa*, the code of laws laid down by Chinghis-Khan, and one of those laws required that no-one, whether rich or poor or even a khan, should wash their clothing. It was meant as a perpetual reminder of the time when the Conquerors of the World had been no more than poor nomads on the steppes of Sibir'ya, where clothing to keep out the cold had more value than gold, and where water was rarer than silver. It also meant that a Tatar encampment could be smelt miles away, though like any who lived amid stench for long enough, Ivan and the others had grown used to it. It was lucky that Batu the Splendid Khan, unlike most of his subjects, had more than enough changes of clothes that no one garment among them smelt especially rank; and besides, he had a fondness for the heavy perfumes of musk and civet, which helped to disguise any lingering aroma.

There were other proximities that gave Ivan more immediate concern, and three of them were staring at him right now. Batu Khan's pets included more than Russians with a talent for story-telling. Besides the herd of three thousand pure white mares that provided milk and *kumys* for the Khan and the court, and the massive bears kept as totem beasts by the shamans, there were animals in Sarai that Ivan had only ever heard of. Huge striped Sibir'yan tigers and indolent blotched leopards kept for no other reason than that they were living, beautiful ornaments; their leggy cousins the cheetahs, who wore little red cloth hoods with holes cut for their ears and worked for their keep in the hunting field; and the *böragut* eagles with a wingspan of ten feet from tip to tip that hunted with them, flying from the Khan's own wrist. The sleepy interest of one wild beast more or less was something Ivan had been forced to live with since his first summons into the Pavilion.

If anyone had bothered to ask, though nobody ever did, he would have preferred the cheetahs. They had blunt cat faces – and he liked cats, at least cats of a reasonable size – that were marked with dark stripes down the sides of their muzzles so that they always had a faintly depressed expression, as if they had cried into their eye make-up. Probably it was the hoods. They looked very foolish with their hoods on, and if there was one thing a cat of any size disliked, it was looking foolish.

Perhaps because all they ever wore were heavy collars, and chains that to Ivan's jaundiced eye weren't anything like thick enough, the tigers and leopards never looked foolish. But hungry, yes; and nothing like as tame as Batu Khan had maintained once he had stopped laughing at Ivan's first ever reaction to their presence. For all their glossy coats and well-fed bellies, these striped and spotted cats always managed to look more than willing to try Tsar as a change of diet from horsemeat. Never Khan, oddly enough, so maybe they were indeed as well-behaved as Batu claimed.

The eagles just stared haughtily at him down their great hooked beaks like the Firebird, and managed to look even more murderously insane.

It was a cheetah and a leopard today, lounging half-asleep with heads resting on crossed forepaws, hind legs and bodies and tails disposed in that indolent, untidily elegant sort of way that cats probably practise while no-one is watching. One of the *böragut* eagles was preening itself on a perch at the back of the cushions, now and again favouring the world in general and Ivan in particular with a yellow-eyed glare that combined arrogance and malevolence in equal measure.

It was strange that the Khan's animals, his wild beasts, personified more of a conqueror's vices than the man himself. The potential was all around him: laziness, cruelty, ferocity or demented rage – Ivan could see all of those just by turning his head. But when he looked at Batu there was no shadow even of ill temper. It was certain that a Chingisid khan had long since trained any betraying flickers of emotion from his facial muscles, but there should have been some trace of where they had been. And there was none.

Their discussions of the world at large could become lengthy and convoluted, Batu dropping into Farsee when his command of Russian failed, but he still demonstrated a grasp of and an interest in what went on beyond his borders that was more than Ivan had expected from a Tatar no more than two generations removed from the howling wilderness of the high steppes. But the Khan had never given Ivan a chance to see what he truly felt or thought about such things. Oh, he smiled, frowned, even laughed out loud, but there was always the sense that these were movements and expressions as studied as those of an actor, appropriate to the moment but not necessarily to the workings of the mind behind the mask. Yet there was a feeling that the Khan of the Golden Horde valued what his pet had to say, and Ivan knew why. It wasn't just the tantalising presence of the Art Magic about his adventures, though he related enough of those both large and small. It was that same reason the ordinary Tatars found him so interesting: because he was different.

He had surrendered, and yet he hadn't; he had submitted, and yet he hadn't. Except for the matter of the Great Crown of Khorlov, he had done all the things that Batu Khan required of a vassal prince from a conquered realm, and yet he personally had managed not to be conquered at all. The normal Tatar response to that was to stamp it out, in case such a habit of insouciance towards authority bred a more serious form of rebellion in other, lesser princes. Yet the stamping boot had been withheld even when the business of the forged crown had made it entirely justified, and now he was as much an object of curiosity and an ornament to the Golden Pavilion as any other strange beast, interesting and – for the moment – harmless.

His own reputation had a good deal to do with that, of course. From what he had overheard – and overhearing was easy enough, since with so many tribal dialects in the city the commonest language was Farsee – the Tatars were fascinated by the Rus magic which was so different to the conjuration performed by their shamans. A lot of that fascination had to do with wondering in a somewhat relieved way why it had never been turned against them during three years of invasion since they, the Golden Horde, could never conceive of a situation where they would fail to use any weapon if it was available.

Ivan had smiled grimly at that. The Art Magic had spells that could be used as a weapon of sorts; in an individual combat, one on one. Not for a battle. Beforehand, yes: that was the proper place for sorcery. But it could not be the obvious things from the old *skazki* tales, fire called from the sky to consume the enemy host, or an army of demons conjured up to oppose them. The sorceror who tried to fight his battles by the summoning of demons would find all his time taken up with trying to control his summonings, while still needing to fight those of the original enemy not burnt by the fire or opposed by the demons – and failing as likely as not to do either. And the other sort of wizard, those who tried to create such ostentatious effects by wands and circles and the direct manipulation of power? They would briefly become an ostentatious effect themselves, blown to bloody rags and tatters by the strain of attempting to channel such energies through a human brain and body that was, when all was said and done, only well-educated meat.

What a sorcerer *could* do was rather more limited and rather less obvious – so much so indeed that few chronicles of battles where sorcery had been involved even mentioned the fact. They were in any case the sort of battles where the Princes in command would not have cared to attribute their great victories to sorcery, so the chronicles were likely rewritten to delete such unpalatable information. Aleksandr Nevskiy had done that very thoroughly with the Battle on the Ice against the Teutonic Knights. By his command, the Lavrent'skiy and Novgorod chronicles ignored the Firebird's presence – and indeed everyone's presence but his own – changed the year in which the battle was fought, and even moved its location from the River Nemen to the River Neva, so that his own nickname of 'Nevskiy' would seem like a battle honour rather than a birthplace. But he could not change the fact that it was another of those battles in which inexplicably convenient things happened. One where a dust storm rose suddenly and blinded the enemy archers, or a sudden downpour soaked the ground to mud and impeded a fatal cavalry charge – or where river ice thought thick enough for safety for no apparent reason suddenly cracked beneath an advancing enemy's feet and pitched them, weighted with their armour, into deep and freezing water.

Ivan knew all about that particular reason, and Nevskiy could rewrite history all he chose.

But all those things had to be there already. It was no use trying to stir up dust after a week of rain; no use calling rain from a cloudless sky; no use cracking ice so thin that the enemy hadn't been enticed onto it. But if the dust, or the clouds, or the ice, were there already, then a sorcerer with any brains at all knew how to use such tools to advantage – provided the commander who placed such reliance on sorcery also had a grasp of tactics, otherwise it would all have been a waste of time. When talking to Batu Khan about them, Ivan always stepped gingerly around such subjects, being careful never to say too much while not giving away that he was holding information back. It was a balancing act, neither to reveal how weak the much-feared magic was where it really mattered to the Tatars, nor suggesting it was so strong as to provoke some sort of pre-emptive action against risk of its further use.

He was always relieved when the Khan sat back and drank, accompanied as always by those damned flutes and cymbals, then leaned forward on his cushions, dismissed the cares of the wide white world and asked yet again for a story of wonders.

At first Ivan had been suspicious even of that. He knew the cool, subtle, convoluted mind working away behind that blunt, seamed face. There was always a fear that the constantly requested repetitions of his own hard-won successes against the Teutonic Knights or Baba Yaga or Koshchey the Undying were being sifted for useful knowledge, and during the third retelling of that time four years past when he had encountered Zmey Gorynyts the Dragon-*boyar* and Tugarin Zmey'yevich, he changed a couple of particulars of the story. They were unimportant, just details of what Tugarin the Dragon's son had looked and sounded like, but he had mentioned them on both previous occasions. It was when Batu called the error to his attention that Ivan knew he had nothing to be afraid of. The Khan was doing nothing more suspicious than committing each story to memory, in order to tell them to others when Ivan had gone back to Khorlov.

Something to boast about, thought Ivan, just a little sourly. Maybe he was doing the old Mongol an injustice, or maybe not. *The only Ilkhan in the empire to have a* skazki *here for a vassal. It must be like having a pet who can do really impressive tricks.*

Then suddenly, with his mind still full of the bright magical images of the past times and past places that had no Tatar invaders in the background, Ivan remembered Aleksandr Nevskiy's taunt about Khorlov living in a world of its own. The recollection hit him like a bucket of cold water, but he smiled at the shock. Nevskiy had meant only an insult, but there were worlds indeed, and to spare – the worlds that existed behind the mirror, of which this one was but a pale reflection. Tsar Morskoy's gratitude had promised him the Blue Kremlin and all its domains, if ever he and Mar'ya Morevna chose to live there. Even now he could smell the salt sea air, and hear the green waves crash in foam against the cliff-face far below.

And then there was the Summer Country. Even when things were worst, there was always the Summer Country.

Ivan grinned at the Khan of the Golden Horde, at his leopards and tigers and eagles, and the Khan, not knowing his mind, grinned back. 'The Great Ancestor Chinghis-Khan Temüchin said that an empire was won from the saddle, but ruled from a throne. Hui! He did not say how much less of that empire you see from the throne. Put an old man back in his saddle, Ivan of Khorlov. Tell me a tale of adventure . . .'

There were three more Russian noblemen residing in Sarai. Ivan had heard the drums and trumpets sounding welcome while out riding on the steppe for the sake of exercise, and to take him out of the increasingly oppressive atmosphere that was hanging over the city of the Golden Horde. He had watched their escort column wending its way down from the steppes and into the Volga basin, but the *arban-ba'atur* commanding his own escort had refused to let him any closer. It hardly mattered. He was considered harmless enough by now that it would be a simple matter of taking a quiet walk through Sarai's muddy streets at some time or other when it wasn't raining, or at least, since the autumn *rasputitsa* was here with a vengeance, picking a few moments when it was raining less heavily. There were never any escorts when he wandered about the city on foot, since no man could run far enough or fast enough to be out of reach before his escape was noticed – and·Ivan preferred that nothing about him be noticed at all.

He didn't trouble with the new arrivals that day, or the next, preferring to let them find out about his presence by other means. But on the morning of the third day a Russian that none of Ivan's people had seen before presented himself at the door of the house, and was duly ushered into Ivan's presence. The man was well dressed in the tall hat and long, flared kaftan of a highly placed house-servant; he was dappled with rain and despite efforts to wipe them, his boots were muddy. But then, in Sarai halfway through a wet September, if he had been dry and clean it would have been more cause for comment.

'Well, fellow? You asked for the Tsar of Khorlov. Here I am.'

The servant swept off his hat and bowed respectfully, with the easy grace that comes only with long practice. 'Majesty,' he said, and Ivan hid a small smile of contentment at hearing the title that had gone so long unused. The man straightened up, returning the hat to his head and pulling a small, sealed scroll from the cuff of his glove all in the same elegant movement. 'I bear an invitation from my master and his companions. They would deem it a high honour if you would take wine with them.'

Ivan said nothing at first; he broke the seals – three of them, none of which he recognised – and scanned the contents of the note. It said little more than the servant had done, except for giving him the names of the new arrivals, all *boyar* noblemen, and those too meant little enough. 'Um,' he said. 'When would be felicitous for the *gospoda* to receive me?'

That a tsar would even consider the convenience of mere *boyaryy* was high courtesy, and the servant flushed with pleasure on their behalf. 'They said, Majesty, that the time is yours to choose.'

'Indeed? Then the gentlemen must be thirsty, and I would consider it remiss of me to keep them waiting.' Ivan stood up, grinning broadly and deliberately both to put the servant at his ease – the man had carried out his duty in a gracious fashion – and to give him some information to bear back to his masters with the accepted invitation. That Ivan of Khorlov was everything gossip reported about him, and perhaps a little more: he was too young to be a tsar, foolishly amiable even to such lowly creatures as other people's servants, possessed of no sense of his own lofty station, and always ready for a drink.

Aleksandr Yaroslavich Nevskiy would have died before allowing such slanders to be associated with his name and reputation, but then Nevskiy was already safe enough, both in his own opinion and that of the Khan. He used Tatar soldiers as his own household troops without a second thought, and more significant still, they obeyed him. That, though he was too blind to see it, said more of what the Tatars thought of him than any number of well-educated histories and chronicles.

And besides, these newcomers were offering wine instead of the interminable supply of *kumys* and vodka that was all the Tatars left him to drink. Even though Ivan made sure he spilled more from his windowsill than he allowed to pass his lips, something that tasted different to fruit-flavoured liquid fire or sour mare's-milk would make a pleasant change.

'You have not bowed before the Khan in hope of gain,' said the *boyar* Stepan Mikhailovich.

'Unlike Prince Aleksandr Nevskiy,' said the *boyar* Andrey Vladimirovich.

'And thus we feel confident in asking you to join with us,' finished the *boyar* Mstislav Vasil'yevich.

Ivan felt a tiny chill run through him at the words. He took a small sip of wine that had suddenly lost its savour, and looked slowly at one and then another of those eager, angry faces. The three *boyaryy* had been working up to saying something like this for a long time now; Ivan had been expecting it a lot sooner, since they obviously held him in as high regard as they disdained Aleksandr Nevskiy and everything the Prince of Vladimir represented. It made his skin crawl. Secretive little cliques like this were common enough among Russian noblemen; those who were not part of a lord's retinue formed mutual appreciation societies of their own, mostly as an excuse for getting together in one or another's home and having drunken parties. There was one difference; such groups were usually younger than the three who sat here, being made up of men whose lives were not yet weighted down with the responsibilities that plagued their seniors. Ivan knew; he had been one of those young men himself, not very long ago. Until now, and with the exception of Konstantin *bogatyr'*, the two children and Ivan himself, there had been no Russians in Sarai under the age of forty – by which time Ivan hoped to have grown into something that even Mar'ya Morevna might concede was sense.

These three noblemen were showing no trace of that useful commodity. To condemn Nevskiy for collaborating so freely with the Tatars was tactless and might lead to a challenge at arms if the Prince heard about it, but since none of the three were liegemen of the principality of Vladimir, it was scarcely treasonable behaviour. But to assume that Ivan was a hero willing to fight against the invaders just because of a fumbled plot to pass off a fake as Khorlov's crown was both stupid and incredibly dangerous. Never mind what Aleksandr Nevskiy might be told: if this trio of hotheads tried anything more violent and Amragan *tarkhan* or the Ilkhan Batu himself learned that Ivan was involved, if only by having spoken to them before whatever they were planning, then he and his family, his friends and the entire domain of Khorlov stood a fair chance of being obliterated. By mistake.

'Join with you?' he asked cautiously. 'In doing what?'

Stepan Mikhailovich looked quickly at the other two. 'We were hoping, Majesty, that you might be able to suggest something,' he said at last. 'Swords are useless against the Tatars; walled cities are no more than a trap for the people inside them. But magic . . .' He let the sentence trail off and gazed expectantly at Ivan.

'Magic?' Ivan repeated, wishing that his ears were playing tricks and knowing absolutely that they weren't. It sounded as though Batu Khan wasn't the only one in Sarai to have heard all about his reputation; but at least the Khan wasn't expecting any more from it than a fund of stories. These three were looking at him as though he was the old hero Il'ya Muromets, stepped straight from a legend to the defence of Mother Russia.

It was horribly ironic that they were sitting around a table at the heart of the Khanate of the Golden Horde, fomenting what amounted to rebellion against the rule of that same Khanate just because Tsar Ivan of Khorlov happened to be here as well, when what had brought them here in the first place was probably the intention to, as Stepan Mikhailovich had put it so succinctly, 'bow before the Khan in hope of gain'. These men were not merchants, so trade was not an objective; nor were they hereditary princes of any of the other lands now held by the Khan. They were opportunists, here to petition for the right to rule one or other of the Rus domains whose ruling family had been wiped out during the Conquest.

Opportunists? They were scavengers, just as much as the crows picking over the skull-mound outside the ruins of Chernigov, and a great deal less honest about their intentions. Yet Ivan suspected that from the very moment he had sat down and accepted the brimming cup of wine held out by Andrey Vladimirovich, he was already in too deep to tell them so.

What he wanted to do right now was fling their wine in their self-satisfied faces and go slamming out of the stuffy room that almost seemed to smell of intrigue, a stink so obvious that it must surely reach the nostrils of the Tatars before long. And that was just what he dared not do. He had been in contact with the conspiracy, like a contagious disease, and it had marked him for both sides to see. An abrupt departure, or even a flat refusal to be a part of whatever plans they had – and if they were asking his

257

advice on sorcery, those plans were already convoluted enough to strangle in – and these three would have no hesitation in killing him. He would be a traitor to their cause, a collaborator with the enemy, a spy for the Tatars, or simply someone whose mouth needed to be shut just in case. Ivan had been in checkmate before; but only on a wooden board. Never in reality, and never so completely as this.

The alternative was to stay, try to control the wilder flights of fancy with a splash of cold reason, and as the source of the magic they were so keen to use, be cautiously willing – and carefully unable – to do anything of the sort. The first thing was to tell them about the gathered crowns of the conquered domains, and why he had put his life at risk trying to avoid handing over another, and after that . . .

But there was no 'after that', at least not straight away. Mstislav Vasil'yevich actually licked his lips with delight at the thought of the massed power of two centuries and more of Russian rulers right in Sarai, and under the Khan's nose. 'The damned Tatars don't understand what they have here,' he said.

Neither do you, thought Ivan. *I've been speaking for ten minutes, and not one of you has listened to more than you want to hear.* 'And I think that's just as well, don't you?' he said.

The *boyar* looked at him sharply, then grinned. 'Oh, indeed. But it's like a mine dug under a city wall. In place and waiting for just one spark to bring everything tumbling down around their Khan's ears. The delight is that even if they did know what power was here, they wouldn't know how to use it.'

'Mstislav Vasil'yevich, what have I said that makes you think *I* do?'

Ivan got another sharp look for that, but no expressions of surprise from any of the others. It looked instead as though they were silently congratulating him for not giving away any information without good reason. In fact it looked to Ivan as though these three, or the other two, at least, would be able to put a favourable interpretation on anything he might or might not do. 'You are widely known as a skilled sorcerer, the Prince who slew Baba Yaga and Koshchey the Undying – '

'In the first case she fell off a bridge,' said Ivan. That was 'through' a bridge, but who cared? His words came out sharply

258

and a little too fast, so that in his own ears he sounded more like someone making an excuse than anything else. 'And in the second, he was trampled by his own horse. Neither instance makes me a sorcerer.'

'Perhaps not.' Stepan Mikhailovich sounded tolerant and understanding, in the worst and most indulgent sense of both terms. It made Ivan feel as though the *boyar*'s next action would be to reach out and pat him on the head for spinning a good yarn, and if he did, Ivan had decided he would break at least one of the man's fingers to teach him respect. 'But you cannot deny – as Aleksandr Nevskiy has done – that when you went up against the Teutonic Knights on the ice – '

'I had a Firebird there to help me. And if you listen to the old tales as much as it seems you do, then I don't need to tell you how little the *zhar'yanoi* fire-creatures care to be involved in the affairs of men. This one owed me a debt of gratitude,' he didn't trouble to explain further, since the affair was both long past and none of their business, 'but I would not care to summon one for such a venture as this. In fact I would not care to summon one at all. They tend not to appreciate it, and in such a situation you might find the Tatars preferable. And anyway, my wife is the sorcerer in Khorlov, and what little I know, I learned from her.'

The *boyaryy* exchanged more of those significant glances and muttered together for longer than Ivan liked, then Andrey Vladimirovich came out of the huddle and shrugged. 'It's a pity she isn't here, Majesty. She would have been a great deal of use.' Now it was Ivan's turn to give the *boyar* a hard stare; he didn't care for the man's phrasing above half, and was within a breath of saying so except that Andrey hadn't stopped talking, and one of the words he spoke drove any thoughts of insult out of Ivan's mind.

'Chernobog?' he said. 'You want to summon *Chernobog*? Are you three out of your minds, or just drunk on too much wine and too many wild ideas? Chernobog . . . Do you truly understand what you're contemplating?'

Andrey Vladimirovich glowered at Ivan, startled and angered by the young Tsar's voice. 'It might surprise you,' he said sullenly, 'but I understand exactly what I mean. Though I wonder if you do, *Majesty*.'

Ivan stealthily braced one foot against the leg of the table, ready to push himself backward or kick it over, and transferred his wine-cup to his left hand so that the right was free for his sword. His right earlobe was throbbing with the memory of an old wound. Ivan had heard his title spoken in that tone before, and he had eventually been forced to kill the man who spoke it. 'Explain that,' he said. It wasn't phrased as a threat, though if the three noblemen took it as such and calmed down as a result he had no objection.

Stepan Mikhailovich did at least. Ivan didn't see, but he heard, as the *boyar* rammed his elbow into Andrey's side. 'Your pardon, Majesty, but we thought you would recognise that we meant nothing but good for Russia.'

'All right.' Ivan forced himself to be calm and listen to their reasoning. 'Tell me how anything to do with That One can be good.' He realised too late that he should have nominated a spokesman, because though their argument was quite simple, the three-part harmony of comment and correction that seemed to accompany any unanimous decision made it difficult to hear.

The trio, armed with their dangerously shaky knowledge gleaned from ballads, myths and legends, had seized on what Ivan had said concerning the pre-eminence of darkness at this time of year. He, like Mar'ya Morevna, had meant it as a warning, but like many fanatics – for so he was beginning to regard them – these noblemen had heard only a potential for destruction that could be turned against their enemies the Tatars. Their explanation had all the enthusiasm that led Western knights to go on crusade; but to Ivan's ear it had been as carefully edited of any unfavourable aspect as one of Aleksandr Nevskiy's court chronicles would be shorn of any mention of heroism besides his own.

Chernobog, the Black God from a time before Russia became Christian, might have fallen from favour over the years, but he was a Russian god, not one imported from outside like the White Christ or the gods of the North People. Since not just the people but the very land of Russia was under threat from the Tatar invaders, they felt sure he would come to the defence of those whose ancestors worshipped him in olden times.

'When the Lord Christ came,' said Stepan Mikhailovich, signing himself with the life-giving cross, 'the old gods were cast down into the fire. But some say they still haunt the empty places of the world, remembering what they were. And if men call on them for help, they listen.'

Ivan repressed a shudder. It seemed to have slipped their notice, or simply not to concern them, that the old Lord of the Dark Places might be less generously inclined than they believed. He had read all those reasons before, and almost exactly word for word. But then they had been written in the book *Enciervanul Doamnisoar*, and since its whole purpose was to aid in and warn about the summoning of demons, it suggested unpleasant things about how a long-forgotten god might have degenerated.

'And what about the God whose sign you made just then?' Ivan asked. He knew what the answer would be, but he wanted to hear Stepan say it aloud, and to hear the tone in which he said it.

'The people have been calling on God and Christ and Mary and all the Saints to save them since the Tatars first rode into Russia,' said Stepan. 'What good has it done them? To be told that the Tatars are God's Scourge on the unrighteous, that all this is a punishment, without knowing what they did to deserve it! Only the bishops and the monasteries have profited, first from being paid to pray for safety, then by being exempted from taxes. Even though the Tatars will slaughter men, women and children, even though they'll burn cities level with the ground, they're wary of offending anybody's god.'

What Ivan heard was regret, anger and frustration; what he did not hear, and had not wanted to hear, was Stepan or any of the others refer to 'the Christian God' as though to something alien. Though he was half-hearted in his own devotions, that would have been truly disturbing. Even though his education in the Art Magic was less than it might have been, Ivan knew about the danger at such a time as this, with the structures of the world stretched thin, of a lack of something to believe in. It didn't have anything to do with religion, neither the Christian Church, nor the Moslems, nor the Jews or even, he supposed, the shamanist beliefs of the Tatars themselves. But without something, even so simple as the blind self-confidence of an undefeated *bogatyr'* champion, there were things in the blackness of Beyond that would slip into an empty space like a bluebottle into a meat-store, and leave all rotten in their passing.

'All right,' he said, 'if you want to call on aid from powers of long ago, then why not call on Byelobog the White God?' He was not expecting the looks of scorn he received from all three *boyaryy*.

'Call on a bright power at the dark of the year?' said Andrey Vladimirovich. 'What chance of success in that?'

'Byelobog is a sky-god,' said Mstislav Vasil'yevich, 'like the one the Tatars bow to. How do we know he would help us, and not them?'

Stepan Mikhailovich said nothing at all. He just smiled, and confronted with that smile and the layers of meaning behind it, Ivan felt the wine he had drunk turn more sour in his stomach than any amount of *kumys*. He was more grateful than ever that he didn't know how to help in this madness even if he wanted to. But it was plain something would have to be done about the crowns in the treasure-house, or they would not need his help at all. Except that he didn't know what to do.

The three watched him slam his chair back from the table, stand up, and walk to the door; all without making any move to impede him. But as Ivan shot the bolts back and flung it open – half-surprised that the corridor outside was not lined with Tatar soldiers sent to kill them all – Stepan called his name.

'Tsar Ivan,' the man said, 'we can rely on you to keep silent, I think. You are one of us now, like it or not, and nothing you could say will make the Tatar Khan believe otherwise. But just in case you think you might – '

Ivan stared at them coldly. 'I do not like threats,' he said. Stepan Mikhailovich shook his head.

'We do not threaten you, Majesty. We promise. Because we know that the Tsar of Khorlov has a wife, and a son, and a daughter. Good day to you, Majesty. Close the door as you leave . . .'

Volk Volkovich strolled through the shadowy streets of Sarai. Sometimes he ambled on two feet, and at other times he trotted on four; but nobody challenged him either way. Even with his drooping false moustache, he would never have passed for a Tatar or one of the squat, bandy-legged Chingisid Mongols. But without it, he was already lean-faced and long-jawed enough to pass once more for a Blue Türk from the high steppes, and one of particularly nasty disposition. There was even less risk of a challenge here than there had been in the siege-camp outside the walls of Ryazan' six years ago. Only in the smallest tribal *bok* might one man know the names and faces of all the others, and Ilkhan Batu's city of the Golden Horde was far too big for that. With a constantly changing population that never fell lower than eighty thousand, and any given fifty thousand of those consisting of the five *tuman* divisions at the Khan's disposal, there was no way in which anyone he might encounter could know every other.

He had been prowling around in one form or another for almost two weeks now, at first shadowing the column escorting Tsar Ivan from Khorlov and then later simply lurking in the vicinity of Sarai to see what could be seen. He had not been missed by Amragan *tarkhan* and the other Tatars of the escort; indeed, they might well have thought that he had been consumed by the wolf that had been tracking them. Now that was a laugh. But he had kept clear of Ivan and all the other Khorlovtsy Russians as well. Pretending to be one Tatar among so many thousand others was a simple matter, but being the one Rus among twenty who seemed able to come and go as he pleased was certain to attract attention. Nothing serious might come of it, but it would curtail his self-appointed activities as Tsar Ivan's spy in the enemy camp.

The Grey Wolf preferred his natural form, which he adopted on the quieter streets. That was not just because he found walking upright as uncomfortable as a man would find stumbling about on all fours, but the wolf-shape had added advantages beside comfort. True, he could no longer see a full range of colours, though after dark and in the deep shadows of the night, that was small loss. But he could see in darkness that would rob human eyes of more than just colour, he could hear farther than most humans could see in better light than this, and what he could not see or hear, he could smell. And he was so much quicker, stronger and more agile in his true shape that no mere human, not even Tsar Ivan, could ever hope to understand the difference.

Just because the streets were quiet did not always mean that they were empty, and with him prowling through them, they were most certainly not safe. The whole city and everyone in it felt uneasy. Volk Volkovich knew it was not because of him, since he had taken such pains to make sure nobody knew he was here. Not even Ivan. But there was a pressure in the air, a tight, hot sensation that left the Grey Wolf feeling permanently uncomfortable. In wolf's shape he was itchy all the time, as though his fur was growing inside-out, and when he took on human form he was prone to skull-splitting headaches. There was no reason for either, except that the whole of Sarai felt like a pot come to the boil and about to overflow – even though there was a weight on top of its lid, holding all that pressure back until – until what? Until the heat beneath it died away? Or the lid was lifted and the pressure released?

Or until something blew that lid clean off and whatever seethed inside came out in a searing rush.

He had been spotted two or three times now, even though he had never been more than a furry shape fading into the broken shadows beyond the doorway lanterns. There had been some slight bewilderment, but so far no alarm. The few men who had seen him were just common soldiers of the Khan, Mongols, Uighurs and the like. They had been intermittent city dwellers for the past few years, still slightly amazed by living among the buildings that their Ilkhan had chosen to build rather than destroy, and steppe nomads for all the rest of their lives. Their eyes told them that they had seen either a wolf, or one of the big herd-dogs that were no more than a well-fed generation removed from wolves. It was very much like Ryazan' all those years ago: since this was a city, what they had seen *couldn't* be a wolf, and therefore *had* to be a dog. A bloody big one, granted, but just a dog.

Volk Volkovich pricked his pointed ears forward and listened to the slurred mumblings of the man who reeled along the street ahead of him, unaware of the fanged grey bulk lurking in the darkness at his back. He was one of the burly, short-legged Uighur tribesmen, and though he was mumbling steadily to himself, all of it was in some Türko-Mongol dialect that made no sense to his unseen listener. Not that much of it would likely have been anything a spy might find of use, since of all the smells that hung in the air, the sharp buttermilk tang of *kumys* was predominant. With enough fermented mares'-milk on board, a steppe Tatar might see wolves anywhere – even when there wasn't one close enough behind him to take out his throat with a single leap-and-snap. The Grey Wolf grinned, curling back his long black lips in a leer that exposed teeth like an ivory picket fence.

It was tempting. Very tempting. Granted, the Tatars were not a clean people, but it wasn't the thought of stained clothing or grubby skin that was making the Grey Wolf's mouth water. There was warm, savoury stuff inside the dirtiest wrapping that . . .

Volk Volkovich closed his teeth silently on the desire to snap them shut and see the Tatar jump out of clothes and skin together. There was a time and a place for everything, and this was neither.

But there would be other times.

The Grey Wolf whined softly at the back of his throat and resumed man's shape in a hurry. It might be weak and gangly, with feeble teeth and a feeling of having wool wrapped round its senses; but right now it had fewer temptations to contend with. He heard another voice further down the street; it was louder and more coherent than that of the drunk soldier he had been tracking, and it said something in Türki. Volk Volkovich pulled his grey wolfskin cloak around his shoulders then up around his neck better to hide his face, and walked quickly and quietly in the opposite direction. Even though he was dressed to look like a Türk and could recognise the sound of their language, he could neither understand nor speak it and made a point of avoiding those who might. If a man who presumed they might both be of the same tribe tried to start a conversation, the sinister looks and sullen, ill-tempered snarls that helped maintain his disguise would only go so far. The voice, having no success with Türki, shifted to Farsee and doubled in volume.

Volk Volkovich smiled thinly and kept on walking. He knew the sound of an officer bawling out a subordinate for drunkenness well enough. A *käshik-jagun* commanding one hundred of the Khan's own guard, was outraged to find one of his own men staggering tipsily through the street – not because he was drunk, since all Tatars from the late Khakhan Ögotäi on down were great drinkers – but that he was doing so at a time when he was supposed to be on duty at Khan Batu's treasure-house.

Treasure-house?

The Grey Wolf froze and flattened against the nearest wall, listening as well as those feeble human ears would let him. The officer's infuriated bellowing helped considerably, since he was one of those junior commanders whose idea of a dressing-down was not merely to list the penalties he intended to award, but to enumerate those duties which should have been performed by the transgressor and which would now be doubled to help him remember them the next time. At least one of his listeners had no difficulty committing them to memory the first time around, and felt half-inclined to thank the man for finally giving purpose to all the creeping around Sarai he had suffered this past while. If a collection of stolen Russian crowns was not kept in the Khan's own treasure-house, then he, Volk Volkovich, wanted to know why.

Finding the place was going to be easiest of all. Still yelling obliging explanations of what he was doing, the *jagun* had begun to haul his swaying soldier towards where the man was supposed to be standing guard, declaring that he would stand guard anyway if the *jagun* had to spike him upright to the door. Volk Volkovich grinned nastily at that, knowing that the officer was both capable of committing such an atrocity, and well within his rights to do so. Discipline in the Golden Horde was brutal; it had to be. In an army of barbaric savages whose response to any opposition was force, superior force was all they understood.

Neither of the Tatars heard the faint sound like an intake of breath as the Grey Wolf returned once again to his preferred shape. He drifted along behind them with no more disturbance than a curl of smoke, listening while the officer's imagination flowered as his voice returned to a more restrained level, and that sharp-fanged smile never left his muzzle the whole time.

It could not have been fear of the various threatened punishments which sobered up the would-be sentry, because he had never been sober enough to hear them in the first place. But the intermittent shaking that punctuated some particularly inventive unpleasantness, and the constant dragging through the dark, wet streets of Sarai by arm or shoulder or by the scruff of the neck, and the tumbles into puddles of standing water and less savoury stuff that happened too often to be accidental, all served to restore some sort of coherence to his speech and movement.

Not that he was fool enough to make use of either. When the *jagun* at last shoved him disgustedly towards a low, squat building, the soldier's flailing stagger and ultimate collapse at the feet of the one guard who *was* on duty would have brought satisfaction to the stoniest heart. Certainly it was effective enough that the officer contented himself with just a single kick before striding off about his own interrupted business, leaving the sprawled Tatar to pick himself up warily, wipe himself off – which the Grey Wolf's nose suggested was a wasted effort – and commence his guarding duties for the night as though nothing had happened.

So this was the treasure-house of the Golden Horde. Like the Ilkhan Batu's Golden Pavilion, it stood alone at the centre of an open square. Torches flared and spat from iron brackets on the doorposts, and there were others at the corners of the four-square building and in the middle of each length of wall. Their pools of yellow light overlapped each other like the scales of a good hauberk, leaving no shadows where an intruder could creep close to the walls. Even if a potential thief could get so close without being seen, there was little that could be done; the windows were small, barred on the outside and closed from the inside with iron shutters, and there was only that single door.

Volk Volkovich lay down in the lee of a house on the far side of the square, laid his head on his paws, and studied the problem. He was not discouraged, just mildly amused that he had not noticed this place before. Probably, he suspected, because it looked like so many other houses in Sarai; with Rus noblemen locked up here and there, guards were not uncommon, and as for houses set off by themselves, the place had been built by so many diverse hands and in so many styles of architecture that no one construction looked much more peculiar than another.

There were only the two guards, each one of which took turns every few minutes to walk right around the building before coming back to the shelter offered by the awning over the doorway. There were the windows, with their bars and shutters. There was the door itself, bolted at top and bottom – but not locked, he noticed with interest. There was no keyhole in the planks. The why and wherefore of that was a conundrum in itself, but not one he wasted much time on. Either the Khan trusted his men not to steal, or they were too well-trained to steal, or they were too afraid of their own commanders. And that was probably the most likely of all.

He could make use of that. Any discipline imposed by fear of a superior could be put to good use by anyone bold enough to be just such a superior – and from the few words that had been exchanged before the *jagun* officer went on his way, neither of these men would be surprised to be addressed in Farsee. Volk Volkovich knew he could speak Farsee as well as anyone in Sarai, and play the harshness of a Tatar officer better than most real ones.

A few minutes later, the two sentries heard footsteps approaching from the far side of the square. They were firm, steady footsteps, the tread of someone with nothing to hide and every right to be where he was. That meant only one thing. A surprise inspection. The sober guard shot a sidelong, accusing glance at his erstwhile drunken companion, before both men gripped their spears tighter and straightened up from the occupational slouch of all sentries on a boring duty late at night.

Volk Volkovich had seen all of it, and was well pleased. For all his dislike of his human shape, its eyes and ears were almost inhumanly sharp, and he had watched the two Tatars convince themselves and each other of what to expect before they saw him emerge from the uncertain shadows beyond the flickering torch-light.

They saw a Türk officer loom over them, six feet tall and looking even more, towering above the stocky Uighurs as he stared coldly down at them from eerie eyes that seemed to be illuminated from within. He was not an officer whose face they knew, but they knew he had to be an officer, to be so heavy-footed; worse, from the grim expression he was wearing, he knew that one of them had been caught drunk when he should have been on duty, and worst of all, he didn't know or care which one.

'Hui! Report!' Volk Volkovich allowed just a little of his own true wolf's voice to edge the Farsee accent, so that there was a snarl like the tearing of metal behind that single word. The Tatars were not frightened as they would have been had he appeared in his true shape, but they were most respectful.

'Nothing to report, Lord,' said the sober one, saluting fist to forehead in the Tatar manner. The drunk one wisely said nothing at all, and Volk Volkovich could hear him breathing shallowly so that any smell of *kumys* couldn't reach the officer's nostrils. He needn't have worried. No ordinary officer of the Horde whether Mongol, Türk or Tatar, could have smelt anything other than the refuse in which the man had fallen on his way to duty.

'Good.' A pause, then a hard stare. 'You,' to the other man, who twitched perceptibly. 'You stink. Stand away.' The soldier saluted in his turn, then gratefully set off on a round of the treasure-house – moving from the sound of his footfalls in no great haste, and probably hoping that this particular officer would have gone by the time he completed his circuit of the building. He was right, since Volk Volkovich had no intention of staying here longer than necessary.

But what *was* necessary was to see the inside of the treasure-house. It concerned the Gates again. One look around inside the building would be enough for him to enter it safely without troubling the guards again, stepping quietly out of this world and then back into it again on the other side of the closed and bolted door. But without that look he stood a more than even chance of sharing the same floor space as whatever golden things were piled up within the Khan's treasury. There would be little satisfaction in finding one of the lost crowns of the Rus domains if the damned thing was embedded in his liver.

'All in order inside?'

'Inside, Lord?'

'Inside.' He glared at the guard as though the man was half-witted. 'Where the treasure is. Where a thief would be.'

'I heard nothing, Lord.'

'Just so. You would not hear a thief. Open the door.' There was just the tiniest hesitation, not so much suspicious as confused and put off-balance by a change in routine. 'Or have you some reason why not, uu?'

That was enough. 'At once, Lord!'

'And quietly. Just in case.' The Grey Wolf gave the man a quick grin to set him back at as much of his ease as he could find, a grin that promised rewards and maybe promotion if anything was in fact discovered, and if not, a report to the man's officer that if not actually good, would at least not be bad.

The bolts, well-greased, slid back in silence, and the door swung open. Volk Volkovich reached up and took one of the doorpost torches from its bracket, and stepped forward into the blackness. It would not have surprised his cynical mind to discover that the place was empty, that all the torches and sentries and thick walls were just a bluff and that real security lay

269

in concealment of the treasure rather than guarding it. He would have been wrong.

For just an instant it seemed as though there was only darkness in the treasure-house, darkness that drank the yellow torchlight like wine. Then he raised its sputtering, smoky flame above his head and the light returned, reflected back from what lay strewn across the floor and heaped like windblown autumn leaves waist-high along the walls, a thousand, thousand glints of icy brilliance, like the eyes of his own people, murderous gemstones embroidered on the sable fabric of the night.

The Grey Wolf had never seen the riches scattered in the *Sira-Ger* at Ilkhan Batu's slippered feet, but if he had, then he would have known why they were discarded. They were merely splendid, as befitting the court of the Splendid Khan, but once set against the magnificence of such a garnering as this, they would have become valueless, cheap and tawdry. What these four strong walls contained were the fruits of the mightiest plundering that the wide white world had ever known, wealth enough to make all other conquerors from Aleksandr the Macedonian and the Roman Caesars gnash their teeth in envy and own themselves defeated.

He had long thought that the Golden Horde was named for the *altan uruk*, the ruling Golden Clan who traced their descent from Chinghis-Khan and from whose family alone the Great Khans were chosen, but he could see now where the name truly had its birth. In this stone nest; from this golden egg. Batu's armies had crushed every realm from the Urals to the Danube, from the Straits of Hormuz to the Baltic, and while much of that wealth had been channelled back to the heart of the empire, all the rest of it was here. It was a golden hoard indeed, a hoard worthy of Zmey Gorynyts and Tugarin his son, worthy maybe of the Dragons of the old times – and perhaps even they might concede that they were satisfied at last.

Volk Volkovich was glad he was not human. A man might not have resisted the lure of so much gold in chain and plate and coin and bar, so many jewels raw and cut, set in their mounts and loose like pebbles, so much sheer power that wealth could buy. But a wolf had little use for precious things, and as for the power, he could feel it dinning at his brain as though he was standing right beneath the great bell of Khorlov's cathedral tower.

And there they were, all in a row: twelve wooden boxes, carved, inlaid, jewelled, each one different, but alike enough as form must follow function. The crowns of twelve kingdoms, taken by conquest and now stacked up and ignored in the darkness. It was all here: the power of untold years of ruling, the strength of laws and armies and successive generations unbroken until now, all humming in his ears and inside his skull like a swarm of monstrous golden bees. Here was the source of the itch, of the headaches, of the pressure grinding down on Sarai like a fist kneading dough. Volk Volkovich thought of that one image, and flinched. What happens to dough when the kneading is done? It goes into the oven. Human or inhuman, the Grey Wolf did not like to dwell on what sort of oven waited for this city and the people in it. Especially when some of those people were his friends.

He turned about and walked from the treasure-house so fast that the torch flame roared softly above his head, almost flung it at the sentry, nodded a curt 'all's-well' at the startled man, then slammed the door and bolted it. Oak and cold iron had some small use in magic, so they said. It might hold back the wild energies that swirled within the treasure-chamber for long enough that he could get to where Ivan and the other Khorlovtsy folk were being held. Despite their differences, despite their arguments and fights, the Grey Wolf knew he had to speak to Mar'ya Morevna. He did not know what was about to happen, but he did know that she was the only person in Sarai who could prevent it . . .

Chapter Ten

The Khanate of the Golden Horde;
September, AD 1243

Mar'ya Morevna ached in all her bones right down to the tiny ones of hands and feet. She had never ridden so far and so hard in such a short time, and had come to understand with a painful clarity why it was that the Khan's *chapar* couriers swathed their bellies with tight bandages. It was supposed to hold their guts in place and cushion them against the jolting of a constant hard gallop; but if the way she felt now was an indication, it also probably saved time in the infirmary later.

The distance between Sarai and Khorlov that had taken Amragan *tarkhan* four weeks, she and the escort had covered in eleven gruelling days. It had become a stubborn point of honour with her to display no more discomfort than the hard-bitten *käshik* horsemen, and she succeeded – though whether she had gained anything approaching their respect was hard to say. They had certainly gained hers.

As members of the Khan's own guard, even the common troopers each outranked a *minghan* commander of one thousand in the ordinary army of the Golden Horde, and when fully trained was reckoned fit enough at need to command a *tuman* of ten thousand. Rather than the furious gallop of the express couriers from one post house and a change of horses to the next, each one of these thousand men had two or three spare horses in tow, and were capable of maintaining a monotonous pace of walk-run-walk from dawn to dusk, changing mounts on the move, eating or sleeping in the saddle, and halting only to perform their hasty eliminations. Even though the roads they travelled were no more than dusty or muddy tracks, the route outlined by wooden poles against those times when the changing weather swept the road away completely, there was never an occasion when they were lost.

The only real relief was now, in the evenings when they halted and made camp. Even that was a double-edged comfort, because Mar'ya Morevna found that her uneasy rest lasted only long enough for strained muscles to stiffen, so that they were doubly painful when the march began again at dawn. But that did not trouble the Tatars. What would have disturbed them more was the prospect of travelling by night, because if the Chingisid khans were afraid of thunder and the anger of Tängri, these ordinary soldiers were afraid of the dark.

For all her knowledge, Mar'ya Morevna could not understand why. Never mind bears, or wolves, or even Volk Volkovich; these Tatars were by far the most dangerous creatures in the area, and there was a twisted feeling of security about riding in their midst. But they were still fearful to be out on the cold black earth of the open steppe after nightfall, and none of them would tell her why.

The old shaman Beyki was a little more forthcoming. Not much, but enough. 'Erlik Khan is lord of the empty places,' he mumbled, chewing on a strip of dried meat and washing it down with swigs of *kumys* as he rode along, swaying, always swaying, but never falling off. One skinny arm waved towards the desolate horizon, a grand, sweeping gesture for all that it was made by a stick wrapped in leathers and furs. 'Huu, places like these.'

Like the movement of his jaws on the meat, his words went around and around and always returned to the same place, chewing sense slowly to pieces. 'We pay him no heed in the daytime, for we pray to Tängri, the Blue Sky, and bright day. Erlik hates that. Hui! He hates us. He dwells in the earth, in the dark, where we give him our bodies. But not our lives. He eats only the dead.'

His old, old eyes gazed at Mar'ya Morevna, cold as frozen flint, glittering with ancient wisdom and ancient wickedness. 'Huu. That is Erlik Khan. That is why they are afraid of the dark. That is why they fear the night. They fear Erlik. It is good that men should have something to fear, uu? Or they might become too bold even for their gods.'

It was all superstition, all stories, all nonsense. Mar'ya Morevna knew that when she heard it, and dismissed it as such. Until nightfall, when the shadows gathered, and she heard the old man's creaking voice in every sound in the dark of her tent. She did not sleep well that night, or for many nights after, and it still muttered at the back of her mind in uneasy dreams.

Mar'ya Morevna avoided Beyki even now, though with more reason. The Great Crown of Khorlov was thumping against her knee, its carrying box wrapped three layers thick in sheepskin and the whole bundle stuffed into a leather bag that hung now from her saddle. There had been a certain wariness among the Tatars when she emerged from the Treasury in Khorlov with it tucked beneath her arm, and they seemed only too happy to allow her to have responsibility for carrying it. That wariness had been much to Mar'ya Morevna's advantage, because there were two other things about her that were not quite the same.

One was an additional pair of saddlebags slung across the withers of her horse, quite ordinary, containing nothing more than the changes of clothing needed by a weak and feeble woman who was not as tough as she pretended. None of them had troubled to unwrap the carefully folded robes and blouses and embroidered shifts to stare in fear and wonder at the books they were concealing.

And none of them had thought anything of it when Mar'ya Morevna's horse went lame. That lameness had been carefully arranged: a handy stone scooped up from the ground and tucked into the frog of one hoof, to make the animal useless for more of the hard riding that had brought them up to Khorlov without doing any lasting harm. It had given her the excuse she needed to take a fresh horse and a remount from the kremlin stables, and the Tatars, who treated their own shaggy ponies better than they treated either their enemies or themselves, had been in full agreement. Though her heart had been pounding up into her mouth the whole time, no-one had scrutinised her choice too closely – and both Sivka and Chyornyy had displayed enough good sense to keep their own mouths shut.

It felt pleasant to hold some of the advantages for a change, although knowing exactly how to make best use of them was another matter.

'What do you mean, she's gone for the real Great Crown? She can't bring that thing back here!'

Volk Volkovich was trying to keep his voice under control, even though Ivan could hear a howl of anguish that was pure wolf trying to break through the human speech. It had been almost midnight when his hammering on the door of the house had sent half-dressed servants scurrying in all directions, but Ivan had been glad to see the Grey Wolf again after so long, and eager to hear what he had been doing. That had been before he learned what Volk Volkovich had discovered in the Khan's treasure-house, and how that long-threatened rending apart of the world's very structure was likely to begin even though the full number of crowns had not yet been gathered together.

'The scheme with the false crown was a failure,' said Ivan wearily. 'The Tatar shaman knew it was a fake from the first moment he picked it up. They sent that same shaman – and an escort of a thousand men – to make sure we can't try the same thing again. She can't *not* bring it back.'

'You know what will happen, don't you?' said Volk Volkovich.

'I can't begin to imagine. But I can guess.' Ivan's mouth twisted in a sort of smile. 'If you see what I'm trying to say.'

'It's as near accurate as you could manage without seeing. And you would not want to see.' The Grey Wolf had been leaning against the wall in another of those studied human postures he liked to adopt, as if taking refuge in something that required conscious thought other than the matters crowding his mind. Ivan watched him straighten up in a way no human ever could, with a disturbing flexion of limbs and muscles that, though he was still a man's shape, served to remind the young Tsar almost more forcefully than a full-scale shapeshift that his companion might look human but was not, and never had been.

'Is there anything that can be done without Mar'yushka being here? Anything at all?' That desperation had begun to infect even his voice, and Ivan had always prided himself on being able to conceal his feelings either in Council or out of it. Volk Volkovich shook his head. 'Because we talked about this before. I had thought if we could somehow – well, somehow get into wherever the crowns were kept, this treasure-house for example, and take one or two of them away . . . No?'

The luminescent yellow-green eyes came up to stare at him for so long that there was almost a feeling of heat at the back of Ivan's skull. 'Yes,' said Volk Volkovich, a low rumble of triumph in a voice gone suddenly soft and speculative. 'Yes.' Then he paused, and Ivan heard his teeth click. 'Or at least, maybe.'

'How did "yes" become "maybe" just like that?'

'A man pulling burning thatch off his roof doesn't know how much good it might do. None, if the house is on fire.'

'But if it's only the straw that's alight, he'll save the rest of the building.' Then suddenly Ivan chuckled, a sound of more wholesome amusement than the warped and bitter laughter he had been uttering of late. 'If even at a time like this we end up speaking in parables, the pair of us have spent too much time in Dmitriy Strel'tsin's company. But we should try it. We *have* to try it.' He grinned wickedly, his always-mercurial mood completing its swing up out of the pit of depression he had dug for himself. '*Bozhe moy!* If it was my house on fire, I'd even climb up and pee on the thatch if I thought it might help.'

'You might get your . . . self singed,' said the Grey Wolf, quite straight-faced, 'and that would scarcely endear me to your lady wife.'

'You might be surprised. If the fire was out.' It was not his place to make Mar'ya Morevna's apologies for her, or even to come right out and tell Volk Volkovich that she had had a change of heart about him; but there were other ways than the crudely verbal to indicate that matters had changed for the better, and his own attitude was one of them.

The Grey Wolf had been his friend for long enough to know that. From master and servant, Prince and chief henchman, Tsar and favoured retainer, they had grown more like elder and younger brother. In her less acidic moments, Mar'ya Morevna had suggested that was borne out by the ease and inventiveness with which they insulted each other when the mood was on them, but Ivan suspected it was more than that. He still wasn't quite enough at ease with the Grey Wolf to regard such a skin-changer as a brother – although this reservation was from a man whose three

276

brothers-in-law were all shape-shifters themselves – but it was good for a man in authority, Tsar, Prince or whatever title the Tatars finally left him, to have a friend whose friendship was not rooted in ambition or profit. It gave him someone whose truth was honest, not slanted for favour, and it gave him someone before whom he too could be honest. Honestly afraid, sometimes, as in the past few minutes, before he was given that straw to clutch at. Ivan smiled to himself. Even if it was a burning straw.

'To business,' he said; then hesitated, looked about, reached for the jug of cooling spiced honey and water *sbiten'* on the dead stove and raised it in a toast. 'To business,' he repeated briskly, and swigged the stuff. His face twisted as he got an involuntary mouthful of the sediment. '*Akh, proklinatyu!*' Ivan swore, bending to spit the gritty stuff through the stove door and into the ashes that filled it. 'Damnit! Unlike straw, this stuff is better when it's burning hot.'

'Of course.'

'Believe me, it is. Now – how do we get at the crowns?'

By the time Volk Volkovich had completed outlining the half-formed idea that had crossed his mind, Ivan had long since discarded the *sbiten'* and was sipping at white wine cut with rainwater. If that idea was successful, and even without Mar'ya Morevna it could well prove so, then a small anticipatory celebration was called for and cold *sbiten'* was not his idea of a proper drink.

'Mar'yushka and even the children know more about the Gate spells than I do,' he said finally. 'But if I understand what you are driving at, then now that you've seen the place, you can come and go much as you please?'

'Without becoming a part of the jewellery collection. Yes, I can.'

'And take one of the crowns away with you each time?'

'No.'

The bluntness of the answer caught Ivan offguard, and he was halfway through an enthusiastic scheme for getting each crown back to its proper domain – if not wearer, since many were dead – before it hit home. 'What do you mean, no?'

'Usually the opposite of yes.'

Ivan Aleksandrovich knew that sharp-voiced reply of old, and knew too that the anger of it was directed in and not out. 'I should have said, why not? Surely once the access Gate has been established, it's a straightforward matter of – '

'Entry and exit, yes, that's straightforward enough. But Vanya, my friend, in all this you're forgetting one very important factor. This.' For an instant, an eyeblink, there was a huge grey-furred, white-fanged wolf sitting in the chair opposite Ivan. It was nothing like a full change of his shape, more an image left on the eye like the aftermath of lightning, but it was still enough to send Ivan bolt upright in shock. 'I am not a man. I'm a creature of sorcery. And I can no more lift one of those crowns and carry it away than you could do so with Khorlov's kremlin. Power has weight, to those who can sense it. Your pardon, Vanya, I mean no insult by this, but even the way that ordinary people speak of such things suggests that they know something of these matters. Do you not speak of, er, the burden of power; or the heavy head that wears a crown; or the weight of responsibility?'

'Those are all figures of speech, nothing more.'

'Are they? Words have a weight and power of their own.'

'I know that, but . . .'

'But?' The Grey Wolf pounced on his hesitation as though it was a careless rabbit.

'But never mind. It's late.' Ivan stared down into his cup of watered wine, then up into those glowing eyes that had been so much more a wolf's eyes tonight than he had ever seen before. 'And getting later all the time. Tell me how I can help.'

'Not you. But the children could.'

Ivan had been half-expecting those words for a long time now. He had been the one who proposed that same idea to Mar'ya Morevna weeks ago. And yet to hear the same thing suggested by someone else was appalling. Especially when that someone, who no matter how good a friend was not a member of his family, had not troubled even to sound regretful. The tone of voice in which those words were spoken could not have changed their meaning one way or the other, and the Grey Wolf didn't bother trying.

Because he was forewarned, Ivan kept his temper on its leash. But because he was their father, he had to know if there was not

278

some other way to circumvent the problem than by putting his own son and daughter at such risk. There was not.

'I can use the Gating spells as naturally as I draw my breath, but because of what I am, I can't take any of the crowns away.' Trying to correct his earlier error, Volk Volkovich spoke softly and with something closer to sympathy. 'You could take as many of them as you could reasonably carry – but passing with them through the Gate might kill you. Nikolai and Anastasya are betwixt and between. They most likely couldn't steal away more than one crown apiece, but they can come and go between the worlds as easily as – ' and he snapped his fingers. 'And that at least would be two coals less from the fire.'

'Volk'ya, they're only seven years old!'

'You are a tsar,' said the Grey Wolf simply. 'A tsar must learn to sacrifice even those he loves the best for the greater good. Your father did not stand in your way when you went against the Teutonic Knights – '

'But I was a grown man!'

'You were twenty-one. About three times the age of the twins. Tsar Aleksandr was almost seventy. Again, about three times the age of the son who was going off to war. The proportions have changed very little, so where's the difference?'

'If you can't see it – '

'I can't.'

'Then you're even more inhuman than you claim.'

'Perhaps. I would have said that one is either human or not, rather than try to measure such things by degrees.'

'Try to understand me, Volk Volkovich. These are children; I was not. I knew what I was doing, and why – '

'And what makes you think that *they* do not? Ivan, I think you do your son and daughter less than justice. Children they may be, but blind and foolish? No. Tell them the problem – if they don't know it already – and ask them to help in its solution. Let them make their own decision. It has been done before. Is there not a tradition that a father may give his only son to die for the greater good?'

Ivan froze as all the spoken and unvoiced meanings bit into him like teeth. Then he signed himself carefully with the life-giving cross and stared coldly at this self-confessed creature of sorcery. 'Blasphemy is hardly an appropriate argument.'

'If you believe that your God and His Son did this to save the generations yet unborn, then where is the blasphemy?'

'That I should dare suggest – '

'You did not. I did.' The Grey Wolf watched Ivan, and behind that gaze, as bestial as anything seen glittering in the shadowed forest, there was a sadness that had no place in the eyes of a wolf. 'Are we enemies, then?' he said.

'No. Damn you, no. I can't make an enemy of a friend who has just been doing what he said he would – telling me the things I need to know but don't want to hear.' Ivan slammed down the wine-cup hard enough that its contents spattered out across the table, but he paid that no heed. Instead he put out one dripping hand, and after a moment Volk Volkovich held out his own so that they met in a gesture that became somehow not a handshake but the wrist-clasp of comradeship from older times. 'I understand. So would Mar'ya Morevna. But even so, I'm glad she isn't here.'

'If she was, we wouldn't need to consider such an alternative. She is not. Your children are. So ask them.'

'When? Now? They're asleep!'

Volk Volkovich glanced at the shuttered window and the windy, rainy night beyond it, and perhaps at something beyond the night that he alone could see. 'The sooner the better,' he said softly. 'I was there. I felt what was building in that place. Tomorrow morning may be too late.'

Nikolai and Anastasya shared a room at the end of the corridor, though each had their own little truckle bed tucked into opposite corners; the Tatars had been that generous at least. There was an oil lamp high up on the wall, clumsily glazed in thick amber glass, throwing dark golden light to keep the worst of the shadows at bay, and each child had the usual two or three toy animals to keep them company at night.

Ivan could see them from the doorway where he stood. A bear of stuffed rabbit fur, loved to shapelessness and premature mange; a woolly lamb so distorted by years of affection that it would have given him nightmares at that age even to have it in the same room; a bird with drooping wings and embroidered plumage so gaudy that it could only represent flames; and two small grey wolves, fuzzy and friendly, with little resemblance that he could see to the sinister reality.

Even though all the toys were scattered on the beds and close to hand, these wolves were the only ones being cuddled. Ivan gazed down at his sleeping children, and through the surge of warmth and love for them, he still felt just the tiniest pang of jealousy, the merest hint of what Mar'ya Morevna must have felt the first time she looked in on her children and saw what they turned to for comfort in the dark.

Though he reached out to stroke their sleeping faces, it was a long time before he dared to wake them. Heavy-eyed and drowsy, neither child was quite sure what was going on at first; and the first thing that registered on either of them was the tall, lean, grey-haired and grey-cloaked figure standing just outside the door. As first Kolya and then 'Tasha scrambled out of bed in a flurry of blankets and long nightshirts, more awake at the sight of the Grey Wolf than their own father, Ivan felt that jealousy return, driving its spike up into his gullet so that for just a second his eyes stung and his choked throat refused to swallow. But its hurt died an instant later when they came back, scampering on bare feet across the chilly floor, to swarm all over him and babble thanks for bringing back their Uncle Wolf as if Volk Volkovich was just another treat given as a present for being good. Ivan looked at them, and at the Grey Wolf, and at the wall, and found that if he closed his own eyes really tightly shut, the tears couldn't escape.

'I am a friend,' said the deep voice behind him. 'A bringer of gifts, a guide to the strange beauties of the worlds beyond the world.' That big hand came down with a reassuring pressure on his shoulder. 'But you are their father, and the *gospozha Tsaritsa* Mar'ya Morevna is their mother, and they know where the difference begins.'

Sitting up after midnight, fully dressed as if it was daylight outside, and drinking their hot milk from real adult's wine-cups, Kolya and 'Tasha were enjoying themselves immensely. They had even seen their father the Tsar rebuild a fire in the stove with his own hands, and swear – though without much originality and no new words at all – at the servants who would have come in to do the work for him. 'This is a family matter,' he had said, among other things. It was all very thrilling and grown-up.

Ivan sneezed twice, dusted ash and bark chips off his fingers and squatted back from the stove, eyed it critically with his hand on one side, then decided it would do one way or the other and closed the iron door with a clank. He eyed the twins sidelong, without being noticed, and watched them grin and giggle and nudge one another with their elbows to provoke still more giggles. *Tell them the problem and ask for their help.* That was easy to say, easier still when you were not the person having to shape the question into something a seven-year-old mind could understand. Who was to say that the prospect of things crawling into the world from Outside would not be just as exciting as being awake after bedtime?

But then, why shape it at all? These two precocious infants already knew more about the sorcerous Gates than Ivan had been able to force into his brain during all of his years of study. They probably knew more than their mother, and had she not said as much? Tsar Ivan of Khorlov stood up, wiped the stove-grease from his hands, considered a drink to give himself some courage – *for talking to your own son and daughter?* – then threw the idea aside. Tonight of all nights, his mind had to stay sharp.

'Nikolai Ivanovich, Anastasya Ivanovna, pay heed to what I tell you.' He watched them compose themselves as best they could, but these were the same children he had once said had all the attention span of a mayfly, or some such insect. Asking them to listen closely was as optimistic as putting a fish on horseback and expecting it to ride. 'In this city of Sarai is a strong place, a treasure-house where the Ilkhan Batu – '

'Old Stinkyfeet,' said Nikolai helpfully.

'Er, yes, him; anyway, that's where he keeps the crowns of twelve kingdoms, and – '

'You found them?' Anastasya burst out, her eyes shining with delight. 'Oh, *batyushka*, how clever you are! Mamma told us they were here, and we knew anyway because they made our heads hurt, but not even she knew where they were!'

The dismissive little flick of one hand that the Grey Wolf made just then was perhaps the most generous thing he had ever done for the Tsar of Khorlov, and Ivan determined to reward his friend and retainer properly. But later. And preferably when the twins weren't around, requiring explanations, elaborations, and all the other things he was glad he didn't need to do right now. There was a certain lack of surprise about the discovery that indicated, as he had suspected, that his children knew as much about matters in hand as he did. And probably more.

'Then do you know what I was going to ask you?'

There was silence; then a pause, and some muttering and nudging of the 'you do it' – 'no, you' variety, before Nikolai sat up very straight, folded his hands in his lap and recited carefully, ' "That one who may shall take away a token of great power and so lessen the gathered weight of that power, so that what remains still laid on the fabric of the world may be made lightened and the render – no, *rend*ing thereof be set aside." ' The boy relaxed a little. 'That's what it says in the book.'

'What book?' Ivan felt certain that he knew the answer already, but there was always the chance he might be wrong. He was right.

Besonyat-vazavat. That was the book. *Enciervanul Doamnisoar*, in its old title. *On the Summoning of Demons*.

'You were reading that?' said Ivan, doing his best not to sound as wild as he felt. There was a momentary rush of relief when both of the children shook their heads. That lasted for no more than the drawing of a breath.

'We couldn't read it,' said Natasha. 'But Mamma read it to us.'

'Not the best bits,' Nikolai added, sounding a little resentful.

There had been no surprise that the twins knew more about the crowns than he did. Hearing where they had learned about the problem was another matter. Maybe it was true what people said, that children's minds were a great deal more resilient when it came to horrors than they were given credit for. Ivan, no child, was not prepared to say one way or the other. All he knew was that *his* children were not among those that the philosophers were thinking about, and that he, though fully grown and adult in most things, had lain awake and sweating after skimming through that particular book for the first time. And even then, he had taken pains to avoid 'the best bits'.

'I can take them to the treasure-house, Vanya,' said the Grey Wolf. 'No need for you to come.'

Ivan blinked once, twice, then turned an empty stare on Volk Volkovich, wondering whether his sudden spasm of horror had been quite so obvious. He shook his head. 'They are my son and my daughter. I'm coming with you. Though I may be nothing more than dead weight, an ignorant, uneducated lump of meat, I go where they go.'

'I didn't mean that.'

'Old friend,' said Ivan, punching the Grey Wolf amiably in the ribs, though hard enough to hurt, 'what you meant or didn't mean doesn't matter. It's the way I feel right now. Mar'ya Morevna would have been the saviour of this undertaking; and her two children are a good second-best. While I . . .' If he had drunk enough to blunt his sense of pride completely, Ivan might have said exactly where he felt he stood amid these cold equations. Instead he walked to the wall and unhooked the *shashka* sabre hanging there, attached its scabbard to his belt, and turned around with the blade half drawn. The metallic sound as he slapped it home again was as sharp as the clapping of hands. 'I can use this, if it's needed. Shall we go?'

Ivan shook the clangour of abrupt passage between the worlds out of his head, and tried not to be sick as what had once passed for equilibrium reeled through his inner ear backwards and upside down. He sniffed through a nose that was trying to bleed from the impossible pressures that had crushed against his body both inside and out, and decided in a detached sort of way that as a form of travel, there was little to recommend this process.

At least – looking sourly from side to side – not unless the traveller was an *oboroten'* wolfling or a child quickened somewhere halfway between Moist-Mother-Earth and the Summer Country. The ordinary route of Gate and circle might have been more dangerous, but it was at least more comfortable. This way was to be like a sheet of parchment folded in upon itself a thousand times to fit through the spaces that separated one world from the next, and then brutally unfolded again at the final destination. Small wonder he had a bloody nose and his ears rang. If the Firebird had felt like this when it was snatched through the world-warp created by the stolen crowns, then no wonder its temper had been fraying at the edges. Ivan would have been grateful had it been just his temper; his mind, his body, the very stitches that held his muscles together were all unravelling at once.

And in the light that someone – not he – had conjured up to see by, the floor was winking at him with a million yellow eyes. Then he blinked, and blinked again, and all those eyes slid into focus with a snap.

The golden hoard of the Golden Horde was everything that Volk Volkovich had said, and more. His disinterest had taken colour from his words, and castrated the lust that such a mountain of gold might have for men of normal appetites. Men like Ivan Aleksandrovich Khorlovskiy.

To be Tsar of Khorlov was one thing; but Khorlov had never been a wealthy realm, and the gold and jewels scattered here could have made it a domain second to none in the wide white world. Ivan went down on one knee and scooped up gemstones in his two cupped hands; rubies like blood, sapphires like a summer sky at evening, emeralds green as grass and pearls like quicksilver tears, all of them shot through with the cold white fire of diamonds.

He poured them like sand back down through his fingers so that they clattered blazing in their myriad colours across the hard stone floor, then lifted another handful. This time it was of gold, minted coins with the heads of dead or conquered kings; and tiny, perfect ingots each half the length of a man's fingers that a highborn lady might wear strung on wires to adorn herself; all of them cold against his skin but the weight of them extraordinary, and each possessed of its own yellow metal inner warmth. Batu Khan was no Dragon, to know the place and the provenance and the value of every last jewel here, and the fill of just one belt-pouch, a quantity so small among all this as to be dust beneath the feet, would secure Khorlov and all the people of Khorlov for generations yet to come.

Then a coin, just one coin, fell to the floor and rolled chiming like a gong to join the snowdrift heaping of its mates.

'No, *batyushka*,' said Natasha. Her pale brows were drawn together as the grinding pressure of the place crushed down on her brain, but there was no disapproval of his action in her voice, no condemnation; more surprise that he would have touched this treasure in the first place. 'Put them down. They're dirty.'

Nikolai came over and crouched down by Ivan's side. He too had the look of a child whose head was aching, and as he put out his own hands to hold his father's, Ivan could see how they shook.

'This is a horrible place, Papa,' he said softly. 'Can't you see the blood?'

Ivan looked; at his son, at his daughter, and at the riches held within his two cupped hands. Riches taken from a hundred conquered cities, riches paid for with a hundred thousand lives. And he saw.

The gold wept congealing drools of sticky crimson down between his fingers, and the smell that clogged his nostrils was no longer that of gold, but the sheared-copper stench of blood. Stealing it to use for Khorlov's benefit would be like building a palace on a foundation of skulls – and Ivan had seen skulls enough since he left home. He opened his hands and the gold cascaded to the ground. Far away he could hear the high, metallic echoes of metal against stone; but closer, the only sound was a repetitive damp thud, like dropped gobbets of raw meat.

'Here,' said Volk Volkovich.

The Grey Wolf had thrown back the lids of all the wooden boxes, and to Ivan's eyes the royal crowns within them glowed with a cleaner radiance than the soiled gold and jewels on the floor. He stood up, wiping off the stains on his hands that now only he could see, and examined the carving and the decoration on each box in turn, in an attempt to learn the origin of the crown it held. 'This, this and this,' he said at last, lifting each one from its padded case as he spoke. 'One each. That should serve to do something at least.'

Volk Volkovich gazed at them, and then at him. 'Why one and not another?' he said. Ivan closed the wooden boxes one after another, a chorus of small, sharp snapping sounds, then touched each of the chosen crowns in turn.

'Because these three I recognise, and know to be stolen rather than surrendered. Maybe stealing them back into Rus hands might ease the warping more than taking any other. I don't know. But here is the Great Crown of the Great Princes of Kiev. The city fell by storm, and its people were slaughtered; this one did not come willingly into Batu's hands. Here, the Crown of Vladimir, the lord so highly thought of that his domain adopted their first lord's name for ever after. And here – one you should know, my friend, since you saw the siege that took it – Ryazan'. It was last worn by Roman Ingvarevich, before the Tatars impaled him outside his own city gates. Old crowns, with much power; and taken, not given. Best we should take them back.'

Nikolai Ivanovich was staring wide-eyed at the three crowns. 'I thought the gold was bloody, father,' he said, sounding just a little sick. 'But these are awful. I know we have to carry one, but can we do it now, and go?'

Ivan saw nothing, and knew that meant nothing. He wondered whether the blood that Kolya saw was all to do with the Tatars, and if it was not, what the boy would see the first time he looked long and hard at the Great Crown of Khorlov. How much blood had been spilled down the years to secure the realm, or the succession – and was Aleksey Romanov's death still dripping warm from the jewelled gold that Ivan had killed him to defend?

'Yes,' he said, lifting the crown of Kiev and tucking it beneath one arm. The thought of wearing it, unmannerly as it had seemed before, had suddenly become revolting. 'Volk Volkovich, do what you need to do to get us out of here. Now. At once.'

The light oozing through the shuttered windows was just as dull and grey as it had been on any day that Ivan Aleksandrovich could remember since he first arrived in Sarai. But it was still far too bright, bright enough to hurt even though his still half-asleep subconscious was certain that he hadn't drunk enough last night to justify the way he felt this morning. The one bleary eye not shrouded by the covers of the far-too-big and far-too-empty bed glanced around the room, looking for empty bottles, upturned furniture, even the boots of a guest not expelled by the servants and sleeping off his skinful underneath the table. None of those. Just three lumps on the floor, two of them wrapped in old cloaks and the third in what could almost have passed for the best outdoor coat. But as for –

Three lumps on the floor?

'*Yezu-Kristos!*'

Even though Ivan's head was still pounding as though someone was using it for a drum with a war mace as a drumstick, he shot out of bed in a swirl of furs and oaths and blankets. The oaths had to do with what it felt like when the cold air of the room hit his naked skin, and he realised that he had locked the door to keep any servant from coming in and seeing the three stolen crowns. That

287

also meant no-one had been able to get in and lay a fire in the stove – but it didn't matter, because that meant his far from pleasant dream had been completely real. Wrapping a fur coverlet from the bed around himself, Ivan squatted down and gingerly unwrapped the first of those anonymous lumps. This was Sarai, the city of the Golden Horde, and they might have been severed human heads for all he knew.

They were nothing of the sort. The Crown of the city-state of Kiev gleamed out at him, three hundred and twenty-seven years of history all wrapped up in a single piece of gold dressed up with fur and jewels. Even though he didn't have even his own son or daughter's talent at sensing such things, Ivan could feel that abstract energy called the power to rule come rolling off it, like heat from an iron taken fresh from the fire. He shivered violently enough to make his teeth rattle together, wished it really *was* heat after all, then bundled his trophy up again and started looking about for somewhere to stow it. There was a loose floorboard somewhere in the room, because he could remember an irritating squeak underfoot somewhere near the window; but exactly where near the window, and whether there would be enough space beneath it when he found it, was something else again. Ivan would have preferred to get the damned and damning things right out of the city, but that was out of the question either by magical or ordinary means. If Mar'ya Morevna had been here, she could have opened a storage pocket in some alternate reality which the Tatars could never know existed, never mind find and search. But then, if Mar'ya Morevna had been in Sarai, they would not have needed to bring the crowns back here in the first place.

They had almost failed to do even that; in fact they had barely made it back to the house. Volk Volkovich had underestimated the strength needed by a seven-year-old child to carry any sorcerous artifact through a Gate, no matter how short the distance or how talented the child. And the third crown, the one that he had been carrying, probably hadn't helped the situation.

Well, never mind.

Ivan lowered the third bundle down into the space beneath the bedroom floor, dropped the floorboard back in place, and secured the whole thing by dragging a clothes-chest on top of it. The unsettling business was all past and done with, no-one had come to any harm – except for some tattering of his own nerves – and both wolf and children had told him that they were already sensing a lightening of the weight that had been hanging over the city. They had staggered off to bed, the twins to their room, Volk Volkovich to the servants' quarters on the grounds that nobody ever noticed an extra servant more or less, and Ivan had simply fallen over almost where he stood.

Now the autumn equinox could come and go as it pleased; tonight, if he remembered aright, so they had probably acted just in time. From what Ivan had seen of the disregarded collection of crowns taken, locked away and forgotten in the shadows at the back of the treasure-house, Ilkhan Batu might never notice anything was missing, except that whatever catastrophe had been threatening to happen never would. And the Tsar of Khorlov could never claim the credit for averting it, either. Ivan grinned at nothing in particular, and crawled back into bed.

Half an hour later he was awake again, listening to the thunderous pounding of fists on the street door and wondering what the hell was going on. Then he looked at the handsome, flower-patterned wall, trying to remember when was the last time he had checked to see if the spyholes were in use, and felt his stomach turn to a cold lump of lead inside him.

He was half-dressed, in shirt and breeches and one boot, when other boots came thudding along the corridor outside and those same fists as downstairs transferred their attentions to his bedroom door. 'Open up, Khorlovskiy!' Now there was a voice he knew and hated. 'Open up or we break the door down!'

Ivan didn't bother with the other boot; he knew the threat was not an idle one, and if Amragan *tarkhan* was going to enter his room, he would do so whether the door was locked or not. At the very least he could take away the Türk's satisfaction in smashing his way in. Ivan pulled back the bolts at the top and bottom, swung back the door, and stepped neatly aside as a burly Tatar who had been just about to ram his shoulder against the timbers came lurching past.

'Well, well,' he said, as casually as he could. 'To what do I owe the pleasure so early in the morning?'

'Whether it's a pleasure or not remains to be seen, Russian,' said the Türk as he strode inside. He was wearing not his usual

289

coat but half-armour, and donned hastily if the misaligned laces meant anything. 'Were you perhaps expecting visitors?'

For an instant Ivan didn't know what he meant; then started slightly when he realised that though he hadn't wasted time putting on his second boot, he had pulled his sabre from its hooks by the door and the sheathed weapon was still in his hand. 'I, er, I wasn't quite sure what to expect. Even you are usually more polite when you come calling.'

'Times change,' said Amragan. 'Circumstances differ.' He sat down on the clothes-chest that Ivan had so recently been dragging about the floor, his own weight and that of the armour making both the chest and the floorboard beneath it creak painfully. Ivan quailed inwardly, but managed to keep any expression off his face. 'Well?' said the Türk. 'Get dressed. You must come with me. At once.'

Ivan perched on the end of the bed and reached for his other boot. Whatever was going on had nothing to do with the theft of any crowns from the treasure-house, at least not yet. If anything had been spotted through the spyholes, Amragan *tarkhan* would not have spent time in playing cat and mouse. Most especially he would not have bothered sitting on the trunk when the most obvious thing was to fling it aside and have his men tear up the floor.

He had still been given no explanation when he and the *tarkhan* went back downstairs at a pace almost fast enough to be a trot, and what made it still more mysterious was that when he had hooked the sabre to his belt, Amragan had said nothing against it. Indeed, the look he had shot at the weapon had been almost approving, as though every sword might help. But help what, and where? Nor was there any comment when Volk Volkovich emerged from the servants' hall beyond the kitchen and fell into step among Amragan's ten soldiers at Ivan's heels. Perhaps it was true that one more servant always went unnoticed, even one so striking as the Grey Wolf, but it seemed to Ivan as though Amragan *tarkhan* simply had too much on his mind, and if he wanted silence rather than idle chatter, then that was what he would get.

But within a few minutes Ivan realised where they were going, and his uneasiness returned with a rush. The last time he had walked along this street and turned at – yes, and turned at this corner, he had been following a well-dressed servant who had come to invite him to take wine with his masters. That had been an afternoon which had soon spiralled downward into unpleasantness and ended with threats, and Ivan was extremely glad that his sabre and Volk Volkovich were with him. Whatever was happening now, the three *boyaryy* he had met before were of a mind to take exception if he arrived in the company of a *tarkhan* and ten Tatar soldiers.

They went into the house at the same raking stride which had taken them through the streets of Sarai, past more Tatars obviously standing guard, and into a low-ceilinged room at the back. Then Amragan *tarkhan* turned on Ivan, gestured at the room and demanded, 'Do you know them?'

Ivan looked at the mess on floor and walls and ceiling that had been Stepan Mikhailovich, Andrey Vladimirovich and Mstislav Vasil'yevich, and realised after a few confused seconds that not even their own mothers could have said 'yes' to such a question. Had he not been introduced to each man by name and known that there were three of them, he would have been hard put to say how many corpses were actually in the room. Or even if they had been human. Usually squeamish in the presence of massacre, this time Ivan did not feel nauseated, any more than he would have done when passing a butcher's stall in the market, because whatever had happened to the trio had been so thorough that there was nothing recognisable as more than just fresh meat. What *did* make him feel momentarily queasy was the unmistakable sound of Volk Volkovich's stomach rumbling.

'If it – they – are, or were, who I think . . .' Ivan cursed briefly and gave up on trying to make sense from case and tense. Whatever he called them wouldn't matter to the *boyaryy* any more. 'We spoke last week. Wine, gossip; they were strangers in Sarai, but they had heard of me. I hadn't met them before. Or since.'

'What did you talk about?'

'I told you: just gossip. Why? Do you think I killed them because of something they said?'

Amragan *tarkhan* smiled thinly and looked him up and down, a slow, contemptuous scrutiny that made Ivan bristle. 'You? Do this? Hardly.'

'Then why drag me over here? Why get me out of bed at all?'

'It was time you were up and about,' said the Türk coolly. 'And this is only a part of what I wanted you to see. Follow.'

He brushed past and headed upstairs to the room where Ivan and the three dead men had exchanged useless opinions of each other. There was another dead man in the middle of the floor, and this one was all too recognisable. He was a Tatar, gagged with a cloth stuffed into his mouth and spread-eagled on the bare wooden floor, secured there by long iron spikes driven through all his major joints. But that had not killed him. It had been done merely to hold him in place, as a cook will do with a roast to hold it steady for carving. And then he had been carved, probably slowly, certainly carefully, until shock or loss of blood had done what his torturers had taken such pains not to hasten.

Carved as a dark gift for a dark god.

There were no magic circles on the floor, no cryptic patterns drawn in blood or cunning arrangements of sliced-off meat. There was just a particularly vile murder, and Ivan's memory of a certain conversation held right here, in which certain Russians who should have known better could not be dissuaded from a certain course of action, and the explosive carnage in the room downstairs that suggested in no uncertain terms that the sacrifice had been rejected.

Or had it been accepted after all? From the little Ivan knew of Chernobog, the gratitude of the Lord of the Dark Places was not likely to manifest itself in warm light and sweet savour. Mar'ya Morevna had a saying culled from years of studying the grimoires in her father's library, books that had as much to do with avoiding sorcerous entities as calling them up. 'Be careful what you wish for; you may get it. And while you may not like it, it may well like you. Raw or cooked.'

He was relieved beyond measure that they had succeeded last night in making away with the crowns. Probably while this butchery was taking place. And that too might explain why the three downstairs had died: the Dark One had been venting his frustration that a door left unlatched had been slammed in his face.

Then Ivan swore under his breath. If they had not stolen the crowns, then this killing and the reason behind it would have been a perfect excuse to tell Batu Khan what was trying to happen, and why it would be wise to overrule the shamans and send each crown back to where it belonged. Except that if they had indeed not stolen the crowns, then the three *boyaryy* might have succeeded after all, and there would have been more to contend with this morning than just a murder. There would have been Hell to pay. Literally. It was the sort of self-replicating conundrum that delighted Mar'ya Morevna, but it was making Ivan's head throb.

'Well?' From the sound of it Amragan *tarkhan*'s patience was wearing thin. Ivan tore his horror-fascinated eyes from the corpse on the floor – all over the floor – and stared at the Türk.

'Well what? I didn't do this either. If I kill a man, I do it quickly. Not – ' he waved expressively at the floor and turned away.

Amragan followed him downstairs and out into fresher air. 'I have seen you kill. I already know that this is not your way. But you know other things, Ivan Aleksandrovich. Was this just a murder, or was it something more?'

If he already suspects, then this is the perfect time to tell him, except he might go straight to the treasure-house, and then . . . oh God, what should I do?

'I know a few other things, Amragan *tarkhan*. But not as many as my wife, whom you in your infinite wisdom sent off to Khorlov to fetch the Great Crown that your orders stated should have come with us in the first place.'

'What?' The sudden attack took Amragan completely off-guard and off-balance.

'You had shamans with you. I know. I saw them. But what good were they? Not much!' Ivan shrugged flamboyantly. 'So anyway, I'm here, and she's somewhere between here and there; and I say that this was just a murder by a group of malcontents who probably lost family and friends to Tatar soldiers just like this one. Though what doing *that* to just one was was meant to achieve is quite beyond me. And if Mar'ya Morevna was here, she might tell you something else. But she isn't, and she can't, so that leaves you with me or nothing.' He had intended to grin in triumph at the end of his little speech, but a spike of pain ran straight up from the nape of his neck to his temples and twisted the grin to a grimace.

Amragan *tarkhan* paid his discomfort no heed. 'All right,

Khorlovskiy. So this was a murder. I can accept that. Just. But what in Tängri's name happened downstairs?'

'Maybe they were trying to make something like the Chin fire-pots shot from siege engines, and it backfired.'

'Hardly. And that's just it. You used the word twice yourself. There was no trace of *fire*. If you ever saw one of those things in use, you would know what I mean. If they got the mix right, this house would be rubble and cinders; and even if not, the room downstairs would be charred. It isn't.'

'Unfortunately. But I can't help. I think, Amragan *tarkhan*, that you want me to say they were working some spell. I won't say that, because I don't know.' That was true enough. If Ivan's suspicions were accurate, there was no spell involved. 'You'll have to wait for my wife to get back from Khorlov. Ask her.'

The sky flickered, and after several seconds thunder came rumbling in over the city, a long, sullen roll on the Drums of Tängri. As if in sympathy with the distant lightning, another silvery bolt of anguish drilled through Ivan's head, this time severe enough that his teeth ached, and even his hair seemed to hurt.

'Investigate your murder mystery all you like, Amragan,' he said, blinking the spasm away. 'I am going back to my house before the storm breaks. And if my head doesn't stop pounding, I'm going back to bed as well.'

'You have a headache?' Once they were out of earshot of Amragan *tarkhan*, Volk Volkovich spoke for the first time; and rather than solicitous he sounded worried. 'From when?'

Ivan's brows drew together in a frown as he tried to remember, then deepened as the lightning flashed far away over the steppes and another jolt stabbed at the backs of his eyes. 'I . . . I think in the house,' he managed eventually, having learned the hard way that grinding his teeth was no use. 'Upstairs.' He looked at the Grey Wolf through glowing red flecks that swam in his vision. 'Where that Tatar was given to Chernobog.'

Volk Volkovich growled something savage low in his chest. 'If the Black One's involved, then the sooner we're away from this vicinity the better. There's a foulness lingering here from last night. You feel it; I can almost taste it.'

Ivan missed what else he said. He was learning things that were more than enough for his senses to cope with, things that he would

294

have preferred not to know. He learned that real, deep pain had a colour and sound all its own. It was sickly glowing purple like the afterimage of lightning, and it sounded like sand poured on parchment. The Grey Wolf took him by the crook of the elbow and started to hurry him away, but after only a moment Ivan pulled free and stopped walking.

'It's gone,' he said, and very, very carefully shook his head. 'Completely. It didn't fade away. It just, well, stopped.'

'That house,' said the Grey Wolf, looking back at it, 'would be better as rubble and cinders. What happened in there was no way for any creature to die, even a Tatar. And as a sacrifice to Chernobog! Why would they be so foolish?'

Ivan explained the *boyaryy*'s twisted reasoning as best he could. What with the echoes of that murderous headache, and his own lack of any desire to be connected with their crazed scheme, he had forgotten most of it; but he remembered enough for Volk Volkovich to grin scornfully at the thought of such amateur enchanters.

'A Russian god, to fight on behalf of Russia? It shows how much they really knew. Nothing. If an entire race can't dare lay claim to a monopoly of good or evil, how can that people's gods claim the prerogative? Chernobog is no more exclusive to Russia than sunlight is. The Tatars know him too. They call him Erlik Khan, the Dweller in the Dark Gulf under the Earth, the enemy of light, Tängri's eternal adversary. But a Russian god? Don't make me – '

The blast from behind smashed both of them flat with a great blunt fist and slapped all the air out of their lungs. For just an instant all their senses were drowned out by a roar of silence and a vast lightless glare. They could smell cold, and taste darkness; and then the torn, tormented world came howling back to haunt them.

Ivan pushed himself up off the muddy street, half-stunned and trembling. 'We were too late,' he said, almost to himself. 'Too late, too slow, too close. We should have got those damned things out of the city no matter what.' He wiped a smear of dirt from his face, spat more onto the ground, turned – and wished he hadn't. Volk Volkovich, whom he had never seen afraid in all the years that they had known each other, was staring back the way they had come. Under the spatters of mud his face was grey with horror, and though still in human shape he was cringing like a dog before a beating.

The house was gone, and in its place a great black column towered up into the stormy sky. But it was not smoke. No smoke could just hang there as this was doing, rising so far and no further, spreading so far and no further. It was like a snake made of snakes, coiling sluggishly in and around itself, shadows within shadows. There was no heat, no fire, no rain of wreckage. Just silence, and cold and that pillar of darkness like a dagger nailing Sarai and every living creature in it to the dark, cold, silent earth.

The Khanate of the Golden Horde;
September, AD 1243

The ground heaved under Sivka's hoofs, so that Mar'ya Morevna swayed in her saddle and had to clutch the stallion's mane or pitch headlong. It was not a jolt, but a smooth rise and fall like a wave on the open sea – except this was Moist-Mother-Earth, supposedly solid and unmoving. Accustomed to such things as no mortal horse could be, Chyornyy and Sivka whinnied more in surprise than fear – but all the other animals, almost three thousand of them, squealed and reared and fought against things they could no longer trust. Tatar riders who had remained securely on horseback through countless bloody engagements went spilling to the ground, adding their yells and curses to the uproar.

Mar'ya Morevna swore as well, and with more reason. Though she knew no more than any other what had happened, she was at least better placed to make a guess – because the crown of Khorlov, wrapped and swaddled though it was, had turned so cold that it almost burned.

The earth rippled again, ponderous and slow, and she felt the fine hairs on her neck and arms stand up in horror as she realised where she had felt that same leisurely movement before. In bed, with Ivan at her side and no longer quite asleep, she had felt the unhurried shift of living bone and muscle as he yawned and stretched himself awake. It was as if the earth itself was waking up.

Or something underneath the earth, down in the cold dark. Something that had slept for a long, long time, ignored and forgotten. And when it woke after such a long sleep, it would surely be –

Hungry.

She looked around her at the Tatars, searching for the shrivelled old man with the wise, cruel eyes. Among a thousand men and three thousand horses, all reeling together in confusion, the task should have been impossible. But Beyki was easily seen, even though he was down on his knees. There was a space around him, growing wide by the minute as those nearby heard what he was chanting and fled for their lives and their sanity. One name and nothing else, endlessly repeated as he gashed his scrawny limbs with a knife, or bowed low to beat his forehead against the shivering ground.

'Erlik Khan! Erlik Khan!' Over and over again, but whether to call or to calm made little difference now, because the glitter of wisdom had gone out of his eyes like light from a snuffed candle. Wisdom, and sanity, and anything else that made meat into Beyki the shaman. There was only the husk of an old man kneeling in the trampled dirt, chanting a name that meant nothing any more.

'So much for advice from you,' said Mar'ya Morevna between her teeth. 'Sivka, Chyornyy – to Sarai and Ivan, as quick as you can. I have to . . . Wait!' She tugged back on the reins, slipped to the ground and picked up a discarded bow case. There was a full quiver of arrows hanging from the other side of its belt. She buckled it hastily around her waist and scrambled back into Sivka's saddle; then pulled the short, heavy bow from its case and nocked an arrow to the string.

'Erlik Khan! Erlik Kha – !' The shaman looked down uncomprehending at the shaft driven to its fletching in his chest, and toppled over sideways.

'Why did you do that, little mistress?' asked Sivka.

'An act of mercy, perhaps. Or an act of revenge. Horse, I don't know myself. But of one thing I'm certain: it wasn't an accident.' She put the bow away. 'Now. Sarai – and *move!*'

Sarai, capital of the Khanate of the Golden Horde; September, AD 1243

And the darkness moved upon the face of the earth, and saw that it was good . . .

That and stranger things went tumbling through Ivan's head as he and Volk Volkovich scrambled with silent determination through a crowd of shrieking people. They had all come pouring out of their homes, and were now struggling frenziedly to get as far as they could from the thing they had come out to see. Ivan had wanted to hear the Tatars make that sound, the sound of the terror they had visited on so many others, but now that he heard it, he wished it would stop. As the street widened and the trampling confusion eased somewhat, he looked back again – then stopped and stared at the unbelievable. Not the vast darkness that was Chernobog or Erlik Khan, but at Amragan *tarkhan*, alive and tottering down the street, his clothing and armour in rags where it wasn't white with a crusting of frost. The man was harder to kill than a cockroach.

There was a slamming explosion at Ivan's back and a brilliant flare of light threw his shadow down the street, as long and black and sinister as the swirling tower of darkness that was Chernobog. 'God damn it, no!' he snarled helplessly. 'Not again!'

The screams redoubled their volume as people scattered in all directions, and there was a metallic hammering sound close behind him that he felt sure he knew. The sabre at his belt came from its scabbard with slick, eager ease, and as he turned to face whatever had appeared this time, Ivan was already swinging out the wicked blade to cut at anything in his path. Its edge stopped a shuddering handspan short of Mar'ya Morevna's leg.

She and the two horses looked down at Ivan, then at the sword, with an expression of such deliberately ordinary disapproval that Ivan could have hugged all of them on the spot. It didn't bring things back into any sort of perspective, because with the Lord of the Dark Places loose in the world, perspective didn't matter a damn. But there was something comforting about it all the same. Mar'ya Morevna swung down from Sivka's high saddle and gave him a quick kiss on the cheek, all the time staring past him at the writhing column smeared across the sky. 'You're like the children, Vanya,' she said in his ear. 'You can't be left alone at all.'

'Less jokes, *gospozha*,' said Volk Volkovich. 'The situation here is hardly funny.'

'But then you never understood my sense of humour, did you?' said Mar'ya Morevna.

Ivan looked from his wife to his friend and back again, his lips pulled back in a tight, crooked grin; it sounded like the old sniping, but the ugly edge had gone. If they survived the next few minutes, everything was going to be all right – because nothing else would ever seem as bad again. 'Later for all that,' he said. 'We should do something. If we *can* do something.'

'Where are the twins?'

Ivan gestured down the street, now almost empty of people. 'In the house where I left them this morning. We were heading that way. After what happened, they'll have more sense than to go outside.'

'This – ' Mar'ya Morevna waved up at the coiled serpentine darkness, and it seemed to shift torpidly at her attention – 'is too recent. What *did* happen?'

Ivan told her, in as few words as he could spare: about the *boyaryy* and their wild scheme for sorcerous intervention; about the crowns and how three of them were no longer where the Tatars thought; and about how he had thought right up to the last minute that the rending between the worlds had been averted.

'If it hadn't been for those three fools, you would have succeeded.' Mar'ya Morevna's voice managed to blend warm approval and cold rage together in the same few words, and Ivan shivered. 'They made their sacrifice, and that attracted attention. They didn't get out of their house in time, and that provided nourishment – ' she caught a question taking shape and shook her head. 'Blood, souls, I don't know. And I don't want to know.'

'Mar'yushka, if Chernobog's power lies in the dark and the night, why did he – it – that thing wait until morning?' Mar'ya Morevna had started rummaging in her saddlebags, and it was the Grey Wolf who answered.

'Because you don't gain strength from a good meal at once. You have to digest it.'

Ivan curled his lip in silent disgust. 'Thank you for that,' he said with massive dignity. 'Would you go to the children, make sure they're all right, and bring them here? Now that we have the horses' – she slapped Sivka and Chyornyy – 'we can at least be sure they're out of this mess.'

'And bring the other crowns while you're at it,' said Mar'ya Morevna briskly, still rummaging. 'You know where they're hidden?'

Volk Volkovich put fist to forehead and bowed low. 'Yes, *gospozha Tsaritsa*. At once, *gospozha Tsaritsa*.' His shape collapsed in on itself, and the Grey Wolf in his true form looked at her with wicked yellow eyes. Mar'ya Morevna looked him up and down and raised one eyebrow.

'There. You do have a real sense of humour after all. Not that anyone in Sarai is going to notice. But stay in man's shape if you can.'

'When I come back is time enough for that,' said the Grey Wolf, and raced off.

'You are all being remarkably calm,' said Ivan, quite aware that his own voice and his hands were developing a tendency to shake. 'Is there any significance about that?'

'Just that panicking wouldn't help.' Mar'ya Morevna patted him on the shoulder. 'You were the one who told me that last time, when I saw Tsar Morskoy and started to scream.'

Ivan chuckled weakly, feeling very much put in his place. 'I still can't believe you did that.'

'Believe it. We all have our terrors. He happened to be one of mine. But look: why panic? Erlik Khan seems content enough just to be here.'

'They thought they were summoning Chernobog. Something Russian. Volk Volkovich says not.'

'He's right. But the Great Crown of Khorlov is here, and that's Russian enough.' She lifted it out of the leather bag and brushed ice-crystals from its sheepskin wrapping. 'And in there I have the sort of books I thought I might need.'

'Grimoires?'

'No, Vanya. Accounts ledgers. What do you think?'

'I think you could be moving faster.'

'No need. We're safe until nightfall.'

'Then what – ?' Ivan shut up and took a small step backwards as Mar'ya Morevna took the books from her saddlebags, because *Enciervanul Doamnisoar* was the least of them. 'You were expecting trouble,' he said weakly, not offering to help.

'I didn't know what I was expecting. But there's enough trouble between these covers to match most things I might have found in Sarai.'

'Even that?' Chernobog was curling heavily in on itself, a

movement less like smoke than ink poured into water, all coils and convolutions of infinite complexity. It looked a mile high, and terrifying.

'Even that. The term is dualism: the existence and attraction – and antagonism – of opposites. Where there is one, there can always be another. Black and white, light and darkness, heat and cold. Good and Evil.'

'Byelobog and Chernobog,' echoed Ivan. 'Tängri and Erlik Khan. Life and death . . .' They were not just pairs of words, because he understood their significance only too well.

The energies contained within Khorlov's Great Crown had played no part in aiding Chernobog's entry to the world of men. Brought here voluntarily rather than under escort, its presence gave Mar'ya Morevna access to a voluntary imbalance of power, and the ability to restore that balance by the Rule of Opposites. The summoning of some entity, some manifestation, some *thing* whose characteristics opposed those of Erlik Khan.

It was completely logical, but as Ivan stared up at the throbbing congeries of shadows that was Chernobog and Erlik Khan, he began to wonder if the cure might not be just as lethal as the ailment.

'Vanya?' Mar'ya Morevna's voice broke into his ugly imaginings and made him realise how little he had been paying attention. The spell books were open, their pages marked with many little strips of parchment, and the muddy ground was covered with a complex series of patterns where if one line curved right, another curved left. Those mirror patterns matched each other sweep for sweep until Ivan's eyes could not make sense of their convolutions any more. 'Vanya, you are the Tsar of Khorlov; its crown is yours by right. Take it in your hands and hold it high.'

The gem-beaded surface of its metal was still white with the frost that had been encasing it when Mar'ya Morevna peeled away the sheepskins, but even though the frost-crystals crushed and melted under the pressure of his fingers, Ivan felt no sensation of cold. There was only a faint coolness, as pleasant as a breeze on a summer day; and that, as much as any deeper chill, made Ivan of Khorlov shudder.

He could hear Mar'ya Morevna murmuring the complicated cadences of a charm of summoning, but did not look down to watch her. Without needing to be told, he stared up at Chernobog, full into the heart of the dark, and tried to visualise it suffused with a warm glow of light. He was imagining the wrong thing.

The dull sky split asunder and something came searing into existence alongside the black column, casting such light that the snakelike spirals of Chernobog's structure might have been carved from jet. It made a sound like the singing of flame, and cast a flare of warmth like the sun coming out from behind a cloud.

And when its coil of light entwined with the coils of darkness, that silent darkness shrieked.

Ivan picked himself up off the street and spat out mud. He might have thought that this sort of thing was becoming something of a habit; he might have wished that Mar'ya Morevna had warned him of what was about to happen; he might have wished to be somewhere else entirely. But he was here, and alive, and watching things no man had ever seen before.

There was a vast stillness in the city of the Golden Horde. Petty differences were set aside, petty human needs were discarded – even flight, for when gods duel for the souls of men, where is there left to run? The structure of the Bright being was like that of the Dark, flickering, dazzling, constantly changing, and as the darkness was most often a great snake made of lesser snakes, so the brightness was sometimes almost human-shaped – though at other times very far from it. But at least once it took on the form of a warrior clad in blue and gold, the colours of the sun and the sky, armed with a spear made of a bolt of lightning, that stabbed through the darkness like a needle in cloth.

To the Tatars, that was Tängri of the Eternal Blue Sky fighting Erlik Khan with his thunderbolt, though Ivan knew that there was at least one old servant who had come with him down from Khorlov who would see Othinn or Thorr wielding spear or hammer against their old adversary Jormungandr the Midgarth-serpent. To some of the Russians, it would be Byelobog struggling with Chernobog, but the rest would see the Archangel Mikhail, come to do battle against the darkness and the Old Serpent, not for them alone but for all the wide white world.

And it was not enough.

'What's wrong?' yelled Ivan through the din. 'Nothing's happening! They're just – '

And then he knew. The Rule of Opposites was too exactly balanced, for while everyone watching wanted the Light to defeat the Dark, there was still enough darkness in their own souls – hidden hatreds, jealousies, a secret desire by either side to turn that power of Light against their enemies whether Rus or Tatar – that the two forces hung in perfect opposition. They could neither win, nor lose, nor even break off the combat once it had been joined.

Instead they remained where they were, a screeching, twisting column of ravening energies, black light shot through with lightnings that was planted all too solidly in the heart of Sarai and the heart of the Khanate and for all Ivan knew, in the heart of the world itself.

It should have been impossible that so small a noise could have been heard above the high, tearing roar thrown off by that swirling vortex, but Ivan heard something behind him. Nikolai and Anastasya were standing there, and what he had heard was a gasp – of fear, or astonishment, or even delight, for all he knew. His twin children were removed enough from the normal concerns of childhood that what he found terrible, they might find strangely magnificent. Volk Volkovich was behind them, restored to human form; and he, at least, looked appalled at what he saw.

'Mamma,' said Nikolai. Just that one word; no greeting, no running into a long-missed embrace. No more than a simple recognition of her presence. It was as if all emotion had been shocked out of the boy – and his sister too, for Natasha didn't even speak. They were carrying the other three crowns between them, sagging a little with the strain of the power they contained, and the look in their eyes was ancient.

'We stole these,' said Natasha. 'Stealing is wrong.'

'It's wrong even when you steal from an enemy,' said Kolya. 'That's why *they* won't go away. The ekwi – ' he fought with the word, 'equilibrium is upset.'

Natasha looked at her parents with old, wise eyes in her child's face. It chilled Ivan to the marrow of his bones. 'We were trying to do good by doing a bad thing.'

'Then give me the crowns,' said Mar'ya Morevna, 'and I'll – '

'No, Mamma. That wouldn't work. You didn't take them. You can't put them back.'

'Neither can Papa.'

'But we can.'

Ivan stared, and heard, and that chill turned to stark terror. 'Put them back? What do you mean?'

The children didn't reply. Instead they looked at each other and then, hand in hand, ran past their father and out towards the flaring, spitting pillar of fire and darkness.

'NO!' Ivan flung himself after them as he might have done had they been running towards a street busy with horses and wagons, but his clawing fingers rebounded before they could close around collars or hems, before he could reach his own children. As though a vast sheet of glass or an invisible, unbridgeable gulf lay between them. He could hear Mar'ya Morevna's heart-rending scream as Volk Volkovich the Grey Wolf sprang past him and slammed against the barrier, hard enough to have dented a kremlin's stone wall, but not hard enough to break through this, and he knew he would hear that scream in his ears for the rest of his life. And still the two small figures ran on, now no more than silhouettes against the black brightness while the heat and the cold swirled out to meet them.

'NO. . . !'

And they were gone.

Through his own helpless sobbing, Ivan could hear even Tatar voices shouting in horror. Those hardened warriors had killed men, women and children in their time, but they had been strangers. There were people in Sarai who had come to know Ivan's twins well over the past weeks. They had not also expected to see them die. The man who had been their father, and who had once been Tsar of Khorlov, collapsed on his face in the mud where his fingers clawed up great useless handfuls of the cold black earth. As if that would help. As if it would hurt those who dwelt in the darkness. As if it could do anything at all.

And then the earth shook. It lurched under his outstretched hands as though he had in very truth touched some exposed nerve. But why now? Why, when it was of no use? Why could something not have happened before –

Before.

Ivan raised his head from the dirt, stood up even though he wanted to crawl like a worm, and watched with tear-blinded eyes as the vortex began to collapse, blackness and brightness devouring each other, spiralling in on itself with a vast howling noise while random pulses of energy sleeted across the sky like the Northern Aurora gone mad. The lofty pillar that had towered into the sky and defied Heaven itself slumped to a sphere no bigger than two men could span with their arms, roiling with incredible light and utter darkness as though those colours or the lack of them were still shining through holes cut into other worlds than this.

And perhaps they were. Ivan no longer cared. The light in his world had gone out.

The howling faded to a rumble and then to an impossibly deep, fading groan, the sound that Ivan's heart might have made in the moment that it broke. With shocking suddenness the brilliant light and deep darkness both vanished, leaving in their wake a perfect outline of the sphere sliced out of everything it had come in contact with. Buildings, walls – even the ground itself had a perfectly curved scoop taken out of it.

Then he heard the sound of laughter, a sound that he had never hoped to hear again in this life, and the darkness in his mind groped out to find a chance for light. Ivan took a tremulous step forward, and then another, and the third one that let him peer over the sharp-edged brink.

Nikolai and Anastasya were there, at the bottom of the shallow depression, looking as unconcerned as though nothing of note had happened, and they were laughing and playing catch with a little, glossy ball that looked like hollow glass, filled with whirling skeins of black and white that never mixed to grey.

Ivan heard footsteps behind him as he slithered down into the pit and swayed there, his heeled boots unsteady on the glass-smooth surface. The twins eyed him curiously as he reached out to take the ball and rest it on the mud-smeared palm of his right hand. Already it was smaller than when he saw it first. He went down on one knee beside the children, their faces pressed alongside his, while up on solid ground Mar'ya Morevna stood with Volk Volkovich at her side, and they all watched in silence as it dwindled away, smaller and smaller, until there was nothing there at all.

He handed son and daughter to their mother, to be caressed and cried over, and taken one by one and then together into a crushing hug, before scrambling up awkwardly himself. He stared at things he had not noticed before. All the walls of all the buildings around the crater cup were white, no matter what colour they might have been before; and on them, starkly silhouetted on the original paint or brick or stone, were the shadows of all those who were not either bowing in terrified supplication or diving for cover.

Mar'ya Morevna was there; so was Ivan, and on the farther side, Amragan *tarkhan* and a few others, even the Ilkhan Batu himself. All could be identified with ease, because the profiles were almost crisp enough to discern individual hairs. But there was one shadow that made no sense to most of those who stared at it.

Instead of a man, it was the outline of a monstrous wolf; and Volk Volkovich had the decency to look embarrassed.

'Hui! Look at my city, Russian! My beautiful golden city! Your demons have wrecked it! What have you to say for yourself, uu?'

Ivan bowed his head in well-feigned contrition. There were a number of things he might have said, but Khan Batu would have appreciated very few, and taken grave exception to the rest. But the old Mongol was right about one thing; Sarai was wrecked indeed. What the fight between the powers of light and darkness did not pulverise had been demolished by their cataclysmic departure.

'It is as well you say nothing, Ivan of Khorlov,' said Batu at length, swigging *kumys* – though without the usual accompaniment of pipes and cymbals. The Splendid Khan of the Golden Horde had let it be known in no uncertain terms that there had been enough noise for one day. 'Excuses only compound an obvious error, uu? But I will not have you killed for what you have done. I should be grateful after all that you dismissed the demons before more harm was done.'

Neither Ivan nor Mar'ya Morevna said anything just yet. It would not have been wise to remind Batu that his policy with the crowns of the conquered domains had been largely responsible for one 'demon', while Mar'ya Morevna had summoned the second. And anyway, they were both waiting nervously for the inevitable sting that lurked in the tail of such statements as these. This one turned out to be blunt.

'No, huu, I shall dismiss you. Completely. I want nothing more to do with you, or your adventures.' He glowered at Ivan. 'When I want such things, you tell me about them. Don't show me unless I ask! Hah! Go back to Khorlov and stay there, the sooner the better. You do not exist!'

The Khan held out one hand and a sheet of parchment was set in it; one edge was tattered, as though it was a page torn violently out of a book. He waved the sheet under their noses, then tore it across and across, flung the pieces into the nearest brazier of charcoal, and watched as they curled, blackened, flared and were consumed. 'Your names are gone. The realm of Khorlov is gone. The page that bore them is gone from the chronicle of the Khanate. Go live in your own little world, and do not intrude on mine!'

Ivan and Mar'ya Morevna looked at one another, then, greatly daring, winked at the Grey Wolf and the children. That could be managed. And though they knew they were hearing the words of Aleksandr Nevskiy again, they were content. If Russian and Tatar both wanted them out of the world, but neither were willing to do it in the brutal, old-fashioned way, then they would be more than happy to oblige in their own fashion.

As he had done once before, Batu Khan of the Golden Horde clapped his hands in dismissal. 'Go!'

They went.

The Independent Tsardom of Khorlov; October, AD 1243

Ivan heard the door of the kremlin library open, then shut; he heard footsteps descend slowly and wearily down the long flight of dressed stone stairs that led out at last into the courtyard; and he stood in the falling snow, and he waited.

Mar'ya Morevna and Nikolai and Anastasya emerged blinking into the pallid light. The children were holding their mother's hands, and all three of them looked tired to the point of exhaustion. That did not stop first one child and then the other from running through the snow and leaping up into their father's embrace. 'Did it work?' he said. 'You promised, remember?'

'It worked,' said Mar'ya Morevna. The last time Ivan had heard such deep satisfaction in her voice had been after the birth of the twins, when the doctors had assured her that all had gone well and – more important – she had at last believed them. 'Whenever you're ready.'

Ivan set the children down with a little grunt of effort; they were sturdy, well-grown, and getting no lighter. He watched as they ran off across the snow-covered courtyard, and that same gaze took in all the hopeful, or nervous, or downright fearful faces staring at him. 'I've been ready for years,' he said softly. 'And never more ready than now. Say the words.'

'Nothing so crude, my loved one. The Great Gate is open and ready.' She smiled, and kissed him lightly on the lips, regardless or maybe because of the watchers. 'What is it they say in the stories? "Just wish, and you're there." So wish . . .'

A sudden gust of warmth swept through the courtyard, a breeze laden with a tingling scent of flowers that was the very breath of summer. The falling snow stopped, and that on the ground began to melt into little, chuckling rivulets of clear water. Ivan looked upwards at an arch of light that had come sweeping from the east like an impossibly swift dawn. It was like a rainbow with no colour but sunlight, and as it advanced across the sky, the grey, snow-laden clouds were driven before it and clear blue was left in its wake.

'They'll say we were running away,' said Mar'ya Morevna thoughtfully. Half the sky was grey now, and the rest was blue.

'Let them say it,' said Ivan, grinning. 'At least I won't have to listen any more. I've spent my life being concerned over other opinions. This is my Tsardom, these are my people, and if this is the way that I choose to protect them, so be it.'

Somewhere away in the distance, among the shadowed green woods, a wolf howled. Though the long, smooth rise and fall of the voice sounded melancholy, Tsar Ivan knew better. There was no heartbreak in this wolfsong, nor threat either. He nodded acknowledgement of the greeting, then reached out for Mar'ya Morevna and they walked hand in hand across the kremlin courtyard, enjoying the warmth of the sun as they awaited the arrival of their first guest. There was only a new-moon sliver of grey low in the west, as all of the realm of Khorlov slipped quietly

sideways, out of Russia, out of the world, and into the Summer
Country.

The steppes of Russia;
October, AD 1243

A single brightly coloured butterfly fluttered for a few confused
seconds in the cold air, its wings spattered with flecks of falling
snow. Where there had been a city, and a fortress, and the great
kremlin palace of Khorlov, there was just a sliver of blue summer
sky against the grey clouds and white snow. A warm scent of
flowers flowed from it, and already the sliver had narrowed to half
of its previous width. With all the stern purpose that an insect
could summon, the butterfly plunged back to the Gate, and
through it, just as the magic winked shut.

With no errant summer heat to interfere, the snow began to fall
again in earnest. Wind sifted it and sculpted it across the open
steppes, and the snow kept falling. Within an hour, or perhaps a
little longer, there was no trace remaining to prove that the
Tsardom of Khorlov had ever existed in the wide white world.

And if the remaining chronicles of the Golden Horde and of
Aleksandr Nevskiy can be believed, it never did . . .

Bibliography

AFANAS'EV, A. N. (trans. Guterman, N.), *Russian Fairy Tales/Narodnye russkiye skazki* (Pantheon Books, 1945/ Random House, 1973)

AL-AZRED, A., *Kitab al-Azif/The Necronomicon* (restricted-print facsimile no. 290 of 348, Owlswick Press, 1973)

BRENT, P., *The Mongol Empire* (Weidenfeld & Nicholson, 1978)

CHAMBERLAIN, L., *The Food and Cooking of Russia* (Allen Lane 1982/Penguin, 1983, 1988)

COE, M. D., *Swords and Hilt Weapons* (Weidenfeld & Nicholson, 1989)

DOWNING, C., *Russian Tales and Legends* (Oxford University Press, 1956)

FENNEL, J., *The Crisis of Medieval Russia 1200–1304* (Longman, 1988)

FRAZER, J. G., *The Golden Bough* (Macmillan, 1978)

FUNCKEN, L. & F., *The Age of Chivalry Part 2* (Ward Locke, 1980)

GOLDSTEIN, D., *A Taste of Russia* (Robert Hale, 1985/Sphere, 1987)

GOLYNETS, S. V. (trans. Kochov, G. A.), *Ivan Bilibin* (Aurora/Pan, 1981)

GRAVETT, C., *Medieval Siege Warfare* (Osprey Elite, 1990)

GRIMAL, P. (ed.), *Larousse World Mythology* (Hamlyn, 1989)

GUIRAND, F. (ed.), *New Larousse Encyclopedia of Mythology* (Hamlyn, 1974)

HALPERIN, C. J., *Russia and the Golden Horde* (I. B. Tauris, 1987)

de HARTOG, L., *Genghis Khan, Conqueror of the World* (I. B. Tauris, 1989)

HASLER, J., *The Making of Russia* (Longmans, Green & Co, 1969)

LAMB, H., *The March of the Barbarians* (Literary Guild of America Inc., 1940)

LONGWORTH, P., *The Cossacks* (Constable & Co., 1969/ Sphere, 1971)

MORGAN, D., *The Mongols* (Blackwell, 1990)

NICOLLE, D., *The Mongol Warlords* (Firebird, 1990)

NICOLLE, D., *Attila and the Nomad Hordes* (Osprey Elite, 1990)

OBOLENSKY, D. & STONE, N., *The Russian Chronicles* (Random Century, 1990)

PAYNE-GALLWEY, R., *The Crossbow* (Holland Press, 1990)

POLLARD, J., *Wolves and Werewolves* (Robert Hale, 1966)

RIASANOVSKY, N. V., *A History of Russia* (Oxford University Press, 1969)

TOMAŠEVIC, N-B. & VARTABEDIJAN, M., *Russia* (Bracken Books, 1989)

TURNBULL, S. R., *The Mongols* (Osprey, 1980)

Von FRANZ, M-L., *Shadow and Evil in Fairytales* (Spring Publications Inc., 1983)

WARNER, E., *Heroes, Monsters and Otherworlds from Russian Mythology* (Peter Lowe, 1985)

WHEELER, P., *Russian Wonder Tales* (The Century Co., 1912; P. Wheeler, 1940/1946; Thomas Yoseleff, 1957)

ZVORYKIN, B. V. (ed. Onassis, J.), *The Firebird and other Russian Fairy Tales* (Viking, 1978)